The Pra
Dramaturgy
Working on Actions in Performance

Konstantina Georgelou
Efrosini Protopapa
Danae Theodoridou (eds.)

Antennae
Valiz, Amsterdam

The Practice of Dramaturgy
Working on Actions in Performance

Konstantina Georgelou
Efrosini Protopapa
Danae Theodoridou (eds.)

With contributions by
Una Bauer
Simon Bayly
Andrea Božić
Nicola Conibere
Guy Cools
Augusto Corrieri
Konstantina Georgelou
Ivana Müller
Betina Panagiotara
Efrosini Protopapa
Joachim Robbrecht
Jonas Rutgeerts
Nienke Scholts
Arabella Stanger
Danae Theodoridou
Julia Willms
Jasna Jasna Žmak

Contents

Introduction

Konstantina Georgelou
Efrosini Protopapa
Danae Theodoridou

Why Dramaturgy Today?

This book is the culmination of a research project that took place from 2013 to 2015, entitled 'Dramaturgy at Work'.[1] Given the growing interest in the notion and practice of dramaturgy, as evidenced by the recent proliferation of texts, discussions, and events on dramaturgy, this book could easily be considered to be 'just another publication' on a 'hot topic'.[2] One of our main concerns, therefore, as editors of this collection of texts and initiators of the research project that preceded it, has been to address the question 'why dramaturgy today?', which has also prompted us to consider what is at stake in our desire to engage with what seems to be a tired or exhausted field.

Already in the 1990s discussions started to emerge on the relationship between dramaturgy, and forms of theatre or dance that did not seem to follow traditional paradigms of performance. Some key ideas on dramaturgy became more or less established at that time, considering what dramaturgy is, how it manifests, and its contribution in the frame of artistic production. One such established idea, for example, is the difficulty to arrive at a concrete definition of the term 'dramaturgy'. Marianne Van Kerkhoven, a central figure in dramaturgical discourses, argued in 1994 that 'dramaturgy involves everything, is to be found in everything', and so to identify what constitutes dramaturgy is not an easy task.[3] Similar views have been repeatedly articulated much later by other dramaturgs and scholars, such as André Lepecki, who has referred to his first dramaturgical collaborations with certain choreographers as situations where, although neither of the two sides knew exactly what they were doing when working together, they perceived this collaboration as necessary — as a not knowing that was 'resolved and dissolved by a practice of doing'.[4]

The attempt to define a term that has proved difficult to pinpoint becomes even more complicated in current artistic frames. Today's fragmented and diverse landscape of artistic production is not the result of a single 'guide' for the making of certain types of work, nor can it be approached through set modes of analysis and interpretation. There are no 'golden' rules for the creation of a 'well-made' performance. Instead of a closed and fixed norm, we see 'a consequence of the process', which directly reflects the dialogue between the people involved in the making of a work.[5] We thus talk about a 'dramaturgy of process' in works that are oriented towards the construction of possibilities and not the establishment of clearly definable and repeatable schemas.

Hence, the possible responses to the question of what dramaturgy is or what kind of work it entails seem to be as many as the multiple and diverse dramaturgical practices that are to be found in the heterogeneous landscape of the performing arts today. In other words, it is now commonly accepted that the way we understand dramaturgy has to do with diverse, multiple, and shifting areas of practice that are extremely difficult to nail down. Yet at the same time, this is why the practice of dramaturgy has become relativized; as Bojana Cvejić has rightly argued, 'the temptation of unfolding the many dramaturgies hides the danger of arbitrary relativization – everything and nothing is or can be (considered) dramaturgy – and one loses a position to defend'.[6] It is for this reason that we need to ask: if dramaturgy today has indeed become a relativized and therefore obscure area of research, if it remains an ungraspable practice, then what exactly could one argue for now when arguing for dramaturgy? In other words, what is at stake when engaging with dramaturgy today?

In this book we seek to respond to the question of dramaturgy's relevance in three interconnected ways that are reflective of our approach at different stages of the research: first, we consider how dramaturgy emerged as a common area of enquiry for us, requiring that we position ourselves towards arguably problematic usages and interpretations of dramaturgy including the emergence of several adjectives to signal different types of dramaturgies, the assumption that dramaturgy is primarily the work of a collaborator called 'the dramaturg', and understandings that link dramaturgy to theatrical coherence and sense making, all of which we question in an attempt to create a common ground on which to offer our proposals on dramaturgy; second, we set out to explicitly propose dramaturgy as 'a practice', and to address through this lens the political stakes that the question of dramaturgy entails for us; and third, in considering what may be at stake in our engagement with dramaturgy today, we take into account that this whole research project was set up in the framework of our collaboration. This last point, we suggest, carries a dramaturgy of its own that also expands our understanding of dramaturgy beyond the solely artistic domain into the infrastructural one, pointing to relations with institutional structures and funding bodies that constitute today's economy of performance theory and practice. These perspectives inform our propositions on dramaturgy in Part I of the book, which we have co-authored;

subsequently, they are also worked through in more or less direct ways in the texts comprising Part II, written by guest authors. These texts tackle a variety of interrelated issues, from dramaturgical practices within artistic work and expanded understandings of dramaturgy, to social matters and political debates.

A Shared Field of Enquiry
The project 'Dramaturgy at Work' that led to this book developed through a series of workshops and roundtable discussions in different cities in Europe that sought to approach dramaturgy from a variety of perspectives. The reasons we pursued this nomadic project, in spite of its great practical difficulties (for example, travelling as well as production and administration work alongside our other jobs), vary and include our need to address artistic, pedagogical, and political concerns that we share and that we *had to* investigate between us and with others who were willing to take part in this venture. This project qualifies as a demand, a 'had to' among us, because the subject matters it proposes feel urgent in our artistic and institutional spheres of work, and in the social and political contexts in which we operate. Our different but in many ways intersecting research concerns and ways of working in choreography, theatre, performance, theory, and higher education, significantly, produce points of tension, which we also felt could be addressed through the question of dramaturgy.

In this frame, the overall project was especially triggered by our shared experiences and reflections on the status of dramaturgy today, as evidenced in a number of publications and related events. More specifically, in order to describe dramaturgy as our shared field of enquiry, we offer here three positions in response to central ideas arising in scholarship on dramaturgy since 1994 and the publication of the special issue of *Theaterschrift* 5 & 6 'On Dramaturgy' in that same year:

a. Dramaturgy as a singular term:
Dramaturgical practices that emerged from the diverse artistic developments of the performing arts in the late twentieth and early twenty-first centuries are usually discussed under terms such as 'new' (Van Kerkhoven, Trencsényi and Cochrane, Turner and Behrndt), 'open' (Van Kerkhoven), 'contemporary' (Lehmann and Primavesi), 'expanded' (Eckersall), 'slow' (Eckersall and

Paterson), 'porous' (Turner), and 'postdramatic' (Lehmann), whereas often dramaturgy is also addressed in plural as 'dramaturgies'. In fact, the workshops and roundtable discussions through which our project evolved were also initially grouped under the title 'Unfolding Dramaturgies'.[7] Our subsequent return to the singular term 'dramaturgy' is not accidental. It partly reflects our desire to work around a certain anxiety, observed in the performance field particularly in the last twenty to thirty years, that emerges from the demand to continually invent yet more 'radical' and 'innovative' terms that will break from the 'traditional' or 'passé', which also unavoidably implies a clear-cut break between the 'old' and the 'new'. By using the term in the singular, and without an accompanying adjective, we seek to delve deeper into an understanding of dramaturgy as a particular process of work that is common to all artistic production (whether 'experimental', 'traditional', 'new', or 'old'), and that sheds light upon the ways in which encounters, work, and creation inside (and possibly also outside) the artistic frame happen.

For this reason, the events that have led to this book addressed a wide range of participants, from performance makers and visual artists, choreographers, and theatre directors, to theorists, writers, philosophers, and dramaturgs. Arriving at the project with their own practices, which could be considered varied also in terms of their aesthetical concerns, tools, and methodologies (again, for example, they could be considered 'traditional', 'experimental', 'site-specific', or 'participatory'), this mix of practitioners participated in the workshops, presented at the roundtable discussions, or participated in both. Invited guests to the roundtable discussions were asked to prepare statements that responded to the themes of each workshop and would offer distinct positions on the matters and questions at hand. Special consideration was given to the varied backgrounds of the selected guests in each roundtable, to secure diverse approaches towards the specific concerns of each workshop preceding a roundtable discussion (ranging, for example, from artistic and educational to institutional and theoretical). Some of these guests' contributions have been further developed for the purposes of this publication, and appear in Part II of the book. Hence, while acknowledging the different backgrounds, practices, and approaches that the various collaborators and we editors have brought to the project, we speak of dramaturgy here as a singular shared field of enquiry among us all, which nevertheless has the capacity to 'hold' and even benefit from different approaches to and positions on performance making.

b. Dramaturgy with or without a dramaturg:
Another relatively common thread in existing discourse is the use of the terms 'dramaturgy' and 'dramaturg' interchangeably. Even when the two terms are clearly distinguished, dramaturgy tends to be understood as the work of a specific collaborator called 'the dramaturg', and topics such as the history of the two terms, the characteristics of dramaturgical processes in contemporary artistic production, and the working conditions of dramaturgs in various contexts seem to be discussed all at once. The focus of this book, however, is primarily on dramaturgy, as we seek to offer an in-depth study of the processes and modes involved in dramaturgical work, whether that involves a dramaturg or not. Although none of us — the editors — identifies as a dramaturg, at least not by considering dramaturgy as her exclusive profession, our common research has focused on dramaturgy as a practice that does not necessarily coincide with the work of the dramaturg, nor with the different practices that each one of us is occupied with (choreography, theatre making, performance theory, philosophy, and arts education). By arguing that this is a book on dramaturgy, rather than on the work of the dramaturg, we suggest a focus on a practice that operates in the common space created among the distinct professional backgrounds that each one of us brings to the work — a practice primarily concerned with our shared questions around modes of production in the arts and in arts theory, how thinking (between many) happens, and what it means to make artistic work public today. Our common research, therefore, is grounded in a simultaneous attraction to and questioning of dramaturgy: what it suggests; when, why, and how it is done; how it differs from other practices (such as choreography or performance making), especially if not seen as the work of the dramaturg; and what it has to offer — particularly in today's sociopolitical context — as a practice shared among the different agents involved in artistic work.

Undeniably, people who work professionally as dramaturgs (such as in-house dramaturgs and production dramaturgs) often have to deal with processes commonly understood as dramaturgy.

Depending on the context, these may include, for example, 'background research, analysis, observing rehearsals, being a first audience, writing program notes and grant applications',[8] acting as a liaison between the artistic team and the audience, writing theoretical texts on the production, or even being responsible for public relations, post-show talks, lobby displays, and social networking — an approach that seems to particularly be flourishing in our new digital information age.[9] However, practising dramaturgy does not necessarily mean doing such work. In fact, practising dramaturgical thinking, at least as we will address it here, may sometimes mean doing very little of what is commonly accepted as the dramaturg's work, or even resisting doing such work and going against the systems it seems to be servicing.

In this sense, the need for a dramaturg suggests a need for one more valuable collaborator in the room and does not arise out of the recognition of any other lack or insufficiency of the work that the dramaturg is then expected to address and resolve; rather, we suggest, one asks a collaborator to join the creative process in a dramaturgical capacity precisely so that they can contribute to the work's disorientations and inefficiencies. 'Wherever there is a performance taking shape there are a set of dramaturgical questions being asked and dramaturgical principles being tested',[10] Adrian Heathfield has posited, regardless of whether a dramaturg is or is not part of this work. This depersonalization of the dramaturgical function renders dramaturgy a shared responsibility for all collaborators involved in the production of a performance. And, even if the suggestion of approaching dramaturgy independently from the work of the dramaturg is not new, what may still be missing is a re-articulation of dramaturgy as a process that sets a work in motion, through a type of operation that realizes its forces and qualities, and is shared among collaborators, whether those include a dramaturg or not. It is this discussion that we seek to contribute to here.

c. Dramaturgy beyond sense-making and theatrical coherence:

Finally, it could be noted that contemporary discourses address dramaturgy mostly as linked to the compositional logic of a work. For Turner and Behrndt, for instance, the 'dramaturgy' of a play or performance can be described as its 'composition', 'structure', or 'fabric'[11] so that 'doing dramaturgy' or 'dramaturging' points to an engagement with the work's composition. Whether this compositional logic relates to more traditional rules, which aim to direct the audience's attention towards a climax in the middle or end of the piece,[12] or whether it negates the aforementioned classical structures in order to create and expose gaps, breaks, contradictions, frictions, and holes, the focus in any case is on *structuredness* and the way that things come to constitute a whole. Aligning instead with views such as those of Heathfield and Pil Hansen,[13] we too, however, feel a certain discontent with general claims that run the danger of considering dramaturgy as a 'feature' of performance reduced to what one does in order to attribute coherence to it. And at the same time, we disagree with what we identify as a tendency of educational and artistic institutions and publications to equal dramaturgy either to performance analysis or to how-to-do manuals. Our approach here, therefore, opposes understandings of dramaturgy as a guarantor of the work's supposed coherence. Instead, our critical suggestion, as formulated in Part I of the book, is to return to the etymology of dramaturgy in order to consider it as a fusion between action and work that operates in a specifically catalytic mode;[14] this we shall arrive at by elaborating on three concrete working principles that aim at activating a process through interruptive and often destabilizing operations, rather than mechanisms that may secure a supposed theatrical coherence.

Departing from the abovementioned positions on dramaturgy, as a term used in the singular and independently from both the figure of the dramaturg as well as processes of composition and sense making, it is important to mention here that we have also been interested in dramaturgical practices placed *before* the event of a performance and during the 'making of' a work, even though 'dramaturgy does not belong to a resolved temporality' and it certainly does not refer only to the moment of creation.[15] The distinct temporalities of dramaturgy have been discussed by scholars and artists alike: some distinguish between what is known as 'the rehearsal' in relation to the event of performance (Heathfield, 2011); some focus on the reflective analysis that accompanies or follows a production (Turner and Behrndt, 2008): and others consider the potential of dramaturgy to exceed the phase of creation of any one particular work and be studied by looking backwards at the work as a system which may provide strategies and perspectives for the creation of future work too (BADco.'s 'post-hoc dramaturgy').[16] All of these distinct temporalities are equally valid and important for a complete understanding of phenomena and processes that relate to dramaturgy. However, here we insist on the present time of a work's creation and focus mostly on dramaturgical processes as these unfold *within* a work's making, instead of looking at them either from a past or a future point. This is because, as we suggest, it is precisely an in-depth study of such a present time — the present time of making when all agents involved in a creation meet and act together — that shows how dramaturgy positions itself in today's working and living conditions as a *shared* field of enquiry and practice.

Our aim to explore dramaturgy as a shared field of research on the basis of our aforementioned positions is reflected also in the way that the project preceding this book was designed: we kept expanding the community at work from the three of us (who designed and facilitated each gathering), to the participants of the workshops (who came with the aim of revisiting their own work through the workshops' focus), to the invited guests of the roundtables (who approached in their own way the questions we had been exploring in the workshops), to the general public who attended (and pushed our enquiry further with their questions and interventions). The book echoes and continues this gesture, by bringing together a writing community and facilitating further exchange with readers. In this way, rather than proposing a dramaturgical method that is specific to certain kinds of performance making, or dealing with dramaturgy as an isolated practice that guarantees success, a professional capacity, or a subject matter for theoretical discussion, the book suggests (and practices) a dramaturgy that attends to the distinct ways through which we activate ourselves, our work, and our communities; moreover, it explores how we may do so precisely from within the diverse but interrelated disciplines that we identify with professionally.

The Practice of Dramaturgy

If this book is the result of specific dramaturgical practices that aimed to experiment with ideas and tasks (with others) in studios and theatres throughout Europe, it could also be argued that in a sense every book is the result of practice — of some kind of practice, be that an investigation into archives or science experiments in laboratories, but even writing itself, or thinking as a practice. Moreover, given the fact that the focus of this project has been on practising dramaturgy, without, however, aiming to produce tools or manuals for such a practice, we would like to suggest here an examination of this term – practice – in the context of dramaturgy and of this book. In particular, our aim is to revisit dramaturgy as a 'practice' – that is, as a term and working mode – so as to claim back its political nuance.

In order to do this, we suggest reconceptualizing dramaturgy by recovering the notions of 'action' (*drama*) and 'work' (*ergon*) contained in its etymological dimension. This perspective points to a dual operation of dramaturgy: how actions work and how one works on actions. Both facets of dramaturgy are acknowledged in this book, but our focus will primarily reside in the second one, due to the insufficient attention we think it has received in literature. As will be argued, this approach could also be seen as paradigmatic of – but possibly at the same time indicating a point of resistance against – the current neoliberal fusion between work and action. We will thus critically investigate the kind of work and the kind of action we may be talking about when we talk about dramaturgical practice today, and in fact suggest that the fusion of these terms in 'dramaturgy' has the potential to produce (art)work and at the same time intervene in the social context. In this sense, our proposed approach to dramaturgy is relevant today not only in the way it conceives dramaturgy as a practice that fuses action and work in performance, but also because of the way in which it rearticulates action as a social and political kind of work *in practice.*

First, then, we maintain that this approach to dramaturgical practice comes in contrast to the way that 'practice' may be understood today as one's individual work – 'my practice' – that is meant to, for example, demonstrate specific features, carry an individual (artistic) signature, follow a particular methodology, and take place in specific settings and certain kinds of conditions. Second, it questions an understanding of practice as opposed to theory. Even when one speaks of the way that practice and theory complement each other, this still implies a pre-existing separation and subsequent coming together of the two; instead, the kind of work that we identify as dramaturgical takes place in thinking, doing, making, and writing, in a way that does not privilege either theoretical thinking or performance making as the site of dramaturgical practice, but rather exceeds and makes irrelevant such distinctions. Third, and most importantly, we aim to resist the use of 'practice' as a flattening term that fits everywhere and concerns every mode of human action; it is important for us that the dramaturgical practice we speak of is indeed the result of the working together that takes place in the performance-making process, regardless of the spheres of life and action that such working modes may have implications for. Tendencies and assumptions such as those listed here can lead to an understanding of practice as something that can be controlled and, therefore, subsequently also taught, disseminated, and exploited as a product; this is particularly true in educational spheres (as in training programmes that focus on specific types of 'practices'), but also especially in the way that dramaturgy is supposedly practised, or 'packaged' and 'sold', through guides or manuals, either on 'how to do it successfully' or on how to practice 'it' so that choreography or theatre making will be successful, coherent, or socially relevant.

Instead of succumbing to an understanding of dramaturgy then as a private, corporate, or individual and necessarily 'useful' practice, the book proclaims practising dramaturgy as a catalytic mode of working that has the capacity to activate processes that in today's sociopolitical and economic context could be understood as indirect, inefficient, interfering, or negatively efficient. In this way, we therefore seek to interrogate and reinvent modes of working (together) in the existing neoliberal contexts, ways of being and acting (together) in a world that currently suffers from social and political upheavals, and ways of addressing artistic practice as a public activity. These intersecting spheres of care and concern suggest our need to consider art as a social phenomenon in a way that distinguishes itself from current neoliberal dominant policies of arts councils and several other organizations that fund arts and research in the arts. In particular, we propose a practice-led enquiry as the ground on which we can discuss the relation of arts to society, not by addressing how arts can be 'successfully' quantified and can 'usefully' contribute to society or address political matters or public affairs, but through the lens of a practice that is already a politicized activity, constantly reconfiguring its relationship to art making and the social. In fact, we understand the inclusion of this book into the series *Arts & Society* by Valiz publications as serving a similar purpose, addressing the social through the perspective of an arts-practice enquiry, but at the same time refusing to claim a particular kind of usefulness in relation to any artistic, social, political, or economic agendas.

In Collaboration

Equally important to our attempt to politicize the notion of practice in dramaturgy is the way in which we have worked *dramaturgically* for this project and throughout our collaboration. If we pursued this nomadic endeavour with determination, this is because through this process we were able to address our various artistic, pedagogical, and political concerns precisely by reflecting on the particular conditions in which the work developed. And we investigated those concerns among ourselves but also with others who took part in our collaboration. One of the main purposes of this book then has been to consider the manifold political articulations of dramaturgical practice also through the process of co-authoring a large part of it. In this frame, we would like to briefly reflect here on the dramaturgy of our collaboration, which means seeking to understand and reveal how the work we do together relates to the infrastructures within which we work and how we make decisions in that respect. This aspect of our collaboration can namely provide another rationale for our suggestion to consider dramaturgy as a practice with political implications, rather than as a service or a toolbox for successful work.

In the year of this book's publication, the three of us will have already been collaborating for over six years 'under the radar', so to say, without ever forming an organization or institute. Each project we have initiated together bears a name, but there is no name that refers to us, as a group of researchers working together in the field of performance theory and practice. Due to this non-institutional formation and despite several opportunities that have come across our way, we have also not been eligible to apply for large funds or European Union projects that usually demand a 'planning ahead' attitude and also often lead to greater visibility. We are, one could say, operating at the shadows of 'big' institutional structures and funding bodies. At the same time, however, we do have individual affiliations with several important institutions in Europe (such as universities, research centres, theatres, festivals, and art organizations) that have often supported our projects, including the various research gatherings that formed part of the project 'Dramaturgy at Work'. In fact, it is often precisely by attending to our professional responsibilities that arise from our positions within institutions, and through our complex relations to a variety of organizations as employees or freelance workers, that we have managed over the years to support our projects while exercising relationships simultaneously inside and outside particular systems. This durational and concurrent engagement and disengagement with institutional affiliations reveals, we believe, the dramaturgy of our collaboration. As would be the case with the 'mafia',[17] the actions taken in the frame of our collaborative work (such as projects and initiatives) are rendered visible, whereas the agents that constitute them (us three and others, as well as the structures that are involved each time) are not easy to track.

And yet, as post-Operaist and post-Marxist theorists have shown,[18] in the current neoliberal conditions of work one is expected to self-manage and to be flexible and virtuosic in how she communicates, collaborates, and networks inter/nationally, which is not dissimilar to how we work. These skills, which concern human experience, affect, and communication, on the one hand comprise basic modes of socialization, and on the other have traditionally belonged to the artistic and educational sectors, as many of these theorists have also argued. This becomes problematic when we suspect that we currently constitute the economy that characterizes all spheres of work and labour in the Western world, as we may have arguably been capitalized and transformed into commodities of service and experience. As expected, the educational, artistic, and research institutions in the field of contemporary performance, many of which we have worked with, largely participate in this economy of skills as well. They namely fund, train, and support such skills by being actively involved in the organization and promotions of conferences, gatherings, talks, meetings, exchanges, festivals, and so on. Short-term appointments, temporary collaborations, the expectation of constant availability, quick and quantifiable outcomes and overtime work are also constitutive of this same institutional neoliberal logic; and such institutional structures therefore generate precarious conditions of work (and, by extension, life) by mainly supporting small and short-term research projects, such as this one, one could claim.

Given the above, our collaboration could indeed then be regarded as being fully immersed in this neoliberal paradigm, wherein work and life have been fused, and flexibility is maintained as one works strategically with an inside-outside relationship to institutional structures. Nevertheless, we would argue that the actions we take while necessarily being part of this paradigm also contradict and in some way even exceed it. If we accept that the conditions set up by institutional and governmental structures that constitute the economy of performance theory and practice today (universities, residencies, art schools, theatre venues, art policies, funding systems, and so forth) exploit cultural workers, then through our work we have been trying to outgrow these structures. We are namely seeking to sustain a durational collaboration that cannot be confined by the logics of a singular project, while at the same time is not marked by a name or title either; moreover, we pursue this with others who regularly join the projects we set up, relations that again may similarly overuse the temporary frames that are available to us in each case and do not allow us to be grouped with those others under a name either. In this way, instead of simply succumbing to the exigencies and logics of the market, we are in fact utilizing the resources available to us in each instance (often through our connection to institutional structures) to set up gatherings and other sites of exchange that generate modes of production and socialization that do not necessarily fit the neoliberal paradigm. The dramaturgy of our collaboration could thus be regarded as a non-institutionalized dynamic undercurrent between and with several other institutional and independent frames; it could be considered as a kind of ongoing struggle to outgrow neoliberal exploitations of artistic and intellectual practice, but from within our various institutional affiliations and motilities.

What Next?

The question of 'why dramaturgy today?' leads us therefore to an urgent demand to reassess how we understand and practice dramaturgy as a mode of thinking and doing together that is not concerned with specific aesthetics or styles of performance, neither obsesses over proving its sociopolitical relevance; rather, it is a politicized practice itself that provides a ground on which to address artistic production by working within structures and reimagining our relation to them at the same time, in order to produce something that exceeds them, a socialization perhaps that cannot be restricted either to the confines of an artistic project or to a collaboration, nor consequently to the logics of the neoliberal market.

In order to speak to this demand, in Part I of the book that follows, which has been co-authored by us three editors, we start by unfolding three key working principles: mobilizing questions, alienating and commoning. These arose out of the workshops and roundtable discussions that formed part of this project. They are principles that lie at the heart of the dramaturgical practice proposed here, and aim to open up, destabilize, and problematize what happens in the encounters between bodies, materials, and ideas that produce performance. We then draw attention to the specific catalytic function that such principles suggest, and in this way introduce dramaturgy as a catalytic operation within artistic creation that produces (re)actions that in turn open up and move a work forward without interfering in or controlling it. This leads us to consider a return to the etymology of dramaturgy (deriving from the Greek *'drama'* = action and *'ergon'* = work), in order to scrutinize the term further through the notions of action and work. We do this by referring to Hannah Arendt and Aristotle, who have drawn distinctions between the concepts of action, work, and labour, but also by engaging with more recent debates on post-Fordist labour that potentially require a renewed understanding of terms such as 'work' and 'action'. Finally, we arrive at our suggestion for an understanding of dramaturgy as a particular type of politicized practice that sets actions in motion within artistic contexts in a more speculative rather than prescriptive way.

Part II of the book opens up to include different artistic, social, and political perspectives that such understandings of dramaturgy may give rise to, through contributions by guest writers with distinct backgrounds and areas of research. This does not only result in an understanding of dramaturgy that somehow borders on different disciplines and modes of thinking — crossing over between the fields of dance, theatre, performance, theory, and the domain of the social — but also in the suggestion of a common ground for artistic and philosophical concerns, particularly, as we will have shown, through the lens of our proposed attention to action and work.

The multiplicity of perspectives that arises out of the individual texts offers, in other words, new ways to readdress the

urgency of our main question of interest: Why dramaturgy today? The texts do this in a variety of ways. Some directly refer to or reflect on ideas and practices that were developed as part of the research exchange meetings that took place in the frame of the project 'Dramaturgy at Work', in order to exemplify a shift in the authors' thinking or practice that occurred as a result of one such meeting. Other authors depart from an initial question or point of concern we offered in one of these events to draw connections to their own particular practices and thinking, or even stage tensions between our main proposal in this book and other understandings of dramaturgy. Some texts therefore complement, counter-balance, or even challenge some of the positions we have offered here, returning, for example, to the role of the dramaturg in particular, or considering different temporalities of dramaturgy from the one we have focused on here. In this sense, this second part of the book is a collection of texts that share a series of interrelated encounters as their starting point, but tackle different topics, present distinct propositions, and take on various formats.

It has always been our aim to include in the project practitioners whose primary mode is writing (academics, theorists, dramaturgs, and so on), but also others for whom writing may be an accompanying practice to the other modes in which they work (choreographers, theatre makers, and so on). The book reflects this in its staging of different relationships to writing itself as a practice. Some authors have therefore pursued an argumentative tone, engaging with critical discourse around dramaturgy and beyond, while others have attempted to practice dramaturgy through different forms of writing. Similarly, just like we as editors do not consider dramaturgy as our sole area of expertise, we have invited here texts by both dramaturgs and researchers who engage directly with the field of dramaturgy, but also others who have often used their texts as an opportunity to explore precisely how their diverse practices may address, resist, or sit next to dramaturgy. These texts therefore operate themselves as a dramaturgical act of a writing community, rather than a curated collection of expert-texts on dramaturgy. It is hoped that readers too will approach the book through their different relationships to dramaturgy and an interest in asking 'why dramaturgy today?' from within their distinct areas of interest.

Even though the texts included in Part II of the book can be read in any order, they have been grouped under certain headings that suggest a potential direction from specific dramaturgical practices to an opening out of thinking in relation to dramaturgy. The first section comprises texts by writers who identify as dramaturgs and have a shared interest in dramaturgy as a relational practice. Guy Cools presents correspondence and ekphrasis as two dialogical practices with choreographers through writing, which also suggests a specific temporality of dramaturgy in relation to the creative process. Departing from a workshop in Brussels, where participants engaged in collaborative tasks that supported them in bringing their individual dramaturgical processes into motion, Nienke Scholts writes on the possibility of a collaboration between two dramaturgs that aims to produce work without, however, serving a particular piece of work, and further examines dramaturgy *of* and *as* collaboration. Jonas Rutgeerts writes in dialogue with choreographer and long-term collaborator Ivana Müller, to offer an understanding of dramaturgy as a networking practice that operates similarly to metabolic systems, constantly adapting in order to digest new information. On the one hand dramaturgy is presented here as having an internal logic that is not uncontrollable but remains speculative in terms of how decisions are made in a creative process, and on the other it is also staged on the page as Rutgeerts offers an argumentative text that is then annotated by Müller who interferes by writing on the margins.

The second section includes texts that engage with questions of otherness in dramaturgy, considering specific instances and experiences of dramaturgical practice in performance making and beyond. Continuing the consideration of dramaturgy as a conversational practice, Joachim Robbrecht focuses on acknowledging the agents engaged in the dramaturgy of a work, as they engage in what he terms 'contagious conversations' that often happen through metaphors, or a practice of 'queering' that requires one to reconfigure what they think they may already know. Jasna Jasna Žmak embarks on a quest to identify what dramaturgs actually do, in the form of a letter to a forensic anthropologist, inviting him (and us) to notice the verbs in dramaturgy, which she claims to be a queer form of practice in the first place. Closing this section, choreographer Nicola Conibere's text stages her own restless relationship to dramaturgy, as the author undergoes a constant process of othering through the very process of writing the text.

A questioning or potential destabilization of dramaturgy is presented in the next section, which includes texts that locate and investigate dramaturgy not only in performance practices, but also in other fields of practice and spheres of life. Simon Bayly tackles the anxiety surrounding the notions of dramaturgy and the dramaturg, as they operate in between knowing, not-knowing, and the navigation of knowledge; the author relates this simultaneous absence and excess of knowledge performed by dramaturgy to artistic practices as well as politics, to show how 'working on actions' could be conceived as an improvisatory method of non-dramaturgy that addresses the relationship between the studio and 'the streets', not by leaving its anxieties behind but by making them the object of its own enquiry. Examining her own anxious relationship to dramaturgy, Betina Panagiotara attempts to tease out the dramaturgical processes involved in her theoretical research on dance that takes the form of scholarly writing. Una Bauer problematizes what she identifies as a dramaturgy of 'impersonal sociability' that arises when art blends with social practices, while Arabella Stanger engages with the concept of sabotage as a particular dramaturgical operation that testifies to the working of actions that seek to destructure a system, whether aesthetical, sociopolitical, or economic, during the live performance itself.

The fourth and final section of Part II considers and imagines different scales in which dramaturgy may operate. Inviting us to undertake an exercise in attention that she devised with collaborator Julia Willms, and to do so through our very reading of the text, Andrea Božić proposes dramaturgy as a cosmology-in-the-making, that is practised through divided attention, aiming to create a space where we may imagine and exercise other possible realities to the one in which we live. Augusto Corrieri questions the anthropocentric bias that is apparent in current understandings of dramaturgy, in order to consider both a cosmic and a microcosmic dimension of dramaturgy outside the theatre and within.

In the concluding epilogue of the book, we stage a written conversation among us editors, in order to foreground and unpack the differences, divisions, and antagonisms between us, as well as the diversity of contexts we are placed in, and the way that the ethical-political-social imperatives we outline here sit within the full range of our 'professional lives'. In other words, this last part aims to revisit through the lens of this project the urgency of the abovementioned 'had to' that set forth this book and the project that led to it as an imperative gesture. Our hope is that in this last section we also offer an instance of practising dramaturgy as a catalytic mode of working, in this case through a particular type of co-writing that attends to our coming and creating together.

Notes

1 For a full list of the workshops and roundtable discussions and the distinct contexts in which these took place in the frame of the project, see: www.dramaturgyatwork.wordpress.com.

2 For recent dramaturgy-related discourse, see indicatively:
a. conferences and other research events and projects: 'PLAY – Relational Aspects of Dramaturgy', Ghent, Belgium, 15–16 March 2012; 'International Seminar of New Dramaturgies', Murcia, Spain, 2010; 'European Dramaturgy in the Twenty-first Century', Frankfurt am Main, Germany, 27–30 September 2007; *Dramaturgies Project*, 2001: www.dramaturgies.net.
b. thematic journal issues: 'New Dramaturgies', *Contemporary Theatre Review* 20, no. 2 (2010); 'Practical Dramaturgy', *Maska* XVI, nos. 131–132 (2010); 'On Dramaturgy', *Performance Research* 14, no. 3 (2009); 'On Dramaturgy', *Theaterschrift* 5–6 (1994); *Women & Performance: A Journal of Feminist Theory* 13, no. 2 (2003).
c. books: Hansen and Callison, *Dance Dramaturgy*; Romanska, *Routledge Companion to Dramaturgy*; Trencsényi, *Dramaturgy in the Making*; Trencsényi and Cochrane, *New Dramaturgy*; Bellisco, Cifuentes and Ecija, eds. *Rethinking Dramaturgy*; Turner and Behrndt, *Dramaturgy and Performance*; Luckhurst, *Dramaturgy*; Rudakoff and Thomson, *Between the Lines*; Jonas, Proehl and Lupu, *Dramaturgy in American Theatre*; Cardullo, *What is Dramaturgy?*

3 Van Kerkhoven, 'Introduction', in 'On Dramaturgy', p. 8.

4 Lepecki, '"We are Not Ready for the Dramaturge"', p. 187.

5 Turner and Behrndt, *Dramaturgy and Performance*, p. 170.

6 Cvejić, 'The Ignorant Dramaturg', p. 4l.

7 Here we borrowed from Cvejić (ibid., p. 41), who uses the phrase 'unfolding the many dramaturgies' to discuss the multiple questions, cases, and affairs involved in the study of dramaturgy today.

8 Bleeker, 'Thinking No-One's Thought', p. 67.

9 Romanska, *The Routledge Companion to Dramaturgy*, p. 11.

10 Heathfield, 'Dramaturgy without a Dramaturge', p. 115.

11 Turner and Behrndt, *Dramaturgy and Performance*, p. 3.

12 Ruhsam, 'Dramaturgy of and as Collaboration', p. 29.

13 For example, Heathfield ('Dramaturgy without a Dramaturge', p. 106) has criticized views that approach dramaturgy as a process of shaping, ordering, cohering, and making sense. And he has argued that it is the necessity of such cohesions of sense and sedimentation of meaning in a work that contemporary dramaturgical functions need to question. Drawing from the work of Bojana Bauer and Bojana Cvejić, Pil Hansen ('Introduction', pp. 12–13) has recently also discussed dramaturgy as a practice that serves the mobilization of a process rather than one that seeks to define it – a practice that insists on creative exploration and research against 'norms and complacency of success that lead to recognizable products'.

14 This notion of dramaturgy as a catalytic operation first emerged in discussions with our advisor for this publication, Ric Allsopp, during a residency in Falmouth, UK, June 2015.

15 Heathfield, 'Dramaturgy without a Dramaturge', p. 105.

16 See, respectively: Heathfield, ibid., p. 105; Turner and Behrndt, *Dramaturgy and Performance*, p. 3; Badco./Medak, 'Post-hoc Dramaturgy', www.youtube.com/watch?v=FIo7Sd1waLQ and Kostanić 'Post-hoc Dramaturgy', bezimeni.files.wordpress.com/2011/10/1_whatever3_kostanic1.pdf.

17 Performance artist Janez Janša, a regular collaborator and interlocutor in some of our research projects, used the term 'Greek mafia' to refer to our co-working modes during our encounter in Syros, Greece, as part of the project 'Syros: A Bet on the Potentiality of Cooperation' (July 2013). See the resulting *Maska* issue with the same title (nos. 169–171, Spring–Summer 2015) for the texts that came out of that project.

18 For instance: Lazzarato, 'Immaterial Labour'; Virno, *A Grammar of the Multitude*; and Hardt and Negri, *Empire*.

Bibliography

- BadCo./Medak, Tomislav. 'Post-hoc Dramaturgy'. November 2010, YouTube. www.youtube.com/watch?v=FIo7Sd1waLQ (accessed: 13 April 2016).
- Behrndt, Synne and Cathy Turner, eds. 'New Dramaturgies'. *Contemporary Theatre Review* 20, no. 2 (2010).
- Bellisco, Manuel, María José Cifuentes and Amparo Ecija, eds. *Rethinking Dramaturgy: Errancy and Transformation*. Madrid: Centro Párraga, Centro de Documentación y Estudios Avanzados de Arte Contemporáneo, 2011.
- Bleeker, Maaike. 'Thinking No-One's Thought'. In *Dance Dramaturgy: Modes of Agency, Awareness and Engagement*, ed. by Pil Hansen and Darcey Callison, pp. 67-84. London: Palgrave MacMillan, 2015.
- Brizell, Cindy and André Lepecki, eds. *Women & Performance: A Journal of Feminist Theory* 13, no. 2 (2003).
- Cardullo, Bert. *What is Dramaturgy?* New York: Peter Lang Publishing, 1995.
- Cvejić, Bojana. 'The Ignorant Dramaturg'. *Maska* XVI, nos. 131-132 (2010), pp. 40-53.
- Eckersall, Peter. 'Towards an Expanded Dramaturgical Practice: A Report on "The Dramaturgy and Cultural Intervention Project"'. *Theatre Research International* 31, no. 3 (2006), pp. 283-97.
- Eckersall, Peter and Eddie Paterson. 'Slow Dramaturgy: Renegotiating Politics and Staging the Everyday'. *Australasian Drama Studies* 58 (2011), pp. 178-92.
- Gritzner, Karoline, Patrick Primavesi and Heike Roms, eds. 'On Dramaturgy'. Special issue, *Performance Research* 14, no. 3 (2009).
- Hansen, Pil and Darcey Callison, eds. *Dance Dramaturgy: Modes of Agency, Awareness and Engagement*. London: Palgrave MacMillan, 2015.
- Hardt, Michael and Antonio Negri. *Empire*. Cambridge, MA: Harvard University Press, 2000.
- Heathfield, Adrian. 'Dramaturgy without a Dramaturge'.

In *Rethinking Dramaturgy, Errancy and Transformation*, ed. by Manuel Bellisco, María José Cifuentes and Amparo Ecija, pp. 105-16. Madrid: Centro Párraga, Centro de Documentación y Estudios Avanzados de Arte Contemporáneo, 2011.
- Jonas, Susan, Geoffrey S. Proehl and Michael Lupu, eds. *Dramaturgy in American Theatre: A Source Book*. Belmont, CA: Wadsworth Publishing Co Inc, 1996.
- Kostanić, Marko. 'Post-hoc Dramaturgy'. *WHATEVER* 3 (2010). https://bezimeni.files.wordpress.com/2011/10/1_whatever3_kostanic1.pdf (accessed: 13 April 2016).
- Lazzarato, Maurizio. 'Immaterial Labour'. Generation Online, 1997. www.generation-online.org/c/fcimmateriallabour3.htm (accessed: 19 April 2016).
- Lehmann, Hans-Thies. *Postdramatic Theatre*. London and New York: Routledge, 2006.
- Lepecki, André. '"We are Not Ready for the Dramaturge": Some Notes for Dance Dramaturgy'. In *Rethinking Dramaturgy, Errancy and Transformation*, ed. by Manuel Bellisco, María José Cifuentes and Amparo Ecija, pp. 181-97. Madrid: Centro Párraga, Centro de Documentación y Estudios Avanzados de Arte Contemporáneo, 2011.
- Luckhurst, Mary. *Dramaturgy: A Revolution in Theatre*. Cambridge, MA: Cambridge University Press, 2006.
- Romanska, Magda, ed. *The Routledge Companion to Dramaturgy*. London and New York: Routledge, 2015.
- Rudakoff, Judith and Lynn M. Thomson, eds. *Between the Lines: The Process of Dramaturgy*. Toronto: Playwrights of Canada Press, 2002.
- Ruhsam, Martina. 'Dramaturgy of and as Collaboration'. *Maska* XVI, nos. 131-132 (2010), pp. 28-35.
- Trencsényi, Katalin. *Dramaturgy in the Making*. London: Bloomsbury, 2015.
- Trencsényi, Katalin and Bernadette Cochrane, eds. *New Dramaturgy*. London: Bloomsbury, 2014.
- Turner, Cathy and Synne Behrndt. *Dramaturgy and Performance*.

Hampshire: Palgrave MacMillan,
2008.

— Van Kerkhoven, Marianne, ed.
'On Dramaturgy', ed. by Marianne
Van Kerkhoven. Special issue,
Theaterschrift 5-6 (1994).

— Virno, Paolo. *A Grammar of the
Multitude*. New York: Semiotext[e],
2004.

Part I

Dramaturgy as Working on Actions

Konstantina Georgelou
Efrosini Protopapa
Danae Theodoridou

Principles for Dramaturgy

The project that led to the writing of this book developed through a sequence of research encounters that took place in a variety of institutional frames for dance, theatre, and performance (university departments, research and residency centres, production houses, independent academies, and a squatted theatre) and throughout different parts of Europe — in Belgium, the Netherlands, Great Britain, Croatia, Greece, and Spain. In a series of two- or three-day workshops followed by public roundtable discussions, dramaturgical practice was explored from several perspectives, including the following: identifying dramaturgical tendencies (formal, aesthetic, structural) in contemporary performance; developing concepts and methodologies for performance making; examining feedback, critical and creative response as dramaturgical activity; pursuing dramaturgy as the creation of actions in artistic work; and devising working frames in dramaturgical processes with an awareness of their relation to institutional critique and their potential for producing social imaginings. For each workshop we prepared and facilitated anew different set-ups that would allow the participants and ourselves to delve into a practising of dramaturgy from the proposed perspective. Departing from the work that took place in these interconnected events, this section of the book starts by outlining three key principles that arose from critical reflection on the workshops and roundtable discussions: mobilizing questions, alienating, and commoning. The examination of these principles will lead us later on to discuss dramaturgy as a catalytic type of operation. Prior to their discussion, we will briefly outline how the workshops were conceived and organized, as well as the ways in which we draw on them here so as to subsequently develop our larger argument on dramaturgy as 'working on actions'.

While task-oriented, the workshops aimed to open a space for individual and collective work to occur starting from the projects that the participants were independently engaged in and wanted to further work on during the workshops. The first day usually focused on 'what is already there', in the sense that participants were given a framework in which to reflect on the relationship between their diverse practices and dramaturgy. The second and/or third day aimed to push participants' work further, often through techniques of distraction, distancing, and interruption. Individually and in groups we practised care and exchange through exercises of conceptualization, writing, and composition, without, however, blending the diverse practices in the room or forcing collaboration in the sense of 'making with' someone whose materials and tools could be different from our own; rather, participants were encouraged to problematize, shift, disrupt, or interrogate one another, and in this way support their peers' working practices. Participants were thus invited to activate dramaturgical modi operandi: practising attentiveness to details and to decision-making while developing working methods for their (artistic) work with an understanding of the ways in which it is meant to be public (that is, to address and concern others as well).

Throughout this process our main intention has been to practice dramaturgy in different circumstances and under diverse conditions (political, social, economic, institutional), while positioning this practice within *and* outside the studio by constantly shifting attention and drawing circles that weave together artistic methodologies and socio-political concerns. On the one hand then, the project as a whole, just like this book, moved between and within artistic methods and socio-political enquiries, in order to explore ways in which we come to meet, exchange, work, and create together. On the other hand, it is important to underline that we consider this as a specifically arts practitioners' endeavour. Even if we did not articulate this as explicitly at the start of the project, it seems that at its heart has always been the question of how we may work dramaturgically today. We question the limits and possibilities, scope, and relevance of dramaturgy as a practice that is both artistic and socio-political by its very nature and in its implications. Hence the methodology of the overall project has not been one of developing a series of situations in which to practically test (pre-formulated) hypotheses and positions on dramaturgy inside and outside the studio. Similarly, the explorations, methods, modes, and means of working, or the range of interactive, interventionist, and interrogative tools that we developed, were not used as a way of arriving at a new definition of dramaturgical methodology, or an instrumental approach to producing or analysing performance work. Rather, the workshops and research exchanges we set up served as a means of identifying and defining key principles in the work of others and our own that inform our understanding of dramaturgy as we perceive its relevance today through a simultaneously artistic and socio-political lens.

For this reason, we will not be concerned here with capturing or reporting what went on in the workshops, but with detecting the main operations initiated through the practical tasks developed during the project, and with identifying the particular quality they brought to both our work and that of the participants. We therefore start by discussing three principles that emerged through the project and through which we will then propose dramaturgy as a catalytic operation that produces what we will describe as a process of working on actions. In the same way that the workshops did not aim to offer tools but frames for working dramaturgically, the book too presents these three interconnected principles as underlying and occurring from a series of dramaturgical tasks, rather than tools or methodologies for dramaturgy. Even if we sometimes refer to workshop tasks, points that were raised in the roundtable discussions, as well as others' practices, this is to help us unfold the details of each proposed principle rather than because such an instance encapsulates or demonstrates one of the discussed principles; in fact, it may be that more than one of these principles underlies a specific task that we refer to. Neither do we propose a practising of these principles in any particular order. Any reference to tasks and exercises in this sense is meant to facilitate a return to specific instances that reveal how our understanding of the proposed principles — namely, mobilizing questions, alienating, and commoning — stems from an engagement with processes of working on actions *in practice* and *with others*.

Mobilizing Questions

One simple rule: you always answer a question with a new question! If desired, a specific topic can be set in order to guide the line of questions.[1]

Inspired by the above instruction — through which a group of artists who participated in the project '6 MONTHS 1 LOCATION (6M1L)'[2] led a Skype conversation — in many workshops we invited participants to practice conversing as a group, through questions only. The task was to reply not *to* the question but *with* a question, which required focusing on what is at stake in the question being asked and thinking through how this question could be further questioned and taken forward. We often offered the starting question, setting the focus of the discussion in a way that was suitable to that particular workshop,[3] and practised for forty to forty-five minutes, to allow the group the time needed to get into a state of questioning, to start thinking through questions. Notably, we usually tried this task after participants had spent some time working individually, as a 'warm-up' to get us all tuned into the group before working together; in other words, this practice marked the passage from individual work to togetherness, the overall aim being to start *thinking together in questions*. Similarly, we sometimes proposed that participants interview either one another or themselves (self-interview), paying particular attention to the kinds of questions they would ask in order to detect the dramaturgical in their practice, from whichever perspective they work (as, for instance, artists, writers, dramaturgs, curators, or pedagogues). There are at least two aspects that interest us here, and that form the basis of the principle of mobilizing questions, through which we propose that a certain type of dramaturgical practice may function: first, the articulation of questions that have a capacity to mobilize a process and, second, the mobilization of questions themselves through certain dramaturgical operations. In this sense, we conceive of dramaturgy not as the mere formulation and asking of questions, but as a process that works with questions as its actual material and in this way triggers their very mobilization. In other words, we understand the activity of dramaturgy as the 'motor' that makes questions appear, while such questions also function to activate the work itself. Furthermore, as we will show, we consider both these two understandings of the principle as potentially connected to exercising modes of togetherness.

The practice and purpose of questioning in processes of performance making is undoubtedly not something new. This is probably related to the ways in which uncertainty, un-knowing, and doubt have been foregrounded as significant, or even desirable qualities in creative processes.[4] And, as we shall see, questions and acts of questioning have also appeared as materials in performance works themselves. At the same time, the notions of togetherness, collaboration, and cooperation have also been at the forefront of discourses on performance and beyond,[5] even though the meaningfulness and validity of such terms have likewise been questioned.[6] While we will return to this latter set of terms as part of the third principle proposed in this section —

that of commoning – a brief reference here to examples that have brought questioning to the foreground of artistic creation helps demonstrate how the principle of mobilizing questions builds on and to some extent departs from these propositions; our aim is to show how we may understand such a principle as proposing a type of *dramaturgical thinking*, but also as seeking to establish *new relations* between the agents involved in an artistic process, as well as between such agents and the work itself.

A key example to look at here is Jonathan Burrows and Jan Ritsema's work *Weak Dance Strong Questions* (2001). This dance performance takes the form of an improvisation, where the two men attempt to dance questions, or else to ask questions by moving – asking question after question, questioning continuously, as they say.[7] Usefully, Bojana Cvejić clarifies that after a series of rehearsals, the two artists changed their focus, from dancing questions, to dancing 'in the state of questioning, which is itself not doubted', in other words 'bringing their bodies to a state in which they make the movement question itself through itself'.[8] Although from a different perspective, one could argue that Deborah Hay's practice of practising a hypothetical 'What if...?' question is not dissimilar.[9] Rather than asking the dancer to move to the question, she asks that the question informs the overall state of the performer whatever action they may be doing.

Both of these two artistic experiments are referred to here not because they exemplify a specific type of dramaturgical approach, but because they already hint at an important distinction with regard to the practice of questioning in performance that is relevant when looking at its function within dramaturgical practice as well. It is perhaps a common understanding that, as a practice, dramaturgy involves asking lots of questions; the dramaturg, for example, questions decisions, actions, stagings, intentions, and through a dialogue with the maker and other collaborators, seeks to unpack the logical connections, necessities, and discrepancies in such artistic choices. But in this case, we would further need to ask: What kinds of questions does dramaturgy ask? How are they formulated? Are there more or less 'useful' questions to ask? Moreover, is there an expectation here that such questions aim at specific answers? And what kinds of actions would such questions produce as part of a process and in the work itself? How would one ask questions? And how would that activate a process? Already in this understanding there is an underlying assumption that questioning in and of itself leads to a desired result, something inherently 'good' that dramaturgy helps the process get to, the unveiling of the work perhaps. Similarly, this approach could run the danger of fetishizing uncertainty, the search for the unknown, or even an aesthetics of failure, an image of productive confusion brought about as a result of constant questioning.[10] It is worth then returning here to Burrows and Ritsema's distinction between 'dancing questions' and dancing 'the state of questioning which itself is not doubted'. Instead of considering a practice of asking questions as a way to find answers, or as perpetual questioning for its own sake, could we instead imagine questioning as an active type of practice, whose certainty and clarity gives it a mobilizing force? In this case, it would be possible to even depart from the precise form of asking questions and instead opt for any mode of doing that exercises a state of questioning *as an attitude*, not necessarily within one's performative actions only (as is the case with Burrows and Ritsema), but within any kind of actions involved in the making process (including that of thinking).

When coining the term 'the ignorant dramaturg', Cvejić already departed from the problematic understanding of the dramaturg as someone who observes a process from the outside and has the right questions to ask that will 'improve' or 'fix' the work, the one who 'knows better', and who can predict how the audience will react to a performance.[11] Instead, she has proposed the figure of the dramaturg as the 'co-creator of a problem' and explained that a problem in this case produces a methodology of inventing constraints that will act as enabling conditions for the work to be created.[12] Furthermore, she has argued:

> As questioning nowadays is a domesticated and worn out truism about almost any intellectual activity, questions by which a problem is posed are distinguished by the answers that they give rise to. So the problem is measured by the solution it merits — if this solution is an invention that brings into being something new, to what did not exist or what might never have happened.[13]

In this sense, for Cvejić, raising a problem implies the construction of terms in which the problem will be stated, but also the conditions in which it will be solved. Herein, however,

lies another distinction we would like to draw in relation to the principle of mobilizing questions as we mean it here. In Cvejić's proposition, there is still some emphasis placed upon the arrival at a resolution of the problem through performance. Questions here work to 'slowly eliminate the known possibilities to enable the production of a qualitatively new problem', 'a new dispositive', as she has claimed.[14] The posing of the problem therefore works as a speculation, as she further suggests, which will lead to a future-perfect tense of a performance, a 'will have had'.[15] Instead, mobilizing questions opens up a space by problematizing and does not expect or anticipate a resolution, even though it may produce both actions, and the conditions in which such actions take place. In a way, Cvejić is primarily concerned with the ways in which (choreographic) problems shape a performance, whereas we would like to draw attention here to the activity of mobilizing questions itself, as part of dramaturgical practice, and regardless of whether and how such a practice may lead to a performance outcome.

Notably, after practising conversing in questions in workshops, participants would often be in a position to recall the moments when the questions had produced new thought and when the task had 'failed'. Dramaturgy, we would argue, emerged when a space for thought was opened up through a process of multiplying or exhausting questions that created a shift. In this case, the questions seemed to activate a process of thinking together, rather than presenting us with a need to answer. Without turning into an exhaustive list created through association, they generated a forward movement, not a lateral or horizontal movement, such as the one we would describe as taking place in brainstorming, for example. Such a movement of thought suggests a particular kind of action that has a specific direction, even though it neither reaches towards a resolution, nor exhausts itself in doubting.[16] Hence the mobilization of questions that we propose as a practice creates, frames, and expands the grounds on which action can take place. In fact, we would suggest that in performance this ground includes the spectator, so that they too are invited to follow the movement from one thought to the next, from one action to the next.

Finally, we would like to suggest that, whereas the process of asking, posing, or answering questions may belong to someone (an author, whether dramaturg or other), mobilizing questions does not (and cannot) belong to anyone by its very nature as a directed movement of thought. Rather, by practising it one comes to disown one's thinking; such challenging of individual authorship does not only lead to a proposition about co-authorship, but allows the work to author itself, to think in its own terms, as it were. This could be an instantiation of what Maaike Bleeker has described as 'thinking no-one's thought', a notion that she has proposed as a general mode of dramaturgical work and to which we shall return again later.[17] Here she understands thinking as 'a material practice that proceeds through enactment', that emerges 'through something that mediates between the people involved' but also 'between people and things'.[18] We would further suggest then that 'thinking no-one's thought' could be achieved through specific (material) practices of disowning and therefore opening up images, tasks, solutions, imaginations. Interestingly, albeit from a different perspective, physicist David Bohm has proposed a form of collective dialogue that seems to be aimed at precisely what Bleeker describes: a 'stream of meaning' between people thinking together, which is capable of producing a collective movement of values, meanings, and intentions.[19] The necessity for such a practice arises, in his view, out of the need for us to identify 'systemic faults' in thinking, given that, as he has claimed, thought doesn't know it is doing something and then struggles against what it is doing.[20] In other words, Bohm has stressed that thinking is already doing and that we need to train producing flows of meaning together, so as to reach the possibility of direct insight that a collective moment of thought can achieve. As physicist Nichol Lee has further noted, while we often associate insight with the 'a-ha!' phenomenon of having suddenly grasped the significance of some puzzle or problem, and even though Bohm does not necessarily exclude this type of instance, what is more interesting, however, is that he extends the notion of insight to a much more general, and generative, level of application, an 'active energy' that reorders thought processes themselves.[21]

And yet, there is nothing to suggest that this process of mobilizing questions and collectively disowning thought, as informed by Bleeker and Bohm, could not be pursued individually. One could read Nicola Conibere's contribution to this book, for example, as precisely that: a piece of writing that arose as if in an attempt to respond to a series of questions and then allowed itself to be further mobilized and disowned through such questions. The text is an expanded version of a statement Conibere offered as part of a roundtable discussion that took place in London (September 2015), before which we had sent her a series of questions to consider. She started her presentation by admitting:

> Whilst it was clear that I did not have to answer all, or any, of these questions, each sent me reeling a little bit. And so, I found myself attempting to answer all of the questions, through a desire to find something like a complete answer to just one of them. This was a mistake, but it is what I have to share with you.[22]

Conibere's statement subsequently staged her attempt to respond to the questions, to approach them again, differently, and through this process to reveal the unfolding of shifting perspectives, a desire to engage with the task as someone or something else, renewing the task itself on the way. As is the case with her text published in this book, one senses here a sense of destabilization, what the author herself describes as 'a form of dramaturgical interference', as she starts writing in the first person, and then moves on to third-person female, followed by third-person male, and finishing in third-person plural. Interestingly enough, she finally suggests that all this thinking, shifting, and constant changing, is capable of producing a 'single form', even if that was not the initial intention. This reminds us of a claim by Hélène Cixous that a writer disowns,[23] which would suggest in this case that this kind of dramaturgical interference produced through the process of mobilizing questions does not resemble a mode of thinking that is one of pinning down an argument — or owning the resolution of a problem, to refer back to Cvejić — but is rather constantly disowning through further questioning. Depersonalizing dramaturgy in this way suggests that questions are to be found in the 'work' that is done, while at the same time it is the mobilization of such questions that produces further work. And it is in this way perhaps that the reader or, in the case of performance, the spectator, is invited to further mobilize the questions themselves and be mobilized by them — in other words, to allow the work to do its work and take them to that place of disowning, letting go of the 'a-ha!' moment in favour of a reordering of thought itself, in Bohm's terms.

Alienating

> *Divide into groups of four. One person from the group*
> *interviews a second person from the group about an*
> *artistic project the latter is currently working on and the*
> *dramaturgical aspects involved in it. A third person interrupts*
> *the interviewee regularly by giving her instructions to:*
> *start (a new sentence); replace (a word); close eyes; open*
> *eyes; reverse (the direction of her thoughts); pause; reduce*
> *(the number of words used); repeat; reposition (words in a*
> *different context); end. At the same time, the fourth person*
> *in the group notes words, terms, sentences, and ideas heard*
> *in the interview, that seem important for them and relate*
> *to the art project discussed, each one on a different Post-it.*
> *When done, this fourth person adds on separate Post-its*
> *their own thoughts, ideas, terms that came to mind while*
> *listening, before eventually offering all their notes to the*
> *interviewee. This lasts twelve to fifteen minutes. Then the*
> *people in the group change roles and start again.*[24]

Philosopher Miika Luoto has described the particularity of the work of art as something that 'stems from human activity but essentially exceeds that activity'.[25] This means that although it is of course one or more people who bring an artwork forth, this work cannot be conceived merely as the 'product' of their efforts. On the contrary, these efforts allow the coming forth of something else, according to Luoto. This 'something else' resides in the work itself and it is its own 'working', its own productivity.[26] On the one hand, thus, an artwork's existence is dependent on the creative practice initiated by those involved in it (such as makers, performers, and dramaturgs). On the other, the creativity of that practice and the final product that derives from it differ from the scope of its creators. It is in this sense, as Luoto has interestingly noted, that a work 'differs from itself' being creative and a beginning in itself.[27]

At the same time, André Lepecki has discussed tensions that derive among those '*who are supposed to hold knowledge*' over the work being created' (authors, makers, performers, dramaturgs), as opposed to the situation of artistic encounters wherein all collaborators work for the piece to come, without necessarily knowing what it truly is about, what it wants, or what it needs.[28]

And he has argued that a work *'owns its own authorial force'*.[29] It is for this reason that, according to Lepecki, dramaturgy should not be understood as a practice connected with notions such as knowledge, authorship, or ownership as may usually be the case. If dramaturgy is not conceived as a set of tools for 'knowing' in the service of the maker or any of the other collaborators, though, then how does it take place in the creative process? Or, as Lepecki has aptly put it, 'How does it inhabit this zone of indetermination that is nevertheless very precise, very concrete, and very rigorous?'[30] In order for dramaturgy to enter a zone of precise, concrete, and rigorous indetermination and *allow* the piece that no one knows to become actual, we should invent anew a mode of experimenting, a mode of rehearsing that will allow us to operate from 'a place of quasi-nothingness' the writer has posited.[31]

During the workshops that took place as part of the project 'Dramaturgy at Work', we became highly attentive to the abovementioned particularities of the artwork and aimed to delve deeper into possible ways to approach, understand, and work with its 'differing'. If, indeed, what is initiated in the frame of a creative process will always differ from what at some later point will be called the 'work' that derived from such a process, how can one move towards this work? If those involved in a creation will never know their work, since this will always exceed their scope, how can they act towards it, how can they relate to and work for it? Placing ideas such as those of Luoto and Lepecki at the centre of our dramaturgical concerns, however, does not mean arguing for the re-autonomization of an artwork that acts independently from its context and the people involved in it. In contrast to such modernist ideas, we rather wish to point to what is common in a work, what all collaborators share outside each one's distinct role and perspectives. In this sense we share Adrian Heathfield's understanding of dramaturgy as a common 'responsibility towards (and response to) that which is immanent in a given performance, its phenomena and forms of representation';[32] a movement distributed across the various performing agents in the room and across various theoretical, critical, and artistic thinking and operating modes – a movement across diverse disciplines and cultural sites, that does not belong to any one of them. In other words, we refer to an attentiveness, responsibility, and response to what emerges from *working together.*

Within this frame, we devised and suggested tasks for the workshops that would assist this working together and open up different kinds of spaces between the participants, their work, and the work of others. With tasks such as the one described above, we put forth a process of continuous transformation of each participant's project as it was developing. As a consequence, participants' understanding of what their work was or could be sometimes became more distant and others came closer to their initial thoughts and expectations. As others interrogated, interrupted, or documented in writing the principles of a participant's project, intervening and positioning themselves in relation to it, participants were (re)introduced to their own work through the eyes and projections of others. This process allowed one's project not to be changed necessarily, but certainly to be revisited and reimagined. In this way, the projects that participants decided to focus on during the workshops inhabited what Lepecki has called 'this zone of indetermination'; continuous and distracting directives made them precise but at the same time unfixed in one position alone. In order, thus, to sustain such elements of unpredictability and estrangement during the artistic process, we shall propose here the principle of 'alienating' as a crucial one for dramaturgy.

The notion of alienation is not new in the context of theatre. Bertolt Brecht was one of the first to use it as a key term in his work. Already in 1935, in his essay 'Alienation Effects in Chinese Theatre', he described it as an effort 'directed to playing in such a way that the audience was hindered from simply identifying itself with the characters in the play'.[33] Spectators, according to Brecht, should not relate to the stage actions via the subconscious or any kind of empathy. For him, acceptance or rejection of these actions and utterances should take place only on a conscious level. Instead of limiting alienation to the audience's reception, considering it once more as a carefully constructed tool in the hands of those who 'know' (the director, the actor, the dramaturg), a tool used to address the ignorant spectator who has to think consciously, we suggest alienating working modes here as an important dramaturgical principle and concrete directive in the making of the artwork, too.

A significant question arises at this point: *How* can such alienation take place in one's own work? There are possibly many ways in which this can happen, which relate directly to the particular characteristics of each artistic project. Instead of imposing concrete tasks or tools that can be applied anywhere, then, we would rather stress the importance of the presence of such processes of alienation in dramaturgical work, as a significant principle in itself. In effect, we shall also draw here on recent suggestions by Lepecki as well as theatre director Eugenio Barba, who proved to be highly influential for the way tasks connected to alienation and estrangement were approached and devised in the workshops. These ideas are also indicative of the diverse ways in which the alienation principle can be approached in different artistic frames depending on their distinct characteristics and needs.

Lepecki has proposed a methodology of work that draws on errancy, erring, and error as a dramaturgical mode related to not knowing and therefore capable of achieving the alienation that interests us here. His argument is that working via mistaken, incorrect, 'wrong' instructions or starting points can allow one to arrive at possibilities otherwise hidden or censored under the imperative of 'proper use'.[34] When talking about error, alienation, estranging, or not knowing as insightful forces in dramaturgical processes, however, we do not suggest an aesthetics of failing or failure as constitutive of the artwork (although failure's value is also often appreciated). The proposal is rather for developing 'broken compasses' that will misguide or misdirect, without revealing a 'proper' or 'expected' destination, allowing one to be lost, but still getting them somewhere; we therefore talk about finding ourselves in a state of 'not knowing where to go next, but nevertheless going'.[35] What happens in this way, to return to Lepecki, is that one challenges one's self with the terror of not knowing where to go, in order to escape another terror, which is actually even more frightening, that of not knowing how to help a work escape the cliché. Estranging one's self from one's own norms can help them remove the preconceived, established clichés that overflow a work even before it starts – clichés that relate to the way we think about what should be done, how, when, and with what outcome. Such alienation can be achieved in different ways depending on the specific dramaturgical actions each work employs. However, allowing the principle of alienation to affect a work means deciding to go for the 'bad advice', the 'wrong direction', the error, until something else, another glance, something possibly altogether different from what had originally been conceived starts to appear – until one's own clichés start to disappear and something *else* (in Luoto's words) starts to emerge.[36]

Barba has arrived at similar propositions, coming at it from another direction. For him, dramaturgy once more plays a significant role towards distilling into a work *'complex* relationships, capable of *overturning* the obvious ones'.[37] By highlighting the importance of relational aspects in a work, Barba has argued for a dramaturgy that dismisses whatever comes as 'evident' in it. Subsequently, it becomes a process that aims 'to shape, merge, multiply and then overturn the relationships' that establish themselves in one's work. In order to describe this process, Barba has aptly made use of the metaphor of the 'earthquake' that shakes things up, disarranges, and destroys logics revealing unforeseen threads, connections, and relationships.[38] The aim of this earthquake, according to Barba, is not so much to bring forth 'original' inventions but to provide a new potentiality of links and approaches different from those already existing, imagined, and imaginable until then. In the place of Lepecki's 'error', Barba has suggested the voluntary imposition of 'constraints' and 'restrictions' in an artistic process, which helps create such an 'earthquake', an act of forcing unplanned solutions that may lead the work elsewhere.[39] Although we mainly approached the notion of 'constraint' in our workshops in the sense of time-restrictions and the devising of rule-driven tasks (such as the ones mentioned earlier), we consider Barba's suggestion useful in pointing to modes that defamiliarize one with and alienate one from one's own work. We too then consider dramaturgy as capable of reversing facts, making them appear strange and difficult to identify, leading to the unrecognizable.[40] Once more in this case the terror of falling into a void where the parachute may not open, as Barba has wittily put it, is seen as preferable to the terror of giving into a 'proper' way of working. What is offered in return for such anguish certainly deserves the trouble, as it opens up one's work, letting go of the horizon of expectation, and allowing us instead to meet alterity. Or, in Barba's words, it has to do with encountering one's own work, 'seeing it approaching from far away, independent and with a proud life of its own'.[41]

And yet, while proposing similar processes to Lepecki and Barba on alienation and the related notions of unknowing and distracting as central dramaturgical principles, we are also highly aware of the complexities of today's working conditions in an accelerated appropriation system, where whatever one argues for can almost automatically be criticized as the 'new trend', leading to contradictions that become deeply frustrating once one loses a position to defend. We could argue that neoliberalism knows how to co-opt and financialize any creative strategy appropriating every possible working mode with great speed. In this sense, 'not knowing' may become the new 'knowing' in discourses that argue for neo-hippie production modes that are meant to free up our creativity from earlier constraints, which supposedly commit us to specific processes or people instead of opening space for the 'unknown', the 'unexpected', or even the 'impossible'. As philosopher Paolo Virno has argued, 'a certain degree of autonomy or freedom is necessary' in today's production systems, given that a work organized directly by capitalism would not be a profitable one. He has noted that: 'to yield a profit and be useful from the perspective of the capitalist, the work needs to some extent to be established through self-organization'.[42] This easily translates as follows: one should feel encouraged today to not pay any attention to dominant knowledge that restricts one's creativity. One does not need 'to know'. By organizing autonomous, no-strings-attached processes of 'not-knowing', spaces where everything is possible and no commitments (personal but also social and political) are involved, one should feel free to do anything they want – and this is precisely so that clever neoliberal mechanisms can immediately turn such 'unknown', 'groundbreaking' work into a commodity and exploit it accordingly.

Within this frame, we would like to proceed against nihilist views that abolish (or respectively fetishize) either processes of 'knowing' or of 'not knowing' and move towards what we hope is a more carefully balanced proposal. According to our suggestion, 'something else' emerges in a work once the force of not knowing and the desire to know appear together – once we stop prioritizing, evaluating, or announcing the relevance of specific aspects in the work, and we instead become attentive to the diversity of the elements present in it and once we alienate ourselves from what it is that we are doing, in order to rediscover it anew each time. This is what drives the dramaturgical processes discussed here and is offered as a working principle. Instead of proceeding via binaries, then, our take on the dramaturgical function of the alienation principle aligns more with philosopher Richard Kearney's discussion of alienation as a process that subverts our established categories and challenges us to think again by threatening the known with the unknown.[43] Kearney has posited that we should work beyond established ideas, already present since early Western thought, that equate the 'good' with notions of self-identity and sameness, and the 'evil' with notions of exteriority, otherness, and alterity that threaten the pure unity of the soul.[44] Instead of seeing strangeness as something that possesses one's most intimate being or as the alien that needs to be eradicated, the delicate balance between knowing and not knowing should be carefully reconsidered and worked with, Kearney has suggested. As he has accurately remarked, if something or someone becomes '*too transcendent*, they disappear off our radar screen and we lose all contact'.[45] We thus stop seeing them or even conceiving them as this or that thing, which means that we become unable to recognize, imagine, or narrate their alterity. On the other hand, if something or someone becomes too '*immanent*, they become equally exempt from ethical relation'.[46] In this case, they become indistinguishable from one's own self and we are again unable to see them, recognize them, or imagine them as different. It is for this reason that, for the philosopher, one should 'not let the foreign become *too* foreign or the familiar *too* familiar' but constantly try out a variety of crossings between the same and the other, that is, between knowing and not knowing.[47]

Kearney has taken his discussion on otherness even further by connecting it to Jacques Derrida's ideas on hospitality, revealing in this way the social and political implications of the issue. Derrida has declared that 'for pure hospitality or pure gift to occur there must be absolute surprise ... an opening without horizon of expectation ... to the newcomer *whoever that may be*'.[48] If one wishes to eliminate the possibility of the newcomer destroying their house, though, if one wishes to have absolute control on their actions and exclude terrible possibilities in advance, then one can never be hospitable, one can never really welcome someone or something. To truly embrace the other as stranger, then, is to accept a certain decentring of the ego, opening one's self to the novel, the incongruous, and the unexpected. Similarly, according to Kearney, in order to be able to rise to a poetics of new images and an ethics of new practices one has to suspend one's defence mechanisms against alterity.[49]

Betina Panagiotara, in the text that appears in this book, looks back at her participation in one of the workshops. She recalls presenting the way she works to the group and mentioning, among other things, that she always writes with her hair up as this makes her feel more safe. When the presentation is done, another participant responds to her by giving her a note written in red capital letters, which instructs her to 'write with her hair loose'. Panagiotara keeps it on a noticeboard above her desk, and looks at it regularly as she works. And regardless of whether or not she does keep her hair up, she considers this note a recurring reminder of a dramaturgy that, as she describes it, generates doubts that make one shiver about one's practices and that intervene and mess up one's work – a dramaturgy that tickles one's curiosities, builds pathways, provokes dialogues, and doubts any overwhelmingly rational approach towards things and others.[50]

It is in a similar way that the principle of alienation is proposed here, as another reminder note that urges the one who works recurrently and in red capital letters to not be afraid of meeting the 'other' work that is on its way, to not be afraid of hosting it in one's creative processes: an urge that risks suspending defence mechanisms and embracing alienation – not too much, not too little – in order to give rise to a poetics of new images and an ethics of new practices, as Kearney suggested above. Not in the sense of the 'innovative' or the 'unseen/unheard before' but more of the unexpected and unfamiliar: the 'other'.

Commoning

— *Give a 'gift'[51] that can help him/her continue working. This gift should have a specific form. It can be, for example: a wrong instruction; a constraint; an action; a directive; a distraction; a question.*
— *Invent a metaphor that characterizes the way you work and describe it for two minutes to the other people in your group. They will then pose questions aiming to detect working modes, strategies, infrastructures, concerns, and challenges in how you work.*
— *Set-up an experiment that will help you 'test' an aspect of your project with others.[52]*

During the research project 'Dramaturgy at Work' we insisted on devising tasks that invite workshop participants to intervene, question, interfere, and engage with their own as much as with others' working processes, mobilizing a dramaturgical way of working *between many*. The aforementioned tasks are only a few examples of what we tried out in the workshops, which manifest such a process of ongoing sharing and exchange. More specifically, the first one asks participants to respond to someone else's presentation of her working process by, in direct or indirect ways, proposing how that person can continue working. The second requires that one self-reflectively transpose her working processes onto an imaginative realm (that of metaphors), which others will need to join from their perspectives and think through in order to detect methods, infrastructures, and modes that are constitutive of one's way of working. And the third task points to a practice of setting up 'experiments' (for example, game structures, try-outs, and fragmented processes) that open up aspects of the project for others to critically and empirically engage and possibly interfere with. Over the course of the workshops, we namely suggested tasks that directly required appropriation of another's ideas, principles, and methods into one's own work or even more radical formats of working together through scores that derived from each one's artistic projects and were then used to create another single project together.[53] Through these tasks, participants were thus guided to a shared responsibility, engagement, and reconfiguration of one another's works, while these were still in a state of transformation.

Conceiving of exercises that activate ongoing processes of exchange between many parties and through which a state of unbelonging of projects and of ideas emerges, may not be unusual in the context of performance making.[54] It is, however, crucial to look at such processes from a dramaturgical perspective, which points to considering dramaturgy as a practice that puts the idea of plurality 'at work' during and in favour of the development of a specific project. In the context of 'Dramaturgy at Work', the aforementioned tasks were not originally meant to create a space of unbelonging and disowning one's own project, although this may have been one of the consequences. One of the principles that we (the editors) shared and that led to the conception of these tasks is that in order to work dramaturgically during an artistic process and to let an idea/project develop, one has to practice it in relation to others (people, sources, objects, and so forth). It is, hence, precisely the multiple ways of working between many that interested us, as well as the ways in which this proposition can be translated into practical tasks that can mobilize dramaturgical working processes.

When critically reflecting on this aspect of our take on dramaturgy, it appears that we have also been facilitating an articulation of what may be considered as 'commons' among everyone participating in a workshop. This is not to say that we were aiming towards isomorphism of projects and ideas. Rather, such tasks strived for a pluralized and differential process of communicating, working, imagining, and experimenting that makes possible the production of common practices, imaginings, and actions. It is this searching for, articulating, and possibly producing what is 'in common' that could thus be interpreted as a practice of commoning, which constitutes our third working principle for dramaturgy.

The writings about 'commons' by political theorist Isabell Lorey are at the backbone of our theoretical proposition here. Interestingly, Lorey has remarked that in the last decades the *'search for commons (in order to constitute the political), has conspicuously taken place more often in art institutions than in social, political, or even academic contexts'.*[55] Commonality does not mean homogeneity for Lorey, and she has specifically claimed that 'the search for commonality begins from differences and does not end in uniformity; rather, it is accompanied by permanent debates about what counts as the common'.[56] More significantly, Lorey has proposed to search for the commons in the various forms of precarization that humans share in the ways they work and relate with one another today. She has therefore discussed the notion of the 'commons' mainly from a social and political perspective, which is worthwhile to take note of and to then closely relate to the dramaturgical point of view that is herewith explored.

As Lorey has explained in her book *State of Insecurity*, the production of commons is crucial because different dimensions of the 'precarious' have been fused in today's neoliberal world and have led to a normalized state of governmental precarization and social isolation, which have become our shared mode of being and working. Starting with 'precariousness' as the socio-ontological dimension of human vulnerability that points to the constitutive aspect of human sociality and intra-dependence (in the sense that humans cannot survive without one another), and 'precarity' as the vulnerability of specific social groups that suffer from social inequality and are therefore more vulnerable than others (such as refugees and minorities), Lorey has introduced the notion of 'precarization' as more apt for describing today's state of affairs. The latter refers to the type of governmental precarization, that is the continuous biopolitical security measures taken by the state in order to protect the socio-ontological human vulnerability.[57] However, as Lorey has shown, this appropriation of human vulnerability by governmental regimes produces inequalities as well as individualistic subjectivities. That is to say, those regimes assume to secure human vulnerability from (the 'dangerous') others and therefore refute social aspects of interdependence, which are otherwise at the core of human precarity. Hence, the state protects citizens from one another and at the same time upsurges techniques of self-government, which suggests a social mode of isolation and mistrust rather than of interdependence.[58]

In this context, Lorey has additionally suggested that current modes of working that are primarily founded on immateriality – that is, communication and affect – result in a type of production that is to a great extent impossible to manage by means of governmental regimes. She has namely stated that in 'processes of precarization, something unforeseen, contingent and also in this sense precarious arises'.[59] That is, an aspect of precarization that

> harbours the potential of refusal, producing at the same time a re-composition of work and life, of a sociality that is not in this way, not immediately, not so quickly, perhaps even not at all, capitalizable.[60]

Against this backdrop, how can we situate the 'commons' in the direct context of artistic processes, which are also founded on immateriality (that is, affect, experience, language, and movement) and are equally conditioned by regimes of precarity (for example, cuts, privatization, valorization of art on the basis of ticket sales, and temporary projects)? In order to move beyond the idea of an a priori existence of (ontological) commons, we suggest engaging with Lorey's approach again, as she argues that today commons need to first emerge and then be constituted within the state of precarization.[61] This is a crucial thesis, because it requires that we surpass binary assumptions about commonalities and differences, and rather engage in a 'search' that is guided by a certain degree of ignorance and investigates our social and political surroundings. Moving to the context of dramaturgy, we can specifically search for the commons in the apparatuses that aim to draw attention to and create relations during artistic processes. These could be, for instance, directives, proposals, words, movements, experiences, experiments, methods, ideas, decision-making, affects, concepts, infrastructures, problems, institutional structures, and so on. Allowing these apparatuses to emerge and be articulated between many also points to a practice of dramaturgy that engages with the search for commons on several grounds stemming from the artistic, which incorporates the aesthetic, the infrastructural, and the social.

Tasks that expose individual dramaturgical processes to others and in this way open such processes up to potential interventions, interruptions, and possibly transformations by others, are thus hereby understood as operating upon the principle of commoning. Reversing this line of thinking, it could be argued that, in order for dramaturgy to be activated, one needs to experiment with modes of working together, so that dramaturgy in the end is a matter of encounter, exchange, and collaboration. A lot has been written in the last few years about collaboration in the performing arts. Many of these writings draw critical attention upon the commodification and overabundance of collaboration in artistic practices and caution against the legacy of the author over the work.[62] Nienke Scholts justly reminds us in her text that appears in this book that dramaturgy is mainly concerned with how people work together, and she describes how developing the dramaturgy of her collaboration with another dramaturg means that they, for example, have been imagining different forms of partnership. As Scholts' reflections on her dramaturgical partnering with Igor Dobričić demonstrate, thinking and searching through collaboration can arrive at affects, ways of working, and modes of socialization that resist the logic of capitalist production because they opt for the durational, the unspectacular, the unproductive, and the elusive.

Our suggestion is close to that of Scholts, although we are deliberately thinking through processes of commoning that could be regarded as a radical extension of collaboration, because the latter is most commonly understood in the frame of current artistic production as bereft of political implications.[63] The principle of commoning on the one hand directly engages with the emergence and constitution of the commons, and on the other enables a critical approach towards human individualism because of conceiving of the individual on the basis of relations and intra-dependency with all others. A highly relational perspective can therefore become socially and politically radical. The increasing individuality and capitalization of human language and subjectivity, where humans are expected to constantly produce and communicate their 'selves' and their innovative ideas, has been noteworthy in the last decades. At the same time, political and social processes that determine which lives (human and nonhuman) are protected and which are not are at play. Lorey also positions her thesis on the commons to a large extent against the phenomenon of individualism today and explains that individualization,

> means isolation, and this kind of separation is primarily a matter of constituting oneself by way of imaginary relationships, constituting one's 'own' inner being, and only secondly and to a lesser extent by way of connections with others. Yet this interiority and self-reference is not an expression of independence, but rather the crucial element in the pastoral relationship to obedience.[64]

It thus becomes apparent that our approach of dramaturgy, not solely dependent on the persona of a dramaturg, is rather conceived as an attentive engagement that is distributed among everyone who is taking part in a process, including the eventual audience. This reminds us once again of the writing of Bleeker, who understands the dramaturg as the one who thinks *no-one's thought*, and argues that dramaturgical engagement with a performance can be understood as a 'complex and continuously changing set of relationships',[65] a suggestion that resonates with the ways in which Heathfield and Lepecki have also approached dramaturgy as a process that belongs to the work and not to a single person and that is shared among many. Dramaturgy as a type of working that belongs to many that are taking part in an artistic process is therefore crucial when proposing commoning as a principle of dramaturgy. And in this sense, the commons can only be envisioned as emerging *between* individuals that are intra-related and intra-dependent.

Dramaturgy operating under the principle of commoning thus puts plurality and relationality 'at work'. Against this backdrop, the practice of dramaturgy translates into a searching for and articulating of what may count as common in the differential apparatuses that are involved in the making of an artwork, which may equally include artistic methodologies, infrastructures, and working conditions.

Notes

1   Participants of 6M1L/ex.c.r.ce08,
    'Questioning', in Ingvartsen, *6 Months
    1 Location*, p. 112.

2   The project *6 MONTHS 1 LOCATION
    (6M1L)* was initiated by choreographer
    Xavier Le Roy and took place at the
    Centre Chorégraphique Nationale de
    Montpellier in Languédoc-Roussillion
    from July to December 2008, with
    the participation of seventeen artists,
    all working in one location over six
    months, each leading a project and
    collaborating in at least one more
    project. The overall aim was to
    explore what it means to work under
    'special conditions' of research and
    education, considered as different
    from the usual conditions of freelance
    independent production.

3   For example, in the workshop in
    Tilburg, the Netherlands (December
    2014), which focused on feedback
    as a dramaturgical activity, we
    formed two groups, each of which
    worked with one of the two following
    questions, respectively: 'What do
    I need when giving feedback?' and
    'What do I need when receiving
    feedback?' The starting question in
    Thessaloniki, Greece (May 2015)
    was 'What do I need in order to co-
    create?' and, in London (September
    2015), where the focus was on
    dramaturgy as 'working on actions',
    we started from the question: 'How
    do actions involve others?'

4   See, for example: Cole, 'In the
    Perfect World of Doubt'; Protopapa,
    'Choreographic Practice and the
    State of Questioning'.

5   See, for example: Laermans, '"Being
    in Common"'; Sennett, *Together*.

6   See, for example: Georgelou, 'Inside
    the Wor(l)d Collaboration'; Kunst,
    'Prognosis on Collaboration'.

7   Burrows and Ritsema, 'Weak Dance
    Strong Questions', p. 28.

8   Cvejić, *Choreographing Problems*,
    pp. 144, 149, 150.

9   Examples of questions Deborah Hay
    may work with are: 'What if every
    cell in the body had the potential to
    get what it needs, while surrendering
    the habit of a singular facing, and
    inviting being seen?', see: Hill, "What
    If?", http://interventionsjournal.
    net/2015/01/22/what-if-digital-
    documentation-as-performance-
    and-the-body-as-archive-in-deborah-
    hays-no-time-to-fly/#_ftn7. Or the
    question, 'What if where I am is what
    I need?', see: Bissell, 'Communities
    of Consciousness and the Begetting
    of Deborah Hay', www.pcah.us/
    media/files/b304ea5e902bb4564f-
    771de3b8b49966.pdf.

10 In fact, we return to the risk of
    potentially glorifying any term and
    practice suggesting uncertainty
    and unknowing in considering
    dramaturgy when describing the
    second principle of 'alienating'.
    See also Simon Bayly's text in
    Part II of this book, who similarly
    problematizes the relation of knowing
    and not-knowing in his discussion of
    'anxious dramaturgy' and the role of
    the dramaturg.

11 Cvejić 'The Ignorant Dramaturg', p. 43.

12 Ibid., p. 41.

13 Ibid., p. 45.

14 Ibid., p. 49.

15 Ibid., p. 53.

16 One could argue that 'Weak Dance
    Strong Questions' does precisely this:
    Burrows and Ritsema seek to remain
    open to all possibilities, as they ask
    'Is it that we try to dance in a way in
    which every movement contains the
    possibility of all directions?' (Burrows
    and Ritsema, 'Weak Dance Strong
    Questions', p. 31).

17 Bleeker, 'Thinking No-One's
    Thought', p. 70.

18 Ibid., pp. 69–70.

19 Bohm, *On Dialogue*, p. 7.

20 Ibid., p. 60.

21 Lee, 'Foreword', p. xiii–xiv.

22 From Nicola Conibere's unpublished
    statement, Roundtable Discussion,
    Sadler's Wells, London,
    18 September 2015.

23 Cixous, in conversation with
    Heathfield, *Writing Not Yet Thought*.

24 Notes from the workshop plans for
    Brussels, Belgium (November 2014)
    and Thessaloniki, Greece (May
    2015). The task is inspired by Lisa
    Nelson's Tuning Scores (for more
    information: http://olga0.oralsite.
    be/oralsite/pages/Testpage_Lisa_
    Nelson_%28general%29/index.html).

25 Luoto, 'Work, Practice, Event', p. 36.

26 Ric Allsopp also refers to 'an affective
    "something else" that emerges in
    performance' (p. 125) in order to

discuss choreographic images that appear between what disappears or is forgotten — images that emerge, as he notes by quoting Jasper John, 'when a thing becomes other than it is' (p. 127). See: Allsopp, 'Something Else', pp. 125-53.

27 Luoto, 'Work, Practice, Event', p. 36.

28 Lepecki, '"We Are Not Ready for the Dramaturge"', p. 187, emphasis given in the original.

29 Ibid., p. 190, emphasis given in the original.

30 Ibid.

31 Ibid., p. 191.

32 Heathfield, 'Dramaturgy without a Dramaturge', p. 110.

33 Brecht, *Brecht on Theatre*, p. 91.

34 Lepecki, '"We Are Not Ready for the Dramaturge"', p. 193.

35 Ibid., p. 194.

36 See also Joachim Robbrecht's text in Part II of the book, who similarly discusses dramaturgy as a tool to fight one's way out of worn-out questions and arguments, by breaking the 'linguacode' one usually works in and bringing elements together in different constellations.

37 Barba, *On Directing and Dramaturgy*, p. 11, emphasis given in the original.

38 Ibid., p. 11.

39 Ibid., pp. 11-12. Barba refers, for example, to decisions such as that of radically limiting the space one works in, or miniaturizing around a table a scene acted out in a wider area, in order to open up other perspectives that extend possible choices.

40 Ibid., p. 12.

41 Ibid.

42 Virno cited in Lavaert and Gielen, 'The Dismeasure of Art', p. 30.

43 Kearney, *Strangers, Gods and Monsters*, p. 3.

44 Ibid., p. 65.

45 Ibid., p. 11, emphasis given in the original.

46 Ibid., emphasis given in the original.

47 Ibid.

48 Ibid., p. 70, emphasis given in the original.

49 Ibid., p. 77.

50 See Betina Panagiotara's text in Part II of the book.

51 In the context of the workshops we often introduced interruptions and interferences by others that we considered 'gifts', in order to signal

their generous 'positive' way of working towards one another's processes.

52 Notes from workshop plans: Brussels, Belgium, November 2014; Amsterdam, the Netherlands, July 2015; London, UK, September 2015.

53 For example, we worked in several instances with Lisa Nelson's Tuning Scores, which we modified for the purposes of this exchange and is also described in the context of the principle of 'alienating'.

54 There are, for instance, several examples of such processes of exchange denoted in the project between contemporary dance artists, which appears in the form of a website called 'everybodystoolbox'; see, for example: http://everybodystoolbox. net/index.php?title=Accueil (accessed 12 April 2016).

55 Lorey, 'Becoming Common' (emphasis in the original) www.e-flux.com/ journal/becoming-common-precarization-as-political-constituting.

56 Ibid.

57 Here we refer to concentration camps as well as to several biometric technologies, such as optic scanners, chipped identity cards, and fingerprints. These show how the state gains an increasing control over the people, using biological identity for political purposes.

58 The dimensions of precarity have been discussed in detail by Lorey also in an earlier article: 'Governmental Precarization', http://eipcp.net/ transversal/0811/lorey/en

59 Lorey, *State of Insecurity*, p. 104.

60 Ibid., p. 104.

61 In *State of Insecurity*, Lorey has made reference to the common as 'a social ontological constitution', which was proposed by Michael Hardt and Antonio Negri, and has contested this approach by arguing that an ontologically grounded common that is based upon the premises of equality is not enough as political agency. Lorey has rather suggested that the 'common' is what must first emerge and be constituted.

62 Ignoring or undermining the political dimension of collaboration has been critically investigated in the last years. See: Cvejić, 'Learning by Making'; Georgelou, 'Inside the Wor(l)d Collaboration'; Kunst, 'Prognosis

on Collaboration'; Van Imschoot,
'Anxious Dramaturgy'.

63 Kunst (ibid.) and Van Imschoot
(ibid.) are noteworthy exceptions in
that regard.

64 Lorey, *State of Insecurity*, p. 13.

65 Bleeker, 'Thinking No-One's
Thought', p. 71.

A Catalytic Mode of Working

The three working principles offered emerged out of the workshops and discussions that took place as part of the project 'Dramaturgy at Work', and, as we have argued, only became articulated as such as the project progressed and we began the writing for this book. Similarly, as we have underlined repeatedly, they are not offered as tools or to constitute a specific type of dramaturgical methodology, but as general principles that convey a certain approach to dramaturgical practice, a way of doing dramaturgy that has a specific force to it, a quality of 'setting into motion' as we will discuss further on. In particular, we would like to propose here that the three principles discussed earlier work as catalysts for dramaturgy, offering an understanding of dramaturgical practice as a catalytic operation, too, which drives the work forward through specific methods that can only be fully shaped at the moment when dramaturgy enters a specific process. If a catalyst can be defined as an element that comes from the outside to speed up a reaction or precipitate an event, then it is striking that during this process the catalyst performs an action that is still *exclusive to and necessary for* that specific experiment or reaction, process, or practice. Similarly, dramaturgy operates through interruption, pointing to what could not have happened otherwise — an alternative direction that was only potentially there before, but needed a trigger to materialize. What mainly interests us here though is not so much the distance and supposed autonomy a catalyst maintains from the procedure going on, but the way in which it intervenes, from the outside, so to speak, and at any stage of an activity, marking an event, a (new) beginning, an initiation, that sets forth a series of (re)actions within the parameters and conditions of a particular process.

Moreover, what is common in all three principles we have offered and is significant for our understanding of dramaturgy here is that, like catalysts, they transform and develop a process *without necessarily controlling it*. It is this forward motion without an end that we have been proposing through the workshops, too, and to which we shall return when discussing the terms 'action', 'work', and 'practice', a force that in our view opens up a space for experimentation and unanticipated effects. The question of how one can create concrete working frames and tasks that will, nevertheless, not point to expected results and outcomes, has therefore been, and remains, at the centre of our attention. Through this lens, we can consider the dramaturgical operations generated through the principles of mobilizing questions, alienating and commoning, as setting forth but not necessarily predetermining a sequence of experiments, leading thereby to a performative process of constant re-initiations, beyond predictions and pre-calculated results.

At this stage the image of Peter Fischli and David Weiss's work *The Way Things Go* (1987) comes to mind, which could be described as a thirty-minute film showing a series of experiments as a single ongoing event, a chain reaction between objects and materials, an endless sequence of catalyzing. Artist Jeremy Millar notes that

> the objects are here able to follow their own inclinations... reacting to the situations in which they find themselves, situations that they themselves help bring about. And so the things are held in anticipation... Everywhere things are transformed into actions, nouns become verbs.[66]

Millar therefore understands the work as a seemingly never-ending sequence of controlled catastrophe,[67] often showing the inevitability of certain (re)actions, a succession of events that reveals a process of increasing differentiation.[68] Similarly, Weiss himself admitted that one of their aims was for 'this energy of never-ending collapse' to be 'harnessed and channelled in a particular direction'.[69] Not only does the idea of a constant, trivial, or even futile process of trial-and-error come through in these accounts, but also the suggestion that the mini-events set up by the artists seem to take their own course, always ready to be undone and be followed upon by the next diversification. Although not bound to the strict laws of cause and effect such as those one finds in physics as shown in this particular film, dramaturgical work based on the catalytic principles we have outlined could also perhaps be understood here through these terms of a constant transformation of materialities into action and vice versa, a sequence of micro-collapses that allow the work to follow its own inclination, persistently diversifying itself from its previous state.

A further capacity of dramaturgy then becomes possible through its catalytic mode of working. By acting as an initiator that does not seek to necessarily control the process but rather aims at constant shifts and mini-breakdowns, we could suggest that dramaturgy opens up a space for imagination, not in the sense of the unconceivable, but as that that could be otherwise. We have been struck by Anthony Dunne and Fiona Raby's remark that several key changes after the 1970s (such as the fall of the Berlin Wall, neoliberalism, and processes of individualization) have made imaginative, social, and political speculation today more difficult and less likely. As Dunne and Raby have noted, while quoting Fredric Jameson, it seems easier for us now to imagine the end of the world than an alternative to capitalism.[70] The same goes for the arts, too. Kunst has argued that the dominant term through which we discuss, approach, and organize artistic production and research today is that of the 'project'. This term aptly describes the dominant working mode in arts (but not only): a projection to the future, a successful calculation between the present and future that will allow us to estimate with the biggest possible accuracy the results of our work; because time is money and there is no time to lose or no space for 'unwanted', 'unexpected' (and therefore potentially also 'risky' or even 'dangerous') outcomes. Artists are therefore asked to pre-plan in full detail their 'projects' and announce their outcomes in advance in order to then be offered the opportunity to simply execute them in a way that's as quick, flexible, easy, and acceptable as possible. Kunst has criticized the 'project horizon of making today' as unable to open to possibilities, arriving always at what is already expected and projected. Artistic work, she has posited, becomes merely an 'administration of the future' — a continuous projection that forgets the present, a horizon that (as we know from physics) can never be reached. By the time one reaches the end of a project, one is already involved in five more other ones. These conditions relate directly also to the reason art often loses its constitutive role in society today and artists' inability to imagine a different political and economic future. In these terms, contemporary artistic project(ion)s that appear to be 'open', 'flexible', and 'innovative' are actually unable to really produce any difference, surprise, imagination, and, eventually, progress for humanity.[71] Against this backdrop, we suggest that considering dramaturgy in its catalytic function that opens up space for imagination, interruption, and action, also has the capacity to disrupt such logics of project-driven work like the one described by Kunst.

At this stage, we should also acknowledge the limitations of the metaphor of dramaturgy as a catalytic mode of working, especially in two respects that seem at odds with our overall positions on dramaturgy: first, one may misunderstand this catalytic function as generally aiming for efficiency and improvement and, second, this understanding could also suggest an exclusion of potential operations that one would align with those of the anti-catalyst, that is, a substance that retards, diminishes, or cancels out an effect. It is important therefore to expand our understanding of dramaturgy as a process that does not aim at an optimization of reality or at the attainment of a future-oriented goal — how could it measure bettering, after all, if it is not concerned with controlling the setting forth of its own doing? — but that may also include a call for standing still, slowing down, reversing, or backtracking.

In this sense, and if the practice of dramaturgy is often associated with aspects of coherency, concreteness, and meaningfulness of a performance, the three principles we have proposed indeed suggest a way to attribute to dramaturgy a sense of efficiency, but interpreted as a negative one. Of course, we consider it crucial to be critically working through the concepts that are nowadays determining most aspects of work and life, such as efficiency, creativity, and usefulness. In response to Florian Malzacher's provocative claim that art needs to be 'useful', we propose that the principles for dramaturgy we have described have the capacity to be negatively efficient in the workings on and of actions (and in this way be useful). Malzacher justly refers to the 'social democratic instrumentalisation of art as a mere tool for social work and as an appeasement strategy' and maintains that art 'needs to be useful in subverting this reality'.[72] Against this background, dramaturgy is likewise expected to conceive, create, and catalyse actions that can be efficient in ways that question, intervene, or undermine habitual logic and the current state of affairs. In this sense, devising and applying strategies, tactics, and tools is often crucial. However, we also maintain that artistic production needs to preserve its capacity for abstraction and poetics and, even more, to develop it in ways that are not manageable for the logic of the capital.

In a similar vein, the type of dramaturgical work that concerns us here does not necessarily limit itself in activist forms of art, such as those proposed in Malzacher's book. Activism points to acts that have very specific goals and are directed to particular problems, whereas dramaturgy as a catalytic operation may also set forth less (or differently) directed aspects of action. We therefore argue that the principles of mobilizing questions, alienating, and commoning perform a dual operation, of concreteness and instability, of working and unworking, which is crucial in our approach, conceptualization, and practising of dramaturgy. Rather than obscuring dramaturgy, our intention here has been to reveal it as an (un)working process operating on the basis of catalytic principles, so that subsequently it cannot be subordinated to an end, in the same way that it cannot be understood outside of its own materiality.

66   Millar, *Fischli and Weiss*, p. 20.
67   Ibid., p. 1.
68   Ibid., p. 31.
69   Fischli, quoted ibid., p. 9. See also
     Georgelou, 'Inside the Wor(l)d
     Cooperation', p. 96.
70   Dunne and Raby, *Speculative
     Everything*, p. 2.
71   Kunst, 'The Project Horizon'.
72   Malzacher, *Truth is Concrete*, p. 25.

Working on Actions

Drama **and** *Ergon*

The catalytic function of dramaturgical practice, as discussed in the previous section, also dwells in the etymological and conceptual dimension of the term, which consists of two notions: action (δράμα, *drama*) and work (ἔργον, *ergon*). Already for Aristotle, *'drama'*, deriving from the Greek δρω (*dro*, meaning to act), was understood as 'things done' in theatre.[73] Before becoming identified with the theatre text during the Renaissance period, drama thus denoted the action or rather the summation of actions that take place on stage within the frame of a live theatre event. Moreover, dramatic action was initially conceived as primary to the dramatic character, which changed from the eighteenth century onwards as drama became ascribed to issues of character and identification rather than action.[74] When returning to the etymological dimension of dramaturgy, therefore, and after disengaging drama from the theatrical script and from the character alike, dramaturgy basically marks a blending between the terms 'action' and 'work', which, as we will demonstrate, points precisely to its catalytic function. In fact, depending on the connection made between these two terms, dramaturgy can be interpreted both as 'actions at work' and as a 'working on actions'.

Barba has taken into account the etymology of dramaturgy as well and mainly approached it as 'actions at work', largely recovering the Aristotelian primacy of action and supporting drama's independence from the theatre text. Barba has thus precisely pointed at how artistic actions function when they are presented on stage, and has proposed dramaturgy as a technical operation related to 'the weaving and growth of a performance and its different components'.[75] Dramaturgical practice, as we have outlined it so far, suggests, however, that actions also need 'to be worked *on*', in order to be able 'to work' in themselves when they become public. As already noted, dramaturgy sets forth constant re-initiations beyond pre-calculated results, and in this sense includes conceiving, experimenting, intervening with, and setting-up actions. Dramaturgy is, hence, a practice concerned with all preparations, rehearsals, exchanges, collaborations, failures, interruptions, try-outs, and so forth that happen in the process of creating actions. It is in this sense that dramaturgy is as much 'actions at work' as it is a process of 'working on actions'. And here we mainly draw our attention to the latter, which has been so far neglected in theoretical approaches to dramaturgy.

What does it mean to 'work on actions'? What kinds of actions need working on? When does one (not) work on an action? And how can one account for the implications of this approach to dramaturgy, considering today's neoliberal fusion between action and work? These questions, deriving from our take on the notion of 'working on actions', require an expanded understanding of dramaturgy. Approaching dramaturgy in this way namely suggests critically discussing what seems to urgently need attention today: the methods and ways one makes use of so as to arrive at (artistic) choices, the care with which artistic processes and materials of interest are approached, the setting up of working conditions, the consideration of what counts as an action, the relevance and the affect of creating actions inside but also outside the frame of theatre, and the ways one acts (or not) in the world today.

The investigation of those matters becomes even more urgent against the backdrop of the current neoliberal merging between life and work and the disappearance of the political nuance of action (the Aristotelian praxis) in general. At this point it is useful to turn to Aristotle's and Hannah Arendt's writings, where action has been discussed in juxtaposition to labour, work, and intellect, and has been primarily conceptualized as the political capacity of appearing in the public sphere, intervening in social relations, and modifying social contexts. Action has thus been understood in performative terms, in the sense that it points to how contexts and norms act upon us as well as to how one acts and deviates from those contexts and norms.[76] In this theoretical context, action is a mode of (un)doing and is dependent upon its publicness. Recent debates, however, have underlined how the boundaries between these categories (work, labour, and action) have been dissolved,[77] and how, as Paolo Virno has specifically stated, 'the world of so-called post-Fordist labour has absorbed into itself many of the typical characteristics of political action'.[78] Action is therefore no longer conceived in political terms only, and not even as exclusively human, while its performance is often subject to measurement. One can talk today about technological, organizational, cultural, and scientific actions that are mostly evaluated on the basis of their performance, which is then measured in terms of efficiency and profit ratios within each such field. The artistic sector more specifically has to comply with funding and production criteria that demand evidence of social benefits and number of ticket sales.[79] The arts are mostly valued and supported today on the basis of their entrepreneurial character, their participation in community projects for social integration, their role in developing cultural diplomacy and tourism, or their scarce ability to make profit for the market.[80] Differently said, the neoliberal logic and post-Fordist principles of work (such as flexibility, uncertainty about the future, mobility, demand for constant creativity, and immateriality) condition the arts, as well as most institutions and disciplines nowadays, which has led to equalizing action with efficient and profit-making initiatives. Similarly, as already mentioned in the introduction of this book, the existing discourse and practice of dramaturgy demonstrates that to a large extent, dramaturgy is also thought in terms of efficiency, taking up the role of bringing sensical order and securing coherence in artistic production. Dramaturgs are often thought to offer the 'right solutions', so that the performance becomes coherent, understandable, or accessible to the audience, eventually leading to more ticket sales. Dramaturgs have also often been called 'guardians' of an idea, 'outside eyes', mediators for success – all pointing to dramaturgy as a way of individualist work (that of the intellectual who 'knows best') that leads to the creation of more-or-less conclusive and 'successful' actions, efficient, and, in turn, capable of making profit. Against this rather limited perspective on dramaturgy, how can we then understand and practice a 'type of' dramaturgy that can still preserve the catalytic function that was earlier outlined?

Setting into Motion

Aristotle distinguished *poiesis* (production) from *praxis* (practice) and, following his thinking, Arendt has spoken of labour, work, and action in a similarly distinctive manner. While *praxis* and action do not lead to any product, *poiesis* and work are said to produce a 'fabricated thing' or an end product, according to Aristotle and Arendt respectively, which leads to Arendt's conception of the whole process of making as 'entirely determined by the categories of means and end'.[81] And yet, as Kunst has rightly pointed out, in today's post-Fordist paradigm, a certain blurriness occurs between such terms where biological labour, work, and production are rendered indeterminate. Work, the artist's work in particular that Kunst discusses, is not restricted to the production of 'material goods', but rather includes immaterial activities, the invention of processes by which such production takes place, as well as the making visible of such production mechanisms. As she has claimed, 'the visibility of work is also connected to the ways in which the production of communication, relationships, relations, affects and non-material goods drives out post-Fordist production'.[82] In this sense, Kunst's remark that artistic practice has to 'return back to the material aspect of work, to the sensuous and material base of any activity'[83] is crucial and, we would argue, so is understanding dramaturgical work today as concerning the whole spectrum of the activities that the 'artist at work' engages with, not excluding immaterial actions. This undoubtedly leads us to an expanded notion of action, too, one that accepts its current fusion with work and understands its significance and implications not only within artistic processes, but also on a major scale, in the way it appears to engage with production matters, social realities, infrastructures, politics, and working conditions. In this sense, the etymological fusion of 'action' and 'work' in 'drama-turgy' is not only suggestive of how dramaturgy operates but, in view of Kunst's analysis, it can even be considered as evocative of the current conditions of artistic work at large.

Using the fusion of 'action' and 'work' as a lens through which to understand dramaturgy as a different kind of process, differently efficient perhaps, attends to the conditions and modes of working for the creation of actions. The notions 'drama', 'action', and 'praxis' (which is a synonym of 'practice'), despite the different (theoretical) contexts they have emerged from, all point to a catalytic process of setting into motion and intervening that contradicts the end-oriented 'poiesis' and 'work' traced back to Aristotelian and Arendtian thinking. Acknowledging and recovering this conceptual contradiction from within dramaturgy may suggest at first that dramaturgical practice is paradigmatic of post-Fordist modes of work. Inserting into this equation the rather neglected aspect of action as 'setting into motion', however, which reveals dramaturgy's catalytic operation, can eventually lead to a going beyond and making irrelevant of the division between such end-oriented and non-end-oriented modes of work. This, we shall propose, eventually articulates a re-politicization of dramaturgical practice. In other words, this perspective may enable precisely the opposite of what the practice of dramaturgy is often perceived as aiming to achieve: an opening up of spaces of dissensus, un-sensing, dis-orientation, and un-knowing that enables a space for interference, intervention, and imagination.[84]

It is noteworthy that already in 1958, with the aim of resisting utilitarian approaches to action, in *The Human Condition* Arendt argued in favour of the politicality of action. Arendt thus foresaw that usefulness and efficiency were in the process of becoming ultimate principles in life, and it could be stated that her observations match today's political and social reality in the Western world.[85] This had already emerged as a concern earlier, notably of the Frankfurt School and Max Horkheimer in particular,[86] explored in his book *Eclipse of Reason*. With a much more critical tone than Arendt's, he attacked the instrumental reasoning that was manifested in his time, which, as he explained, rationalizes, mechanizes, naturalizes, and streamlines concepts and ideas, but also artworks, rendering them into ends, commodities, and products.[87] Such formalization of reason, he considered fatal for social and political action. In his words, 'efficiency, productivity, and intelligent planning are proclaimed the gods of modern man; so-called "unproductive groups" and "predatory" capital are branded as the enemies of society'.[88]

It was against this backdrop that Arendt specifically noted the double meaning of the verb 'to act' in both ancient Greek and Latin, one that contained two different and yet interrelated significances: the notion of initiating, beginning, setting into motion, and that of seeing through, achieving, finishing.[89] Initially then, even though this distinction indicated an interdependence between these two parts of action, it seems that the strength of the action lied in the setting into motion rather than the seeing through, Arendt has remarked. To further understand such 'setting into motion', it is crucial to notice actions' main constituent aspects that Arendt has retained: initiation, plurality, boundlessness, and unpredictability. These, in effect, resonate with the principles of dramaturgy that we have previously outlined and similarly show a catalytic function. In light of Arendt's properties of action, 'working on actions' points to a setting into motion of processes that, although immersed in the post-Fordist conditions of work that aim towards efficiency and profit, may not be as easily regulated or productive for the logics of the capital, precisely because of the unpredictability, ambivalence, and complexity they entail.

Overall, Arendt has highlighted the unequal separation between '*vita activa*' (life of action) and '*vita contemplativa*' (life of contemplation) that form what she has called 'the human condition'.

And since the life of contemplation was generally considered as more significant than the life of action in Arendt's times, a crucial purpose of her book was to demonstrate that these two are different but not hierarchically related. She has specifically defended action as a human activity that, due to its inherent properties, resists principles of commodification and efficiency. As she has explained, action constitutes a sort of beginning,[90] an initiation of the individual into the public world of appearances, and so initiation becomes the first property of action that she brings forth. In addition, Arendt has pointed out that action is an initiative that takes place in a pluralized world. Notably, for her, human beings are conditioned by plurality, which is to say that action can only be conceived and actualized in its appearance among others. Arendt has therefore rightly shown that actions reveal agents who initiate those actions in the public sphere. When introducing the organizational principles of the ancient Greek *polis*, she additionally noted that 'the political realm rises directly out of acting together, the "sharing of words and deeds". Thus action not only has the most intimate relationship to the public part of the world common to us all, but is the one activity which constitutes it'.[91] Arendt's public realm thus precisely concerns an acting together, an initiation that takes place within an association (*koinonia*) between those who are different and unequal.

Similarly to the dramaturgical principles previously discussed, the above two Arendtian aspects of action point to a radically relational practice of activating issues or questions without the anticipation of any resolution. Initiation and plurality, akin to mobilizing questions and to commoning respectively, make the catalytic function of 'working on actions' even more explicit. In this light, working on actions is specifically rendered a setting in motion of differential beginnings from within a relational and pluralized context. Dramaturgical practice thus appears as dependent upon its context while maintaining its capacity to trigger action (to activate). Dramaturgy should not, however, be regarded as something abstract and only dependent on other humans. Rather, we would like to insist that it is also bound to the material conditions, economies, and infrastructures in which it operates. In that regard, Judith Butler has rightly pronounced the significance of the material aspects of action in her reading of Arendt. In a lecture she specifically explained that Arendt's action is located in what she has called the 'public space of appearance', which has only been depicted as an abstract public space. However, as Butler has justly claimed, public space cannot emerge without the media today and action is fully dependent on infrastructures (that is, streets and squares for assemblies to happen).[92] In other words, the aspect of plurality, and by extension dramaturgical practice as such, needs to be extended to material aspects and conditions that enable or disable it such as infrastructures, space, time, and budget.

Arendt has proposed two additional aspects of action, pointing to action's capacity of 'setting into motion': boundlessness and unpredictability. Boundlessness concerns the consequences of actions, which are not necessarily bound to the initial action but are nevertheless bound by the sphere of human relationships in which it appears. Through its mediality, an action can produce a chain of reactions that are not dependent on the initial one; action 'acts in a medium where every reaction becomes a chain reaction and where process is the cause of new processes'.[93] Within this chain, Arendt has also located the capacity of action to establish relationships and has, subsequently, denoted its inherent unpredictability. Contrary to the product (the 'end') to which work arrives, action is unpredictable in terms of its outcome. As she has explained, 'this is not simply a question of inability to foretell all the logical consequences of a particular act, in which case an electronic computer would be able to foretell the future, but arises directly out of the story, which, as the result of action, begins and establishes itself as soon as the fleeting moment of the deed is past'.[94] In other words, an action leads to the formation of complex relations and unanticipated consequences, forming a grid of heterogeneous connections and nonlinear temporalities.

Boundlessness and unpredictability also resonate with the formerly retained principles of dramaturgy, and especially to that of 'alienating'. Described as a process of estrangement from one's expectations and plans regarding their artistic project, alienating basically suggests that the effects of one's choices and actions cannot be fully controlled or assimilated. Instead, they operate in unpredictable ways and may lead to entirely unexpected or seemingly 'faulty' places. It also needs to be recognized, however, that unlike action, as discussed by Arendt, artistic work most often does arrive at a 'final work', that takes the form of a performance or an event, for instance. In this sense, the practice of dramaturgy is not entirely boundless. It is perhaps more alike another conception of action that Arendt has retained from Aristotle, that of 'entelecheia' (*en telei echei*). This conception precisely exposes how the 'end' (*telos*) of action is not to be pursued elsewhere but exists in the activity per se, in its own actuality (*energeia*).[95] In this regard, an action, just like the artwork, is complete in itself but it also marks the unpredictable beginnings of its own presence into the public. This is exactly the point at which dramaturgy as 'actions at work', which Barba has also insisted on, becomes more apt for discussing and practising dramaturgy. This aspect of the artwork, however, is equally crucial during the process of its creation, where attention is constantly drawn upon and dared by those unpredictable beginnings of its eventual presence in the public sphere.

Arendt's analysis of action consequently sheds light upon the catalytic function of activating, intervening, and setting into motion that has been previously discussed. By conceiving dramaturgy as that that 'sets into motion' processes rather than predetermines them, and that can initiate while remaining plural and unpredictable, we seek to remain attentive to our capacities for artistic, but by extension also – social and political practice. This, however, should not be confused with an insistence on unfinished-ness in the sense of a disavowal of product and a glorification of process. Rather, what is suggested here is a journey towards production that is assisted by an opening out of our imaginative and evocative capacities – a kind of process that can perceive, unfold, and dream differently, arriving perhaps at the not-yet of its own potential. By extension, we would argue that the catalytic attributes of dramaturgy that have been so far discussed from within the fusion between action and work, also prepare the ground for an attempt to (re)articulate the political dimension of dramaturgical practice that is often obscured by current neoliberal conditions of work.

73 Aristotle, *Poetics*, p. 10.

74 As Christopher Balme has explained, it was on the one hand the 'ruleless' legacy of Elizabethan drama and on the other the neoclassical homogeneity of French playwriting that led to the shift from the primacy of action to a primacy of character. *Cambridge Introduction to Theatre Studies*, p. 71.

75 Barba, *On Directing and Dramaturgy*, p. 8.

76 Here we are mainly following Judith Butler's interpretation of performativity, as it has been explained in her books since *Bodies That Matter* (1993).

77 For instance, political theorists Giorgio Agamben, David Hardt, Maurizio Lazzarato, Isabell Lorey, and Paolo Virno have shown how human subjectivity is produced by this fusion.

78 Virno, *A Grammar of the Multitude*, p. 50.

79 In her book *Artificial Hells* (2012), Claire Bishop has illustrated in detail how the British and Dutch art scenes in particular have been altered in recent years by neoliberal policies that specifically demand that the arts are socially effective in community-building and social integration.

80 Characteristically, Sigrid Merx has discussed how the value of the arts is not entirely denied in the Dutch context, but is expressed in economic terms and is therefore subjected to the reality of the market. As she has pointed out, 'artists and cultural institutions are addressed as cultural entrepreneurs. In order to qualify for money they have to demonstrate their shrewdness in exploring new financial sources and strategic partners as well as ability to attract large and broad audiences and generate, at least partly, their own funding. The legitimacy of art is understood purely in neoliberal terms. Whoever is able to create or find their market has a right to exist' ('The Argument of Autonomy', p. 26).

81 For Arendt, labour also produces an end, a 'thing to be consumed', but in this case it refers to biological capacities and it is the exhaustion of labour power itself (*The Human Condition*, p. 143).

82 Kunst, *Artist at Work*, p. 144.

83 Ibid., p. 146.

84 Our understanding of the political is greatly influenced by Chantal Mouffe's book *Agonistics: Thinking the World Politically* (2013), where she has acknowledged that conflict and disagreement are inevitable in politics and they should be dealt with through radically democratic practices that are counter-hegemonic.

85 For instance, Florian Malzacher has stated that 'especially in recent years, after the rise of Tony Blair's New Labour, for example, the idea that positive effects of art should be measurable has become a common trope' (*Truth is Concrete*, p. 25).

86 The Frankfurt School that appeared in the 1930s sought to develop philosophy alongside social theory, considering that theory and the practice of citizenship are intrinsic to each other.

87 Horkheimer, *Eclipse of Reason*, p. 40.

88 Ibid., p. 151.

89 Arendt, *The Human Condition*, pp. 212-15.

90 This initiation is not one of ruling but one of 'setting into motion'. Arendt (ibid., p. 189) nuances this distinction by historicizing the Greek verbs *archein* ('to begin', 'to lead') and *prattein* ('to pass through', 'to achieve').

91 1Ibid., p. 198.

92 Here we refer to Judith Butler's lecture *Vulnerability/Resistance* that took place in the international conference 'How to Act Together: From Collective Engagement to Protest' in Belgrade, Serbia, on 20 November 2015. This lecture emerged out of her book *Notes toward a Performative Theory of Assembly*.

93 Arendt, *The Human Condition*, p. 190.

94 Ibid., pp. 191-92.

95 Ibid., p. 206.

Towards a (Re)Politicized Practice of Dramaturgy

The three proposed principles for dramaturgy discussed here as catalytic ways of 'working on actions' inform our overall suggestion for a dramaturgical practice understood as ongoing and shared in the process of artistic creation. How such practice materializes differs in each case, but we can quite safely claim that (any type of) dramaturgy, including the approach we have suggested, assumes a point of encounter, either among collaborators, or between artists/collaborators and spectators, an invitation to attend, and a process of making something public. Hansen has specifically argued that dramaturgy relates to a heightened mode of awareness of the systems that generate interaction in a work and expand the perceptual capacity of those involved in it. She has pertinently described such work as 'dramaturgy-driven'.[96] In this sense, and even though we could argue that every work has its *own* dramaturgy (given the fact that each work involves certain aesthetic, structural, and collaborative actions), it is not necessarily the case that the type of awareness that Hansen refers to constitutes a major concern of every kind of creative process. In other words, not all works are 'dramaturgy-driven'. It is precisely this important distinction that we have attempted to foreground through a consideration of dramaturgy as a particular type of practice that focuses on the way Hansen's heightened mode of awareness of a work's systems operates. And more than that, we have expanded upon Hansen's approach, by discussing how the practice of dramaturgy is in effect a shared process that sets into motion modes of such heightened awareness in artistic production and beyond.

The notion of 'practice' needs special attention here as it suggests a particular connection to 'action' and 'praxis' discussed earlier, pointing towards dramaturgy-driven work that initiates concrete but at the same time plural, boundless, and unpredictable actions. Chrysa Parkinson has also discussed distinctions between 'practice' and notions such as those of 'training', 'process', and 'product', in a self-interview. She has identified three different definitions and usages of 'practice', considering it as 'an active thought', as 'a habitual or regular activity', or as 'a try', a repeated attempt at something until one gets it right. For her, however, it is the first of these definitions that is the most relevant. As she has explained, practice as an 'active thought' is what underlies the decisions one makes in the training, processes, or products that one is involved in. Resonating with Hansen's views, this practice concerns the way one gives and receives attention and the specific ways through which one processes information. Practice, in this sense, is understood as the volatile substructure one develops in order to navigate, according to Parkinson. As she has aptly explained, one's ideas and thoughts create a place that one inhabits, and operate as scores that direct one to specific actions. For Parkinson too, then, practice as an active thought is closely intertwined with the notion of 'praxis' understood as 'an action that enables that thought', in the sense that it is one's thoughts that create one's actions, whereas one's actions also enable one's thoughts. In this way, Parkinson has suggested practice as something that is not static and remains unstable enough to change — that is volatile enough to escape becoming a marketable object with an author or owner. Quite significantly for our argument here, she has concluded too that, in this way, practice becomes a chemical reaction that acts catalytically on one's experience but without being goal-oriented.[97]

Viewed as such an unstable and volatile practice (of 'active thought', for example), dramaturgy then becomes the creation of the common thinking space that all involved agents construct in order to navigate towards the making of actions within the frame of artistic creation. We argue that this construction is significantly assisted by the three working principles mentioned earlier, which function catalytically not in order to control or stabilize, but in order to enable the work that is to come, activating processes that in today's socio-political and economic context could be understood as indirect, inefficient, interfering, or negatively efficient. By acting as an initiator, we argue, dramaturgy operates beyond predictions and pre-calculated results and opens up a space for imagination, not in the sense of helping us think the unthinkable, but as allowing us to conceive of and do things differently. It is in this sense that dramaturgical practice could also be considered as a speculative one, as discussed by theorist Stefano Harney as well as Cvejić.

Focusing primarily on how study takes place in the university, Harney has discussed the notion of 'speculative practice' as a practice that produces new kinds of intensities by neglecting normative ways of doing things. Influenced by his earlier collaboration with Valentina Desideri,[98] in an interview he described it as a practice that one or more people do when, instead of caring for university credits or any other sort of recognition or completion, they stick to something they do together, deepening their relationship to each other and to the processes they are involved in within the frame of their study.[99] Because this action occurs in a different register than that of capitalist productivism, according to Harney, it can become a preserving activity. It concerns a type of practice that is delicate, gentle, and relaxed, providing a kind of preservation, a social rest from dominant working intensities. It involves, for example, walking around and talking to one another in public, or considering ideas that take place in public, coming into contact with our bodies as we walk, sharing a feeling of being in a space with others. And while this happens, we begin to experience this way of using space as a kind of speculation, pointing to something that is a bit idle, not evidenced correctly, and that involves a kind of conspiracy, a kind of wildness. In this way, speculative practice sets itself up very directly against capital, according to Harney, suggesting alternative ways of using space in our encounters, less 'properly' and more imaginatively. While gentle, it also gently works against what is expected of people when they work together. By developing ways to meet and work that are opposed to the ways in which public space is supposed to be used, ideas are meant to be exchanged and people are expected to be together, a set of complicities can be developed, Harney has posited. And this is because one can begin to imagine that there are others doing this all the time too on the street corner, in the café, and the park, that is, we imagine a kind of speculative practice that is going on around us all the time. From thereon, other social imaginaries can pop up.

From a different perspective, Cvejić has also discussed dramaturgy as a speculative rather than a normative practice. Drawing on the philosopher Isabelle Stengers, who refers to Nobel-prize winning physics experiments and American witch-feminists as equally valuable practices, Cvejić has argued for speculations that place belief or faith in uncertain outcomes without firm evidence.

The key words to extract from such speculation, for her, are 'uncertainty', 'risk', and 'daring'. It is in this sense that in dramaturgy one practices 'standing-under' and supporting before 'under-standing', according to Cvejić. One learns to do and say 'let's think again' because one doesn't know now, but will have known by then.[100]

Once again, aligning with such ideas does not mean equating dramaturgy with open-ended modes of encounter that glorify process for process's sake. On the contrary, we consider our proposal, as described earlier through the three working principles, as a more concrete, forceful, and forward-moving operation. In this sense, the type of speculation that we are suggesting here entails setting concrete processes in motion by means of interruptions, unfamiliarity, and the search for commons. However, this practice needs not be risky and daring (Cvejić), as it is not necessarily idle or directly against productivity (Harney). Instead, we would argue, the practice of dramaturgy at stake here can be any of these speculative practices, as well as less and more than those. Most importantly, it is a systematic practice that, beyond or alongside speculation, activates and invents itself from within the co-presence and relationality of human and nonhuman bodies, material conditions, protocols, infrastructures, positions on publicness, and working modes. In this sense, we suggest that the principles of mobilizing questions, alienating, and commoning facilitate an expansion of the perception of all agents involved in a process, so that they can attend to the complexity of such relationality, and work with all such aspects that for us constitute 'practice'. Dependent on the conditions and the contexts that are set up for each work, dramaturgy is therefore the reconfiguration of agency within those conditions.

Within this frame, how can we more precisely conceive and pursue dramaturgy as a (re)politicized practice? Our reference point here is political philosopher Chantal Mouffe's claim that the domain of 'the political' refers to antagonism, while 'politics' to the 'ensemble of practices and institutions whose aim is to organize human coexistence'.[101] As she has explained, democracy is constituted by 'social division and the impossibility of a final reconciliation',[102] which is to say that division and antagonism need to be taken into account when activating any type of political processes in that regard. It is also noteworthy that, according to Mouffe, radical democracy requires (new) institutional formations and practices that do not exercise hegemonic power. Her 'agonistic' approach to politics, which she has developed against this backdrop, is therefore a plea to render visible and articulate various and conflicting views in the public space, without the desire of a final consensus. Mobilizing counter-hegemonic political and social frameworks are at the core of Mouffe's take on political practice today.

On this basis, we propose that the politicality of dramaturgical practice resides on an attitude of a pluralized interference and reconfiguration of hegemonic organizations of coexistence and co-work. This is not to say that dramaturgical practice is about deciding what such configurations are and then 'teaching' them or selling them to others. Rather, the politicization of dramaturgical practice we are defending here is more concerned with setting into motion actions that work towards the formation of spaces of negotiation, agonisms, dissensus, dis-orientation, and un-knowing. Such actions enable a space for interference, intervention, and imagination, wherein it is possible for the construction of social and political imaginings, art's foremost aspiration, to actually take place.

96 Hansen, 'Introduction', p. 19.
97 Parkinson, 'Self-Interview on Practice', https://vimeo.com/26763244.
98 Harney and Moten, *The Undercommons*, p. 118.
99 Harney, 'Part 6: On Speculative Practice in Theory', www.youtube.com/watch?v=UxZP2cucRXg.
100 Cvejić, 'The Ignorant Dramaturg', p. 53.
101 Mouffe, *Agonistics*, p. xii.
102 Ibid., p. 15.

Bibliography

- Allsopp, Ric. 'Something Else: On Latency and Composition'. In *Practicing Composition: Making Practice: Texts, Dialogues and Documents 2011-2013*, ed. by Kirsi Monni and Ric Allsopp, pp. 125-53. Helsinki: University of the Arts Helsinki, Theater Academy, 2015.
- Arendt, Hannah. *The Human Condition*. Chicago: University of Chicago Press, 1998.
- Aristotle. *Poetics*, trans. Kenneth McLeish. London: Nick Hern Books Limited, 1999.
- Balme, Christopher. 'Theories of Theatre 1: Historical Paradigms'. In *The Cambridge Introduction to Theatre Studies*, pp. 65-77. Cambridge: Cambridge University Press, 2008.
- Barba, Eugenio. *On Directing and Dramaturgy: Burning the House*. Oxon: Routledge, 2010.
- Bishop, Claire. *Artificial Hells: Participatory Art and the Politics of Spectatorship*. London and New York: Verso, 2012.
- Bissell, Bill. 'Communities of Consciousness and the Begetting of Deborah Hay'. The Pew Center for Arts & Heritage, 2012. www.pcah.us/media/files/b304ea5e902bb4564f-771de3b8b49966.pdf (accessed 14 December 2015).
- Bleeker, Maaike. 'Thinking No-One's Thought'. In *Dance Dramaturgy: Modes of Agency, Awareness and Engagement*, ed. by Pil Hansen and Darcey Callisson, pp. 67-84. New York: Palgrave Macmillan, 2015.
- Bohm, David. *Thought as a System*. London and New York: Routledge, 1994.
- Bohm, David. *On Dialogue*. Oxon and New York: Routledge, 1996.
- Brecht, Bertolt. *Brecht on Theatre*, trans. John Willett. London: Eyre Methuen, 1974.
- Burrows, Jonathan and Jan Ritsema. 'Weak Dance Strong Questions'. *Performance Research* 8, no. 2 (2003), pp. 28-33.
- Butler, Judith. *Bodies That Matter: On the Discursive Limits of 'Sex'*. New York and London: Routledge, 1993.
- Butler, Judith. *Precarious Life: The Powers of Mourning and Violence*. New York: Verso, 2004.
- Butler, Judith. *Notes toward a Performative Theory of Assembly*. Cambridge, MA: Harvard University Press, 2015.
- Cixous, Hélène, and Adrian Heathfield. *Writing Not Yet Thought*, a video recording by Hugo Glendinning [my transcription of the conversation]. Paris, 2010. DVD published by Performance Matters, a project by Live Art Development Agency; Goldsmiths, University of London; and Roehampton University, 2010.
- Cole, Helen. 'In the Perfect World of Doubt'. *The Doubt Guardian* 2, no. 2 (2005), p. 8.
- Cvejić, Bojana. 'The Ignorant Dramaturg'. *Maska* XVI, nos. 131-132 (2010), pp. 40-53.
- Cvejić, Bojana. *Choreographing Problems: Expressive Concepts in European Contemporary Dance and Performance*. Basingstoke: Palgrave Macmillan, 2015.
- Cvejić, Bojana. 'Learning by Making and Making by Learning How to Learn'. In *Academy*, ed. by Angelika Nollert et al., pp. 193-97. Berlin: Revolver Verlag, 2006.
- Dunne, Anthony and Fiona Raby. *Speculative Everything: Design, Fiction, and Social Dreaming*. London: MIT Press, 2013.
- Georgelou, Konstantina. 'Inside the Wor(l)d Collaboration'. In *Inventing Futures*, ed. by Emilie Gallier, Konstantina Georgelou and João da Silva, pp. 86-96. Arnhem: ArtEZ Press, 2013.
- Hansen, Pil. 'Introduction'. In *Dance Dramaturgy: Modes of Agency, Awareness and Engagement*, ed. by Pil Hansen and Darcey Callison, pp. 1-27. London: Palgrave MacMillan, 2015.
- Harney, Stefano. 'Part 6: On Speculative Practice in Theory'. YouTube, 2011. www.youtube.com/watch?v=UxZP2cucRXg (accessed 12 April 2015).
- Harney, Stefano, and Fred Moten. *The Undercommons: Fugitive Planning and Black Study*. New York: Minor Compositions, 2013.
- Heathfield, Adrian. 'Dramaturgy without a Dramaturge'. In *Rethinking Dramaturgy: Errancy and Transformation*, ed. by Manuel Bellisco, María José Cifuentes and Amparo Ecija, pp. 105-16. Madrid: Centro Párraga, Centro de Documentación y Estudios Avanzados de Arte Contemporáneo, 2011.
- Hill, Linden. "What If?" Digital Documentation as Performance and

the Body as Archive in Deborah Hay's No Time to Fly'. *Interventions Journal* 4, no. 1 (2015). http://interventionsjournal.net/2015/01/22/what-if-digital-documentation-as-performance-and-the-body-as-archive-in-deborah-hays-no-time-to-fly/#_ftn7 (accessed 14 December 2015).

— Horkheimer, Max. *Eclipse of Reason*. New York: Oxford University Press, 1947.

— Ingvartsen, Mette, ed. *6 MONTHS 1 LOCATION*. n.p.: everybodys publications, 2009.

— Kearney, Richard. *Strangers, Gods and Monsters: Interpreting Otherness*. London and New York: Routledge, 2003.

— Kunst, Bojana. 'Prognosis on Collaboration'. In *Prognosen über Bewegungen*, ed. by Gabriele Brandstetter, Kai van Eikels and Sibylle Peters, pp. 336–47. Berlin: B-Books, 2009.

— Kunst, Bojana. 'The Project Horizon: On the Temporality of Making'. In 'Projected Temporality'. Special issue, *Maska* XXVII, nos. 149–150 (2012), pp. 64–71.

— Kunst, Bojana. *Artist at Work: Proximity of Art and Capitalism*. Winchester: Zero Books, 2015.

— Laermans, Rudi. '"Being in Common": Theorizing Artistic Collaboration'. *Performance Research* 17, no. 6 (2012), pp. 94–102.

— Lavaert, Sonja and Pascal Gielen. 'The Dismeasure of Art: An Interview with Paolo Virno'. In *Being an Artist in Post-Fordist Times*, ed. by Paul Gielen and Paul De Bruyne, pp. 17–44. Rotterdam: NAi Publishers, 2009.

— Lee, Nichol. 'Foreword'. In *Thought as a System*, David Bohm, pp. ix–xvi. London and New York: Routledge, 1994.

— Lepecki, André. "We Are Not Ready for the Dramaturge": Some Notes for Dance dramaturgy'. In *Rethinking Dramaturgy: Errancy and Transformation*, ed. by Manuel Bellisco, María José Cifuentes and Amparo Ecija, pp. 181–97. Madrid: Centro Párraga, Centro de Documentación y Estudios Avanzados de Arte Contemporáneo, 2011.

— Lorey, Isabell. 'Becoming Common: Precarization as Political Constituting', trans. Aileen Derieg. In *e-flux*, Journal #17, 06: 2010. www.e-flux.com/journal/becoming-common-precarization-as-political-constituting/ (accessed 26 November 2015).

— Lorey, Isabell. 'Governmental Precarization'. In *Transversal eipcp*, trans. Aileen Derieg. 2011. http://eipcp.net/transversal/0811/lorey/en (accessed 29 November 2015).

— Lorey, Isabell. *State of Insecurity: Government of the Precarious*, trans. Aileen Derieg. London and New York: Verso, 2015.

— Luoto, Miika. 'Work, Practice, Event: On the Poietic Character of the Work of Art'. In *Practicing Composition: Making Practice: Texts, Dialogues and Documents 2011-2013*, ed. by Kirsi Monni and Ric Allsopp, pp. 34–57. Helsinki: University of the Arts Helsinki, Theater Academy, 2015.

— Malzacher, Florian, ed. *Truth is Concrete: A Handbook for Artistic Strategies in Real Politics*. Berlin: Sternberg Press, 2014.

— Merx, Sigrid. 'The Argument of Autonomy: The Missing Link in the Discursive Arena'. *The Walking Theory: Art and the Public Good* 8 (2012), pp. 23–29.

— Millar, Jeremy. *Fischli and Weiss: The Way Things Go*. London: Afterall Books, 2007.

— Mouffe, Chantal. *Agonistics: Thinking the World Politically*. London and New York: Verso, 2013.

— Nelson, Lisa. 'On Scores'. *What's the Score? On Scores and Notations in Dance*, ed. by M. Van Imschoot, *Oral Site* 1 (2013). http://olga0.oralsite.be/oralsite/pages/Testpage_Lisa_Nelson_%28general%29/index.html (accessed 21 March 2016).

— Parkinson, Chrysa. 'Self-Interview on Practice'. Vimeo, 2008–2009. https://vimeo.com/26763244 (accessed 21 March 2016).

— Protopapa, Efrosini. 'Choreographic Practice and the State of Questioning'. *Dance Theatre Journal* 20, no. 3 (2004), pp. 6–8.

— Sennett, Richard. *Together. The Rituals, Pleasures & Politics of Cooperation*. London: Penguin Books, 2013.

— Van Imschoot, Myriam. 'Anxious Dramaturgy'. *Women & Performance: A Journal of Feminist Theory* 13, no. 2 (2003), pp. 57–68.

— Virno, Paolo. *A Grammar of the Multitude*. New York: Semiotext[e], 2004.

Part II

Working on Actions and Beyond

Dramaturgy as
Conversation

Correspondence
and Ekphrasis

Guy Cools

Dramaturgy as a Dialogical Practice

During the years that I have been working as a dance dramaturg, I have always preferred to understand dramaturgy as the reflection process of the artist addressing critically how she wants to develop her language and discipline. As such, the artist doesn't need a dramaturg to do this.[1] Dramaturgical reflection becomes externalized in the figure of the dramaturg only at the moment when the artist engages in a dialogue with a dramaturg. I, too, therefore participate in the dramaturgical reflection of the artist, mainly through dialogical practice. Even if the choreographer alone is capable of dramaturgical reflection, Maaike Bleeker sees in dialogue the moment where it becomes exteriorized through another person, the dramaturg.[2] Dramaturg André Lepecki in his collaboration with Meg Stuart defines this dialogical practice as an 'act of translation' from 'Meg to the dancers; from the dancers to the dancers; from Meg to Meg; from the dancers to Meg; from myself to Meg; from myself to the dancers; and from all of these to all the other collaborators'.[3] In his enumeration of dramaturgical activities this is just one of many. For Meg Stuart herself, however, it is the essence of their collaboration: 'A dramaturgical process begins with a dialogue with someone you trust. ...They [that someone you trust] are also a big ear with whom I share my initial questions and later my doubts, so as not to spill them all over the studio.'[4] The same approach is echoed in the way that Ruth Little describes her collaborations with different choreographers:

> At the beginning of our relationship, the choreographers I have worked with expressed to me their desire for an evolving exchange, and they were looking for a dialogue that is testing, supportive, challenging and sensitive to both process and to the nature of the work.[5]

Other artists, such as the Dutch theatre director Jan Joris Lamers, define dramaturgy as the 'continuing dialogue'[6] between all the participants of the creative process, regardless of whether there is a dramaturg present or not. In a similar way William Forsythe and his then dramaturg Freya Vass-Rhee, at the Tanzkongress in Düsseldorf, Germany, in 2013, described their collaboration as embedded in a larger dialogue in which all the company members participate.

Although different kinds of dialogic exchanges take place in the frame of performance creation, I have until this point defined my role as a dialogue partner primarily in relationship to the choreographer. I am therefore mainly there for her and I only engage with the other collaborators when invited to do so in order to moderate between them and the choreographer. This is also a strategy to avoid the risk of turning a productive polyphonic conversation into a cacophony of voices that overlap, distract, or confuse.

Similar to how Jacob Zimmer describes the importance of conversation before the start of the rehearsal process, my work as a dramaturg happens as much outside of the studio as inside.[7] Whereas inside the studio the witness role is the most dominant one, outside of it I meet with the choreographer on a regular basis (from daily to weekly depending on the needs of the process) to discuss what is happening in the studio. These conversations ideally start as early as possible, when the first ideas for a new creation germinate (sometimes while the choreographer is still working on the previous piece) and they intensify over the course of the rehearsal process. These discussions don't so much focus on the material that is developed but on what is needed to further nurture the process. This may, for instance, include the communication with the performers, what kind of input they need, how to plan best and organize the time of the rehearsals, and how to start thinking about possible ways to organize the material in parallel to its development. The time and the place of these conversations are crucial and change with each choreographer and/or production. Their distinct forms also require some reflection. A number of times we conversed for instance by writing letters — an actual 'correspondence'. In all cases, these conversations are also very different from so-called feedback processes. They are much more open-ended and purposeless. In them, the act of listening/reading is as important as that of talking/writing.

In what follows, I would like to focus on two particular forms in which dramaturgical dialogue happens in a written form: through correspondence (that is, through letter exchange) and through the practice of *ekphrasis*.

Correspondence
In *Making: Anthropology, Archaeology, Art and Architecture* (2013), Tim Ingold offers a valuable semantic alternative to the term

'dialogue', by reintroducing the notion of 'correspondence', which takes place not only between humans but also between humans and their animate or inanimate environment, as well as between the craftsperson/artist and her materials. Ingold borrows the term 'correspondence' from the increasingly obsolete art of letter writing. He defines its two fundamental qualities. First, it is always 'a movement in real time', which takes time and that 'may go back and forth, without a clear starting point or end point'. Second, this 'movement is sentient' giving rise to an exchange that manifests itself as

> lines of feeling, of sentience, evinced not — or not only — in the choice of words but in the manual gestures of the writing and their traces on the page. To read a letter is not just to read about one's respondent, but to read with him or her. It is as though the writer was speaking from the page, and you — the reader were there, listening.[8]

The act of letter writing always implies a certain intimacy. In January 2007 I accompanied as a dramaturg the improvisation project *R.A.F.T.* (*Remembering and Forgetting Together*) of the Québécois choreographer Marc Boivin. I was present at all the rehearsals/improvisations of the three-week-long rehearsal process, as well as at the first series of five public performances. For this project I preferred seeing myself more as an 'outside body' instead of the more often used 'outside eye', which may feel too reductive since it tends to diminish the somatic experience of the dramaturg to that of sight and rational reflection.[9] In the studio, most of the time I was a silent witness and due to practical circumstances (such as a lack of time to meet outside of rehearsals or Quebec's severe weather conditions), Marc and I decided that I would give my daily thoughts in the form of a handwritten letter, which I would write in the evening and post myself in his mailbox the next morning, while he was doing his daily training. This form of correspondence allowed for a dialogue that was different from an oral one. It created short but important delays between observing, reflecting, writing, reading, and reusing the relevant parts in the ongoing dialogue between Marc and the other performers. Different kinds of information seeped in: for instance, quotes or references I would look up in my library and add to my observations, or straightforward deviations that happened in my own stream of consciousness, not being interrupted by the actual presence of my dialogue partner. Reading my letters (which often also meant deciphering my handwriting) offered a very different stimulus to Marc's own creative thinking. At the same time, because we kept practising the correspondence on a daily basis, it stayed embodied and connected with the physical practice. Since I was present at all of the rehearsals, I also witnessed how Marc used the information I sent him in the letters in his dialogue with the other performers, but also, which part of my writing resonated most with the physical research they were involved in. When relevant I would also actively participate in these conversations with my oral voice complementing the written one. Finally, it also offered the possibility for a very different kind of archival practice. Where my usual rehearsal notes were only intended for myself, to remember the previous stages of the process, the letters were written for a particular reader, the choreographer, and as such gave an insight into the dialogical practice we were engaged in, recording at least one voice.

The Practice of Ekphrasis

It was the Italian painter Tobia Ercolino who introduced me to the concept of ekphrasis. The Greek word '*ekphrasis*', which means expression or description (from '*ekphrazein*', to recount, to describe) is mainly used for poetry that describes and is directly inspired by visual works of art. More broadly, it could also be used for any work of art in any medium that directly dialogues with another work of art.

A recent example of such a practice of ekphrasis are the poems of the Indian poet Karthika Nair in her debut collection *bearings* (2009), which opens with *Zero degrees: between boundaries*, her poetic translation of the 2005 dance duet by Sidi Larbi Cherkaoui and Akram Khan, and contains plenty of other examples of ekphrasis of other choreographies by Sidi Larbi Cherkaoui (for example, *Tempus Fugit*), music by Pierre Henry, or sculptures by Alberto Giacometti. In a footnote she comments on this practice:

> These experiments in ekphrasis started with *zero degrees*, the 2005 duet choreographed and performed by Akram Khan and Sidi Larbi Cherkaoui. ... This opening piece, a sestina, took its underlying themes and the visual lexicon — woven in through the six key words, borders,

end, walls, being, will, hands – to create another fable
from an incident that dominates the dance.[10]

The practice of ekphrasis resonates with the American semiotician
Charles Sanders Peirce's notion that every 'sign' we create or utter
in the world is an open invitation for another 'sign' to respond to
it. It also underlines the ideas Elaine Scarry develops in *On Beauty
and Being Just* (2006). Scarry opens her essay with the question:
'What is felt experience of cognition at the moment one stands
in the presence of a beautiful boy or flower or bird?' Referencing
Wittgenstein, she answers the question herself: beauty 'seems to
invite, even to require the act of replication', often across the senses in a synaesthetic and interdisciplinary act of copying and translation. This act of 'copying' or 'translating' is accompanied by 'an
impulse towards a distribution across perceivers',[11] in order for one
to share the experience with as many people as possible.

All through my career as a dance critic, curator, and dramaturg, I have also practised forms of ekphrasis as a way to dialogue with choreographic works and their creators. As a critic for
the Flemish newspaper *De Morgen*, I developed the practice of
writing, next to the published review, a second more personal and
poetic reaction to the work, using the words I had scribbled down
in the dark while watching the performance. Most of the time
these musings would remain completely unread, but occasionally
I would have them circulate in my circle of friends or even send
them to the artists whose work had inspired them.

When I became the curator of the theatre and dance
program of Vooruit Arts Centre in Ghent, Belgium, I continued
this practice and my poetic musings ended up being read more
often by the artists. One example of that period is a rendering of
a public performance talk by Yvonne Rainer and Steve Paxton
at the Montpellier Festival in the 1990s where the European
dance scene was rediscovering the Judson Church heritage. The
talk started as an intimate dialogue between two old friends and
became more and more performative as it went on:

> Privileged witness of an intimate
> Dialogue between two Grand
> Masters of flopping who touch – 'arms'
> Who look for words – 'demolish'
> Who remember what they shared &

The Practice of Dramaturgy

Who share remembrances I realize
Our transition will never be over

Jonathan Burrows was another artist that inspired me regularly in my practice of ekphrasis. All through the 1990s I would invite Jonathan to present every new work and even co-produced and premiered some of these works such as *The Stop Quartet* (1996). After each new piece, I would send him my scribbles, which were not always intelligible, not even to myself, as, for instance, in the case of the premiere of the live version of *Hands* (1995), which was originally made for a dance film, and may be considered a pre-study for *Both Sitting Duet* (2002), the first of a series of iconic duets with composer Matteo Fargion:

Hands (live version)

In my own language
It is rule of fist
In your language
It is rule of thumb
Which you so generously
Offered me tonight
Without restriction
Without a lot of force
So I ask myself
Who is translating who
& why is paar-d
the translation of hors-e

It was only some years later that I found out that my scribbles intrigued Burrows, that he would put them on the notice board in his kitchen and that his attempts at deciphering them would sometimes inspire him in the next step of his choreographic research. As such the unintended dramaturgical dialogue that my writings initiated expanded in time and space and over genres: from dance to literature and back to dance.

The practice of ekphrasis is as an example of how in the history of art many works have been created as 'translations' of existing works, often in other disciplines and media. In one of my early essays, 'Dance: A Translating Art' (2001), I described how in the second part of the twentieth century, translation theory shifted its focus from issues of faithfulness to its original sources towards practices of renewing the target language by introducing 'foreign elements' to it. The practice of ekphrasis could be considered a particular form of translation and a very creative type of dialogical practice where a work of art dialogues with another work of art across the borders of disciplines. As such it has always felt my most accomplished form of dramaturgical dialogue, even when it wasn't originally intended as such.

In the end, I would argue that one of the main tools or rather attitudes in the dialogical practice of the dramaturg is the playing with distance: the oscillation between proximity and distance towards the creative process that one accompanies. Written forms such as correspondence or ekphrasis create a particular distance in time, a delay in the dialogue, which offers the artist a different freedom of use, interpretation, and reaction on the dramaturg's thoughts and reflections. In other words, written forms of dramaturgy as a dialogical practice 'keep their distance whilst in the thick of the labours of proximity'.[12]

Notes

1 See also Cools, 'Who Needs a Dramaturg?'
2 Bleeker, 'Dramaturgy as a Mode of Looking', p. 166.
3 Lepecki, 'Dramaturging', p. 66.
4 Stuart, 'The Big Ear', p. 134.
5 Little, quoted in Trenscenyi, *Dramaturgy in the Making*, p. 223.
6 Lamers, 'A Continuing Dialogue', pp. 286-87.
7 Zimmer, 'Friendship is No Day Job', p. 17.
8 Ingold, *Making*, p. 105.
9 See also Van Imschoot, 'Anxious Dramaturgy'.
10 Nair, *bearings*, p. 6.
11 Scarry, *On Beauty and Being Just*, p. 6.
12 Ingold, *Making*, p. 72.

Bibliography

– Bleeker, Maaike. 'Dramaturgy as a Mode of Looking'. *Women & Performance: A Journal of Feminist Theory* 13, no. 2 (2003), pp. 163-72.
– Cools, Guy. 'Dance: A Translating Art. The Body as a "Transmuter" of Identity.' In *Dance: Distinct Language and Cross-Cultural influences*, ed. by Chantal Pontbriand, pp. 31-40. Montréal: Parachute, 2001.
– Cools, Guy. 'Who Needs a Dramaturg?'. *Aparté/Arts Vivants*, no. 3 (May 2014), pp. 86-91.
– Cools, Guy. *In-between Dance Cultures: On the Migratory Artistic Identity of Sidi Larbi Cherkaoui and Akram Khan*. Amsterdam: Valiz, 2015.
– Ingold, Tim. *Making. Anthropology, Archaeology, Art and Architecture*. London: Routledge, 2013.
– Lamers, Jan Joris. 'A Continuing Dialogue.' In 'On Dramaturgy', ed. by Marianne Van Kerkhoven. Special issue, *Theaterschrift* 5-6 (1994), pp. 278-303.
– Lepecki, André. 'Dramaturging, A Quasi-objective Gaze on Anti-memory.' In *Are We Here Yet?* ed. Jeroen Peeters, pp. 64-71. Dijon: Les presses du reel, 2010.
– Nair, Karthika. *bearings*. Noida: Harper Collins India, 2009.
– Scarry, Elaine. *On Beauty and Being Just*. London: Duckworth Overlook, 2006.
– Stuart, Meg. 'The Big Ear.' In *Are We Here Yet?* ed. Jeroen Peeters, pp. 134-35. Dijon: Les presses du reel, 2010.
– Trencsényi, Katalin. *Dramaturgy in the Making. A User's Guide for Theatre Practitioners*. London: Bloomsbury, 2015.
– Van Imschoot, Myriam. 'Anxious Dramaturgy'. *Women & Performance: A Journal of Feminist Theory* 13, no. 2 (2003), pp. 57-68.
– Zimmer, Jacob. 'Friendship is No Day Job: And Other Thoughts of a Resident Dance Dramaturg'. In 'Dance and Movement Dramaturgy' ed. by Hansen Pil with Darcey Callison, and Bruce Barton. Special issue, *Canadian Theatre Review* 16, no. 155 (Summer 2013), pp. 16-20.

Dramaturgs That Do Not Work for a Work

Nienke Scholts

In November 2014 I joined the workshop 'Unfolding Dramaturgies' in Brussels, Belgium. The previous year — having been
working as a dramaturg and collaborating with different artists in
various projects since 2007 — I had been questioning and exploring what my individual dramaturgical practice is or how it could
be seen as a whole in itself. Apart from being occupied with the
projects I was involved in, I was trying to take distance and look
at how this practice was and could be formed and developed also
independently. The question of what my practice as a dramaturg
is may not necessitate a fixed answer, but it serves as a motor to
stay critical towards my work. As such it was also underlying my
partaking in the workshop in Brussels. During the first day an
important shift occurred in relation to my abovementioned concerns. This was due to the fact that while we were asked to individually be mentally busy with a case study from our own practice, at
the same time we were also given pragmatic assignments in small
groups that involved simple sets of actions like formulating questions, filtering keywords from answers, and mapping thoughts
in relation to the work of others. This way of encountering one
another resulted, I strongly felt, in a dramaturgical process that
everyone in the room contributed to and was attentive towards,
although we were not working on one nor on the same project.[1]
The particularity of this dramaturgical experience of collaboration, or co-working, got amplified in contrast to the second day of
the workshop where the focus laid on more expected types of collaboration such as that of working together towards the creation
of one common performance outcome, which confronted us with
several struggles and problems and actually appeared much less
productive. Collaborating on 'setting processes in motion' (day
one) thus stood next to collaborating on 'creating content' (day
two). These experiences fuelled a new curiosity in me about the
relation between collaboration and dramaturgy/dramaturgical
processes.[2] I became interested in the possible ways of looking at
and creating dramaturgical processes in my own practice through
different modes of collaboration.

The dramaturg is generally the 'co-' of some sort (co-
creator, co-imaginator, co-worker), alongside the work of someone
else, and she is also perceived as such. As I see it, however,
through the work that is done for another work, a dramaturg still
develops an autonomous practice, which remains intrinsically
intertwined with those collaborations but also stands on its own.

What exactly constitutes this independent dramaturgical practice then remains a complex question, but the practice of collaboration is, I would say, fundamental in it.

While delving deeper into such concerns, I realized that I was already involved in a very specific mode of collaboration, existing within the frame of my practice for years, which I just never perceived as such: my long-term ongoing dialogue with dramaturg Igor Dobričić. In reaction to the invitation to write about how my experience of the workshop reflected on my practice, I take the chance to have a closer look at this exchange as a collaboration, as 'work' that we 'do together'. In this text I, therefore, explore and try to define what kind of dramaturgy can develop from the collaboration between two dramaturgs that 'do not work for a work'[3] and what this does to the approach of dramaturgy *of* and *as* collaboration.

Igor Dobričić and I met in Amsterdam in May 2011. 'We have to discover it together', he wrote in his response to my email in which I expressed my desire to find some kind of guidance further into the performance and dance scene that I had started to enter. As Igor refused quite quickly the idea of me becoming his trainee or assistant, guidance soon became an alliance. Since then, our roles and what we are to each other has been shifting throughout our meetings: collaborators, dramaturgs, agents, business partners, friends ... in any case, we are two people who share certain interests. We meet in different European cities when our paths happen to cross, about five times a year, often various days in a row and each time for a few hours at least.[4] We speak about the projects that we work on and question and advise each other on *how* we deal with certain dramaturgical issues. Through that we reflect on dramaturgy as a practice. Our collaboration does not exclude how we each work but it exists outside the artistic processes of others. Although we have been relating to the practice of a few particular artists, their practices function rather as another type of material through which we continue to work.[5] They are part of the larger context we have been creating for our dialogue to unfold. A context to 'find it out together', that is, finding out *how* we collaborate. Soon enough our main topic became and remained collaboration itself, or more precisely: 'the way of *working together*: the *dramaturgy of collaboration*', which is, as choreographer Martina Rusham writes: 'the very core of a working process'.[6] Developing the dramaturgy of our collaboration means, for example, that we have been imagining different possible relations and contexts for collaboration between (two) dramaturgs. For example: partners in a business, agents in an agency, or performers of an autonomous dramaturgy. These concepts were possible answers to a search for frames that would playfully question certain dominant tendencies in the art field in relation to the organization of a dramaturgical practice. Mainly, sharing our practice would resist the idea of the dramaturg that is 'working for a work'. We would be already a 'co-', even before starting to co-work or co-create alongside someone else's practice.

At first, a recurring question in our exchange was the actualization and visibility of our concepts: how to bring them into a public realm, and to what extent. How to appear as an agency, for example? As a real business, like two lawyers that start a firm? Or just by using the name 'Scholts&Dobričić', having it pop up now and then as an art-frame? We started experiments with this name on a website but never launched it. In another attempt to make visible what we do as an autonomous work, we decided to invite someone as a witness, but here too we hesitated, and did not arrange the meeting. The periods in between our encounters are long enough to make our thoughts move into other directions and transform initial ideas. This may be thought of as undetermined, lazy, or an excuse not to produce something. But I feel it is a (unconscious) choice and an important mechanism of co-doing that shifts the focus away from the actualization of these ideas back to the process itself. 'These intervals and silences', writer and performance artist Myriam Van Imschoot writes, 'feed what is at work in every contact: the *fantasma*. Distance is a good friend of imagination.'[7]

In 'Prognosis on Collaboration' performance scholar Bojana Kunst describes how contemporary collaborative artistic practices are suffering from a total focus on the value of immediate actualization and finalization, leaving no space for potential, which can only become visible if not actualized.[8] Her only hope for the use of the word 'collaboration' to survive in the future is for us to find ways to put the 'imaginative potential of collaboration into practice'.[9] Aligning with Kunst's ideas, I do recognize an imaginative potential in what Igor and I practice: the imagination of what a collaboration 'can both be and not be',[10] our persistence in finding it out together, and the patient commitment to our dialogue. Through that focus we eventually and unconsciously (but inevitably) created for ourselves a dramaturgy of collaboration along the way; a practice that, while being busy with thinking about how to collaborate, we already did in fact collaborate. Or, as Kunst has described it: 'We didn't take into account that we were already collaborating, encountering and challenging each other through many situations; conditioning our future together, with no visibility required.'[11] The dramaturgy of our collaboration has therefore shifted: it is not concerned any more with considering or finding the way we could work together, or how to actualize it for others, but focuses on the further development of the practice and discourse that form the nature of our work together.

I do not want to romanticize this collaboration, nor claim that it is more genuine than any other type of exchange. It is in fact very *unspectacular*. If one could witness our meetings, one would just see two people in conversation while they are perhaps involved in some activity that definitely doesn't look like work: walking, cooking, eating; in a city, in a kitchen, in a rehearsal room. There is some 'non-utilitarian' and 'inconsequential' quality to our way of working. What we do doesn't make sense from the perspective of productivity or achievement. But that doesn't mean that nothing is accomplished. Theatre theorist Joe Kelleher speaks of 'inconsequential acts that do actually matter; things that keep erasing themselves, as forms of resistance'.[12] Such actions have their own functionality. They should not 'make sense'. The unspoken proposal Igor and I made to each other was not to pay attention to a specific result. Yet, along the way something is accomplished nonetheless, which may even be: being emancipated from a focus on the outcomes of our work. Instead, our practice increasingly serves as a tool for sharpening thoughts and skills in exchange, and as a platform through which dramaturgical practices can be understood and improved both collectively and individually at the same time.

I remember that after our first shared project in Maribor, Igor said he 'gained a friend'. Indeed, the type of relation through which our dialogue unfolds does not resemble a (business) partnership, but a friendship. We do things all friends do, celebrating New Year, exploring foreign cites, and sitting in each other's kitchen while the other is cooking, for example. This 'hanging out' in a time and place that does not belong to either of us just for the sake of sharing it, as only friends can, has been beautifully described by Giorgio Agamben, when he wrote that the friend is 'the other self', and friendship 'the ability to feel pleasure in feeling yourself shared'.[13] Igor naming me his friend, and thereby our friendship became fundamental to the specific dramaturgy of our collaboration. A dramaturgy of friendship. The quality of the exchange between Igor and me both as a friendship and as a collaboration is that kind of sharing in which we don't share something particular, but we 'are shared by the experience of friendship',[14] by the experience of collaboration. Myriam Van Imschoot refers to the collaboration between the two philosophers Gilles Deleuze and Félix Guattari, and to Deleuze's description of it as 'not so much the work of two different people' but 'more like two streams coming together to make a third stream, which I suppose was us'. 'When one plus one is not any longer two, but three', Van Imschoot writes, 'then maths becomes chemistry'.[15]

Imaginative potential, the unspectacular, and friendship, are the main elements that result from the 'maths' that Igor and I do. In our case, the chemistry is the particular dramaturgy that develops from the work of two dramaturgs that do not work for a work. Not only does this allow certain understandings of our own dramaturgical practice as a 'co-': as shared, as a plurality, a mutual commitment and so forth, it also allows for a broader approach to dramaturgy, seeing dramaturgy *as* collaboration. And, even more specifically, as a particular type of collaboration that generates and serves the dramaturgical process itself; the interactions between all those (people, elements, thoughts, et cetera) shared through and in collaboration. Producing other types of outcomes that do not relate to product or object making, but to the constitution of different types and practices of 'co-', like friendship, dialogue, and imagination: dramaturgy as 'co-'collaboration, one could say.

André Lepecki has proposed the notion of *co-imagination* to refer to the work of someone (often the dramaturg), who is imagining alongside an artwork. This imagining is not a 'personal hallucination', but done 'in consideration to all the elements at hand'.[16] Although Lepecki seems to relate this process mainly to temporary alliances and the production of certain artistic goals; for me his definition of co-imagination also applies to the process of interactions that take place in 'working not for a work': 'a dialogical procedure, of which the agents co-responsively participate in all that the work proposes already as a field of potential'.[17] In dramaturgy as 'co-'collaboration, imagining takes place not alongside the creation of an artwork but at the very core of the collaboration itself.

The work that is done together is quite literally 'a work on, or the creation of actions' (as is the proposed understanding of dramaturgy in this book), yet a creation of actions co-responsively to one another. These actions may seem not very productive from the outside, just like the exchange between Igor and me. Yet, this apparently unproductive, inconsequent, unspectacular 'space' is, as I experienced it, fundamental to co-doings like friendship and imagination, as well as interaction, dialoguing, discourse, the common, and other experiences of being shared. Dramaturgy as 'co-'collaboration then could be understood as a practice of co-doing sets of (seemingly inconsequent) 'dialogical acts', actions that matter *differently*.

In retrospect, my experience during the first day of the workshop 'Unfolding Dramaturgies' is very much an example of this type of dramaturgy in a broader context. Taking the exchange between Igor and me and, on another scale, the workshop, as microcosms of what is shared at large,[18] autonomous dramaturgical practices could be regarded as catalysts for similar elusive and non-manifested collaborative forms and processes. If through collaboration 'we condition [or imagine] our future together',[19] as Kunst wrote, then the unintended accomplishment of co-imaginative practices that work not for a work may even be the improvement of our shared skills to act upon that future.

Notes

1. The dramaturgical process served a specific mode of collaboration; a series of very simple acts brought in motion a thought process, that was not necessarily done for a particular work but a co-doing done in favour of the common work, the 'co-laboration' itself. Collaboration happened on one level through our actions, and generated all kinds of different thoughts/served multiple goals on another mental/subconscious level.

2. Here I choose to follow the understanding of dramaturgy proposed during the workshop by the editors of this book, as 'the working on actions' (stemming from the etymological meaning of the Greek term).

3. 'Not for a work' meaning here not in service of an artist's work/artwork.

4. In our meetings there is time to catch up, ask, reflect, be critical, think, exchange, watch something, imagine, be silent, eat, drink, advise, have a personal talk, make agreements, make another appointment that week, decide on things to do until we meet next time. One could say that is just an image of two friends hanging out. Which in a way is true.

5. Where Igor is dramaturg/co-creator of these works, I get involved subsequently as another voice, and as an observer. Mirroring my questions and observations gives both Igor and the artist a different understanding of how they work (together). In this case being 'the double' allows for an extra feedback loop in the dramaturgical process.

6. Rusham, 'Dramaturgy of and as Collaboration', p. 31, emphasis given in the original.

7. Van Imschoot, 'Brieven over samenwerken', p. 13. Translated by the author.

8. Kunst, 'Prognosis on Collaboration'.

9. Ibid.

10. According to Giorgio Agamben, that which is potential can both be and not be. If actualization is bringing things into the light, the potential maintains itself by remaining in the dark. The very core of potentiality is its *impotentiality*. To be potential means to be in relation to one's own lack, to one's own incapacity and non-being.

For more see: Nadal, 'The Concept of Potentiality, on Agamben'.

11. Kunst, 'Prognosis on Collaboration', *Post Scriptum.*

12. Joe Kelleher, during SPECTRA lab at WE LIVE HERE summer academy, which took place in 2015 in Amsterdam, the Netherlands.

13. Agamben in De la Durantaye, 'Friendship & Philosophy: An Interview with Giorgio Agamben', p. 53. Agamben says: 'In friendship, we do not share some specific thing; we ourselves are shared. To experience this is to experience friendship. ... I would argue that the first alterity is that of the friend. The enemy comes quickly thereafter and is the man who refuses to feel himself shared, refuses to feel himself divided. ... For this reason, friendship has a political meaning, for when we are able to perceive this threshold something like politics first becomes possible.'

14. Ibid.

15. Van Imschoot, 'Brieven over samenwerken', p. 13, translated by the author.

16. Lepecki in Crunteanu, 'The Power of "Co" in Contemporary Dance'.

17. Ibid.

18. As Hannah Arendt has pointed out, friendship participates in both realms of the private and the public: 'In its plurality it is a microcosm of a shared macrocosm.' Arendt cited in Nixon, 'Hannah Arendt and the Politics of Friendship', p. 173.

19. Kunst, 'Prognosis on Collaboration'.

— Crunteanu, Larisa. 'The Power of
"Co" in Contemporary Dance.'
Revista-ARTA online Magazine 16
January 2016. http://revistaarta.ro/
en/the-power-of-co-in-contemporary-
dance/ (accessed 11 June 2016).
— De la Durantaye, Leland. 'Friendship
& Philosophy: Interview with Giorgio
Agamben'. *Cabinet Magazine* 45
(Spring 2012), pp. 53–54.
— Kunst, Bojana. 'Prognosis on
Collaboration'. www.ivanamuller.com/
contexts/bojana-kunst-prognosis-on-
collaboration/#_ftn17 (accessed 11
June 2016).
— Nadal, Paul. 'The Concept of
Potentiality, on Agamben'. *Be Late
Blog*, 2010. https://belate.wordpress.
com/2010/04/04/agamben-on-
potentiality/ (accessed 11.06.2016).
— Nixon, Jon. *Hannah Arendt and
the Politics of Friendship.* London:
Bloomsbury Academic, 2015.
— Rusham, Martina. 'Dramaturgy of
and as Collaboration.' *Maska* XVI,
nos. 131–132 (2010), pp. 28–35. http://
sarma.be/docs/2873 (accessed 11
June 2016).
— Van Imschoot, Myriam. 'Brieven over
samenwerken'. *De Witte Raaf* 130
(December 2007), pp. 13–16.

Notes[I] from the Margin[II]

Jonas Rutgeerts and Ivana Müller

Prelude[III]

Instead of co-authoring a joint text about dramaturgy we, the authors of this text, decided to adopt a specific approach to work on it together: the marginal notes. This approach has resulted in a text that is composed of two elements: on the left page Jonas Rutgeerts has written a text discussing dramaturgy and on the right page Ivana Müller has annotated fragments of the text, which are marked in bold. This strategy constitutes a continuation of our shared dramaturgical work over the last years, during which we have been using and discussing the strategy of marginal notes in different formats. As such, the text can be read both as a reflection on dramaturgy and as an actualization of our specific 'dramaturgical work'.

The Dramaturgical Work

This text originates from a question that I asked myself when I started writing: what is my **artistic practice as a dramaturg**?[IV] The text in fact takes its cue from my inability to answer this question. I don't seem to have a clear 'practice'. My practices are multiple and constantly fluctuating. They constantly shift and always need to be constructed along the lines of a specific creation or research process. For this reason, rather than focusing on 'my' dramaturgical practice, this text sets out to explore another set of questions: How does dramaturgy work? What does it produce? And, what is the role of the dramaturg in the overall production of a performance or research? By focusing on the work of dramaturgy, I aim to shift the attention from an understanding of practice as a set of fixed methods that can be applied to — or imposed on — a performance, to 'practice' as something that always has to be created and maintained, and, as such, is constantly renegotiated and re-actualized.

Before I start discussing the work of dramaturgy, however, it is important to make a distinction between what I would call 'the dramaturgical work' and 'the work of the dramaturg'.[1] The dramaturgical work basically refers to the dramaturgical process that constitutes the piece, or research. It is the creation and maintenance of structuring principles, ideas, and problems around which a performance or research is *organized*. Dramaturgical work thus constitutes the heart of every performance or research, and is shared by everybody who is involved in it. The work of the dramaturg refers to the specific task of the dramaturg, who plays

I   *13 November 2015 15:29*: I would prefer it if 'M. Word' would have an option 'insert note' rather than 'insert comment'... because these short pieces of text that I'm going to leave on the margin of your text are rather questions, thoughts, impressions, and intuitions than 'comments'.

Also, while doing this peculiar exercise of formulating thoughts on the margin, in the 'comments' area, I started to be aware, even more than when writing on a 'page', of the limitations and frames that a computer programme puts on my thinking.

I also got annoyed by the fact that you, and everybody else, will be able to see at what time and on what day I was writing what I was writing.

I tried cheating on this (which I could if all of this was written by hand) ... but I didn't manage to.

II   *13 November 2015 15:33*: I couldn't help noticing that the title of this text resembles the title of the piece 'Some Notes On the Margin(al)' that we worked on together last year in BUDA in Kortrijk. I was wondering if there was any direct reference to the practice of working on that piece or to the piece itself, or if it is purely by accident that the title of that piece is so similar to this one. In any case, for that previous work I had asked you to do exactly what you have asked me now: to make some kind of notes to the text/texture that I was working on. In that work also other colleagues participated. One of them was Paula Caspao. She had brought to my attention an article in *The New York Times* that speaks about a practice that was used in the nineteenth century (probably because that was the historical moment in which a certain sort of 'democratization' of reading happened), but that already existed from the Middle Ages. The practice was called 'Marginalia' and it contained all sorts of 'gestures', notes, drawings, thoughts, and interventions on the edges of a book that were shared from one reader to another. For example, a lover or a friend would offer a book with the notes that s/he previously wrote in the margins of the book ...

III   *13 November 2015 15:50*: Interesting that you used a term that comes from music ... and not 'introduction' or 'preface'. I like the sound of 'Prelude' and I also like the set of associations it brings ... It creates a much nicer promise :)

Etymology: mid-sixteenth century: from French *'prélude'*, from medieval Latin *'praeludium'*, from Latin *'praeludere'* (play beforehand), from *'prae'* (before) + *'ludere'* (to play).

IV   *13 November 15:40*: I don't know why this surprised me, but it did. I never thought that you had an 'artistic practice'. I saw you more, in your diverse roles and positions, as a theoretician, as an artistic collaborator, as a thinker ... but never really as an artist. So this mentioning of 'artistic practice' made me curious. I started wondering if you sometimes see yourself as an artist. And then the question appeared: how to define 'artistic' in the 'artistic practice', and extending from this, is it possible to see a dramaturg as an artist? Also, why is it important to say, in this case, 'artistic practice' and not only 'practice', or 'practices of dramaturgy' since you say that they are 'multiple and constantly fluctuating'?

only a 'minor role' in the dramaturgical work.[2] In order to understand the specific work of the dramaturg, however, it is important
to first explore how the overall dramaturgical process **works**.[V]

The Dramaturgical Network

To come to a better understanding of the way the dramaturgical
process works, we could look at the notion of the 'network' that
cultural sociologist Stephan Fuchs develops in his book *Against
Essentialism: A Theory of Culture and Society*. Starting from the
assumption that persons are not the 'source or origin of society'
but rather the 'outcomes of some networks',[3] Fuchs sets out to
analyse the different 'networks of society and culture'.[4] In this
analysis, he focuses on the way networks control how and what
we observe. After all, what, according to Fuchs, distinguishes
networks from one another is not their internal composition
but the modes of observation that they produce. To understand this, Fuchs compares networks to '**metabolisms**'.[VI][5] Like
metabolic systems, networks cannot handle pure or raw data.
Networks need to **digest**[VII] the data. They need to decompose
and recombine them according to their 'blueprint' or 'internal
modes of operations'.[6] As such, networks constantly construct
their own 'chains of causality, their own perception of time and
history, and their own basic elements or building blocks'.[7] This
construction, however, and this is crucial, should not be understood as something fixed or stable. On the contrary, as the
network evolves and is confronted with new information, its
internal operation or **metabolism**[VIII] is constantly readjusted.
Fuchs calls this the moment when 'networks go to work'.[8] Confronted with new information networks work to readjust their
metabolism in such a way that they can take in, or **digest**,[IX] this
new information.

The conceptualization of the network as metabolism can
help us to rethink the dramaturgical process. This process now
becomes the collective work of a network that structures itself
via the creation of a specific mode of observation or metabolism.
As such, the dramaturgical process should not be understood
as the creation of new material, but rather as the creation of an
internal logic, or blueprint, which controls what 'raw material'
enters (the network of) the **rehearsal space**[X] and how this material is transformed — restructured and recombined — **into the
material that 'makes' the performance**.[XI]

V   *13 November 2015 16:01*: following this 'pas de deux' of 'dramaturgical and artistic' I went back to this part of the text and instead of using the word 'dramaturg' I changed it to the word 'artist' and instead of using 'dramaturgical' I used 'artistic'. This resulted in the following, confusing, but in some strange way interesting piece of text: 'Before I start discussing the work of dramaturgy, however, it is important to make a distinction between what I would call the "artistic work" and "the work of the artist". The artistic work basically refers to the artistic process that constitutes the piece, or research. It is the creation and maintenance of structuring principles, ideas and problems around which a performance or research is *organized*. Artistic work thus constitutes the heart of every performance or research, and is shared by everybody who is involved in it. The work of the artist refers to the specific task of the artist, who plays only a 'minor role' in the artistic work. In order to understand the specific work of the artist, however, it is important to first explore how the overall artistic process works.'

VI   *13 November 2015 16:13*: the idea of dramaturgy as metabolism is probably the most exciting idea of this text (and to me also the central one). Wikipedia has it that: 'The term metabolism is derived from the Greek Μεταβολισμός – "Metabolismos" for "change", or "overthrow".' The first documented references to metabolism were made by Ibn al-Nafis in his 1260 AD work titled *Al-Risalah al-Kamiliyyah fil Siera al-Nabawiyyah* (*The Treatise of Kamil on the Prophet's Biography*) that included the following phrase: 'Both the body and its parts are in a continuous state of dissolution and nourishment, so they are inevitably undergoing permanent change.' After reading this I thought that in order for dramaturgy to work, just as choreography, it needs to contain a notion of 'a movement' ... and by extension the notion of rhythm and some sort of musicality.

VII   *17 November 2015 15:21*: between the previous comment and this one there is a leap of time of almost five days. During this leap of time, the city I live in got attacked, the country I live in officially entered the war, and life as we knew it changed in a dramatic way. This new situation obviously influences my ways of thinking enormously, how I look at the reality surrounding me and respond to it.

VIII   *18 November 2015 14:38*: this is not directly related to your text, but, since Friday the thirteenth I am having a hard time reading this text without thinking of 'dramaturgies' of evil, 'dramaturgs' of war, 'dramaturgies' of media, and also 'dramaturgies' of love ... and the kind of metabolisms that construct them, comprehensible or not, tangible or not, visible or not.
I was thinking about different tools and methodologies to create 'behaviours', the way we structure order, the way we structure 'chaos' ... about rules, logic, and protocols we use to deal with the visible and the invisible ... and I thought a lot about the 'dramaturgies of the monstrous'.

IX   *20 November 2015 10:48*: many months ago, when we started talking about 'the margins' and 'marginal' connected to the piece 'Edges', we also talked about the idea of 'debris' or 'waste' or 'trash' ... you even started to articulate some thoughts around the 'theory of trash' ... we also spoke about 'ecologies' in the processes of making artwork, we spoke about the 'ecologies' of representation as well as of the 'ecologies' of gaze. I think these could be useful terms to think through in relation to dramaturgy today. I also thought about the idea of 'trash' in relation to the situation in which we are living now and the paradigms that are produced by it. I see a parallel between the states of (physical) bodies, the states of society, and the state of nature. The parallel between, for example, a cancer invading a singular body, the formation of the Islamic State invading social, economic, and political structures, and the formation of huge structures made of concrete physical garbage, such as The Great Garbage Patch in the Pacific Sea. These three phenomena were created by the 'occidental way of living' and through the 'metabolisms' these ways of living were supported by and perpetuated with.

X   *17 November 2015 15:22*: I would rather say: 'what enters into the process of making the piece' because 'rehearsal space' is too much of a physical space for me ... or maybe we should redefine it.

Two things characterize this creation of an internal logic. First, it is created at the level of the network. The dramaturgical process should not be understood as the creation of one person or a group of persons (the choreographer, the dancer/performer, the ensemble, the dramaturg, and so on), but as an outcome of the assemblage between all — human and inhuman — actors that take part in the dramaturgical process:[9] the choreographer, the performers, the technicians, the venue, the promotional apparatus, the technical apparatus, **and so forth**.[XII] Second, the dramaturgical process constantly rethinks itself at every moment of the process. The evolution of the project is not so much driven by the original ideas that initiate the process. Rather, the process transforms with every decision that the network takes and the original ideas are very quickly contaminated by decisions that are taken along the way. In other words, if one starts a dramaturgical process a hundred times, one will get a hundred different outcomes.

However, the fact that the dramaturgical process is not to be understood as a project that follows a specific plan, but rather as the constant renegotiation of the internal mode of observation on the level of the network, doesn't imply that the dramaturgical process is **uncontrollable**.[XIII] The process can be directed, but this directing should be understood in terms of *governing*, described by Michel Foucault as a 'mode of action' that 'structure[s] the possible field of action'.[10] Directing is thus not something external to the process and does not externally control it. Rather, it is a way of structuring the networks from within.[11] One can never be in control of the process but one can direct its course, in the sense that one can speculate on or imagine — to use a word that is closer to performative practice — how decisions taken in the present will influence future outcomes of the **process**.[XIV]

The Work of the Dramaturg

The dramaturgical process could be regarded as the work of the network that reproduces a specific mode of observation or internal code, through which 'raw information' is restructured and rearranged. This work cannot be controlled by one of its actors, but can only be 'governed' in terms of its future possibilities.[12] If dramaturgical work is understood in the abovementioned way as the work of a network, the following question arises: What is the specificity of the dramaturg's work within such a network?

What is interesting in this idea of 'entering' (*Enter Ghost*) is the level of 'conscious' and 'unconscious' ... this is what we are aware of and this is what we are not.

XI   *20 November 2015 18:53*: it is interesting that this process in which 'the material' (which is often not that 'material') is again a process of going from the invisible to the visible ...

XII   *20 November 2015 16:08*: ... the weather, the light in the room, the political and social situation, the emotional state of the participants, the food we are eating ... and also all of the ideas that we ever talked about during the rehearsal period (whether they are or aren't directly connected to the 'official' ideas of the show). I always think, as you know, that when we speak together or do things during the rehearsals we produce or call to life ideas that are then pending in the space in which we rehearse — like clouds or like invisible smoke. They stay with us all the time. They are invisible but very present ... and as they are part of the collective awareness (intelligence), at any given moment any of the participants in the process can reach towards them and bring them back into work(ing)... or simply be affected by them without even noticing it. In that respect we do behave like an organism (or like a metabolism, if you prefer). At the end, any interesting piece of work is a reminiscence, or a memory of the movements produced by those ideas.

XIII   *20 November 2015 16:22*: working on a piece is like going on an expedition towards a place that you know might exist (or at least you have a strong intuition about its existence) but you cannot be entirely sure about. The process of going towards that place is exciting but also dangerous ... you also have to keep on fuelling your belief, and also the belief of those that go through this with you, that at the end you will get there ... or at least that you will get somewhere. So it is better if you are equipped accordingly and it is even better if you do it in a company of good co-adventurers. The performance itself will finally take the spectators on a guided tour to that same expedition.

XIV   *20 November 2015 16:26*: it is important to be concentrated in order not to miss those 'switchers for imagination', keep an eye on the 'main road' but at the same time look there, where we are not expected to look ...

Before trying to formulate an answer to this question, it may be useful to unsettle some traditional assumptions on the work of the dramaturg. A first assumption is the idea of the dramaturg as the *guardian of the concept*, the one who needs to keep the work loyal to its original ideas. The problem with this assumption is that it fails to acknowledge the fact that the original ideas are always contaminated by the decisions that are taken in the process. Dramaturgy is a process of **autopoiesis**,[XV] in which formation and transformation are two sides of the same coin. As such, guarding the original concepts is frustrating, since these ideas will never come back in their original form, as well as counterproductive, as it fails to recognize the actual work that takes place in the dramaturgical process. A second assumption is that of the dramaturg as an *outside eye*. Although the dramaturg most of the time takes up a role in the network that is rather **peripheral**,[XVI] this does not necessarily mean that his position coincides with an outside perspective. This idea misses the specificity of the dramaturgical process, which is exactly the creation of and engagement in a specific mode of observation or point of view. Rather than being distant from the process of constructing and maintaining this mode of observation, the dramaturg engages in this process and figures out what it produces. He does not think about or interpret the process from a distance, but rather thinks through the internal codes of the network and tries to figure out its lines of operation, its consequences, its blind spots, and so forth. This brings us to the last assumption: the idea that the dramaturg functions as the **first spectator**,[XVII] the one who, to quote Bojana Cvejić, 'can predict what the audience see, think, feel, like or dislike'.[13] The implicit assumption here is that the audience is a stable and passive entity, whose only job is to observe and decipher the piece. However, as Marianne Van Kerkhoven points out, a production only 'comes alive through its interaction, through its audience'.[14] The audience is no passive consumer but an active participant, a co-worker of the network. As such, the task of the dramaturg is not to create some kind of interpretation of the audience's experience, but to open up the network and enable the spectators to actively engage with it.

So far, I have tried to **debunk**[XVIII] some of the dominant assumptions regarding the work of the dramaturg. **In this final part then, I want to delve deeper into what actually constitutes the work of the dramaturg.**[XIX] For this I need to turn once more to Fuchs'

^{XV} *20 November 2015 17:33*: Francisco Maturana and Humberto Varela, *Autopoiesis and Cognition: The Realization of the Living* (1980), p. xvii: 'It was in these circumstances ... in which he analysed Don Quixote's dilemma of whether to follow the path of arms (praxis, action) or the path of letters (poiesis, creation, production), I understood for the first time the power of the word "poiesis" and invented the word that we needed: autopoiesis. This was a word without a history, a word that could directly mean what takes place in the dynamics of the autonomy proper to living systems.'

^{XVI} *20 November 2015 17:38*: here I see the point of the title: 'Notes from the Margin' ... the word 'peripheral' performs very well ... being on the edge of the 'visible', yet not completely 'invisible' ... somewhere on the edges of the stage, somewhere between the stage and backstage, somewhere between the stage and the auditorium ... In fact, there is another figure from the world of theatre that comes to mind and is, on a more 'metaphorical' level, comparable to a dramaturg — the figure of a prompter (*souffleur*) ... It is funny that in French the name comes from the word '*souffler*', which means 'to blow'. In some metaphorical way the dramaturg can 'blow' new ideas into the work or 'breathe' those that got left in the air and forgotten back into the process.

^{XVII} *20 November 2015 18:02*: it is maybe interesting to think about the place of the spectator in different moments of the process of working on a piece. I guess that the 'first spectator' is the artist her/himself. S/he 'sees' (or maybe rather 'feels') if the ideas s/he is working with or is inspired by can potentially make a piece. The second 'spectators' are the collaborators that the artist invites to the process (performers, dramaturgs, sound/ light/costume designers, and so forth) ... their views on the ideas proposed by the artist construct the structural tissue of the piece ... then there are 'third spectators' which are colleagues, friends, 'outside eyes' that come in the studio to see the process (in its different stages and in their different functions) ... their point of view also 'feeds' the piece ... and then finally there are the 'real spectators'

who come on the premiere night and who keep on coming as long as the piece is being performed and who keep on influencing the piece each night of the show.

^{XVIII} *20 November 2015 18:21*: what a funny word! Apparently, it also means: Explode, deflate, puncture, quash, knock the bottom out of, drive a coach and horses through, expose, show in its true light, discredit, disprove, contradict, controvert, confute, invalidate, negate, give the lie to, prove to be false, challenge, call into question, demystify.

^{XIX} *20 November 2015 16:26*: it is weird that this now all of a sudden starts to sound like an academic paper.

conceptualization of the network. According to Fuchs, networks always tend to create 'self-similarity'. When the network matures it starts to repeat or resemble — itself and creates a clear and fixed identity. The network 'becomes institutionalized' and 'gradually sets variable limits on what is possible next'.[15] This institutionalization is not a problem in itself, as it is only through becoming self-similar that the network is able to establish and maintain a particular mode of observation or point of view. However, the danger is that these self-similar networks become self-referential. As the self-similarity of the network becomes stronger, the network may close itself off from the outside and make its internal dynamics absolute. The network then becomes rigid, as it forgets all the options that aren't actualized by the network but are nevertheless equally possible. This danger brings us to the task of the dramaturg. The specificity of the dramaturg's work lies exactly in countering this forgetting that is inherent in the actualization of the network. Rather than guarding the original concept, he is the caretaker of that which is not actualized. The dramaturg opens up the metabolism towards what is not a part of the network. His work is akin to the work of the marginal note, which is used to amend, support, critique, associate, link, and so on. It isn't part of the core of the text, but rather an interruption, an excursion, a small detour, a *fait divers*... As such, the marginal note does not destroy the main argument, but disrupts, amends, and opens it up to what it is not. It pokes holes in the text, without destroying its corpus.

The dramaturg's work can thus be understood as the creation of marginal notes. Notes that do not dissolve the dominant mode of observation, but augment it by expanding the possibilities and multiplying the codes. Rather than the guardian of the concept, the dramaturg should be understood as the guardian of the margins. He occupies the margins and opens up the network to what is not included. The dramaturg is thus able to amend and **subvert codes**,[XX] to keep the work open and to **postpone**[XXI] the process of self-similarity. To conclude I can go back to the beginning of this text, where I noted that the dramaturg only plays a minor role in the dramaturgical process. Referring to Gilles Deleuze and Félix Guatarri's concept of 'minor' we can understand this 'minor role' in a dual fashion: on the one hand it indicates the rather marginal and limited role of the dramaturg, being situated at the outskirts of the dramaturgical process, but

XX *20 November 2015 16:28*: I think that the artist should do this as well ... As an artist you have to move the point of view as well in order not to get 'stuck' in one vision. A friend of mine once said that when working on a piece you should at least have two ideas ... and your work is, in fact, organizing the space between those two ... maybe the artist's position is not as 'peripheral' as the dramaturg's, but even if you look from a more central point you are still able to, and you should, look left and right ... or even behind you.

XXI *20 November 2015 18:34*: or even avoided ... but that, of course, depends on how you define 'fixing'.

on the other hand it relates to the fact that the dramaturg is at the service of the minority, or 'force of variations' instead of the side of the majority, or 'power of constants'.[16]

As such, the task of the dramaturg could be understood as the seeding of 'crystals of becoming whose value is to trigger uncontrollable movements and de-territorializations of the... **majority**'[XXII][17]

Postlude

After receiving Ivana's notes I would have changed a lot: I would not have talked about my artistic practice, I would have questioned the academic character of the text, I would have elaborated on the idea of indigestion and marginalia... But, I decided not to cover up these differences in search for a common ground. Rather, I kept the little frictions in the hope that they perform a dialogue in which new ideas can arise. In the hope that the reader takes these frictions, conflicts, augmentations, and associations as an invitation to again rethink the text.

XXII *20 November 2015 18:36*: very
interesting turn into the 'politics' of
ideas and movements ... and a slightly
romantic, 'Robin Hood' way of seeing
a dramaturg :)

Notes

Bibliography

1 The dramaturg is not understood here as a person, but as a position in the overall network of the creation. Several people can take up this position at the same time, or different people can occupy it at different times.
2 I will return to the specificity of this 'minor role' later.
3 Fuchs, *Against Essentialism*, p. 8.
4 Ibid., p. 2.
5 Ibid., p. 264.
6 Ibid., p. 268.
7 Ibid.
8 Ibid., p. 269.
9 In connection to this we can also refer to Rudi Laermans' article 'Dance in General', in which he describes dance as 'the assemblage or force-field [that] consists of the shifting associations between light rays, sounds, bodily movements and non-movements, images, objects and the operations of technical artifacts', p. 12.
10 Foucault, 'The Subject and Power', p. 790.
11 However, this doesn't mean that directing should be understood as something that doesn't involve power. Quite the contrary, directing is always still synonymous with power, but as Laermans clearly points out, this power is not connected with the forbidding of actions, or with repression, but with a 'strategic acting on possible actions and interactions'. In 'Dance in General', p. 12.
12 This approach does not dismiss the difference between the different members of the network. The fact that all the actors in the network always share the work does not imply that one, or several members of the network cannot take the lead. It only means that all of the members are always at least partially co-responsible for the creation and maintenance of the mode of observation.
13 Cvejić, 'Dramaturgy', p. 47.
14 Van Kerkhoven, 'Het theater ligt in de stad en de stad ligt in de wereld en de wanden zijn van huid: State of the Union', p. 7.
15 Fuchs, *Against Essentialism*, p. 207.
16 Deleuze and Guattari. *A Thousand Plateaus*, p. 101.
17 Ibid., p. 106.

– Artistotle. *Nicomachean Ethics*. Trans. Martin Ostwald. Indianapolis: Hobbs-Merrill Educational Publishing, 1983.
– Cvejić, Bojana. 'Dramaturgy: A Friendship of Problems'. In 'Dance/Theories: Reloaded', ed. by Bojana Cvejić and Ana Vujanović. Special issue *Journal for Performing Arts Theory* 18 (December 2010), pp. 46–53.
– Deleuze, Gilles and Félix Guattari. *A Thousand Plateaus: Capitalism and Schizophrenia*. Minneapolis: University of Minnesota Press, 1987.
– Foucault, Michel. 'The Subject and Power'. *Critical Inquiry* 8, no. 4 (1982), 777–95.
– Fuchs, Stephan. *Against Essentialism: A Theory of Culture and Society*. Cambridge, MA, and London: Harvard University Press, 2001.
– Janša, Janez. 'From Dramaturgy to the Dramaturgical: Self-interview'. *Maska* XVI, nos. 131–132 (2010), pp. 54–61.
– Kunst, Bojana. 'Prognosis on Collaboration'. In 'Exhausting Immaterial Labour in Performance', ed. by Bojana Cvejić and Ana Vujanović. Joint issue of *Le Journal des Laboratoires* and *TkH Journal for Performing Arts Theory* 17 (October 2010), pp. 23–29.
– Kunst, Bojana. *Artist At Work: Proximity of Art and Capitalism*. New York: Zero Books, 2015.
– Laermans, Rudi. "Dance in General" or Choreographing the Public: Making Assemblages'. *Performance Research* 13, no. 1 (February 2008), pp. 7–14.
– Monni, Kirsi and Ric Allsopp. *Practicing Composition: Making Practice: Texts, Dialogues and Documents 2011-2013* . Helsinki: University of the Arts Helsinki, Theater Academy, 2015.
– Profeta, Katherine. *Dramaturgy in Motion: At Work on Dance and Movement Performance*. Wisconsin: The University of Wisconsin Press, 2015.
– Rancière, Jacques. *Le spectateur émancipé*. Paris: La Fabrique, 2008.
– Van Kerkhoven, Marianne. 'Het theater ligt in de stad en de stad ligt in de wereld en de wanden zijn van huid: State of the Union. *Etcetera* 12, no. 46 (October 1994), pp. 7–9.

Queering
Dramaturgy

Contagious Conversations

Joachim Robbrecht

'Must be something incredible inside there generating it (looks up from console). We're transmitting linguacode friendship messages on all frequencies', says Commander Branch in *Star Trek: The Motion Picture*.[1] A tensed crew is peering into the universe's darkness, trying to communicate with an unidentified object in a friendly manner. To me, the practice of dramaturgy bears a strong resemblance to this type of conversation – a practice of proximity generated by an encounter with 'something incredible' and 'unidentifiable', as if from outer space.

As a theatre maker, performer, and artistic collaborator,[2] I consider dramaturgy as immanent to the process of creating an artistic work and I practice it by means of conversation. More often than not, none of the collaborators would label herself as a dramaturg in the processes I have been involved with, and yet 'it' is happening. There are 'eyes' but there is no external eye that moves around the work like a satellite. All collaborators are intimately involved in the work. Hence, dramaturgy is relational and processual; it is that web of talks, thoughts, images, and sensualities that brings us towards the conceptualization of what we are actually doing ('the work'), and often resembles an 'unidentifiable object' during an artistic process. The creation and realization of the concept are synchronized. Consequently, dramaturgy is the conversation that pushes the work along while affecting it on many layers. It is unpredictable and has an improvisational – and sometimes dilettantish – quality. It is less a matter of strategy than of tactics. Strategy is 'clean'; it is detached from 'the battlefield' and requires plans and the conceptualizing of things far ahead. Tactics, on the other hand, are 'dirty'. Tactics involve being in the process, inventing tasks, reacting on the spot, playing around, and recalling experiences and productive practices.

Dramaturgy does not come with the dramaturg. Moreover, the dramaturg's reason of presence in a process is not to provide a concept. In the first place, the dramaturg is a conversationalist. She is an observer and a connoisseur of how conversations in an artistic process can be practised, fed, and made productive for the work. She is an expert in 'linguacode friendship messages'. In the collective process of dramaturgy, we discover the concept together. As Bojana Cvejić points out, artists and dramaturgs establish a relation of equality while the work itself stands in between them as the place of research. To work dramaturgically then means, as Sandra Noeth has rightly observed, 'to open up a space for reflection and creation inhabited by a temporary community'.[3]

In order to discuss dramaturgy, I will then explore three distinct but intra-related aspects of conversation that appear in artistic processes, a conversation that in general I understand as a 'contagious' one, because it spreads exponentially and affects multiple layers and aspects of the work. The first part focuses on acknowledging those agents (present and absent, human and non-human), who, through their multiple conversations, unfold the dramaturgy of the work by spreading it to one another. In the second part, the poetic elements of such conversation are stressed by proposing a consideration of dramaturgy as a practice of thinking through metaphors. In the third part, the dramaturgical force of such conversation is brought forth through a practice of 'queering' and reconfiguring what one thinks one already knows. Together, these parts seek to not only suggest dramaturgy as a practice of conversing, but also to propose conversation as a plural, poetic, and queering practice that puts at stake an artwork's coherency and 'identifiability'.

Who's There?

The space that opens up in an artistic process is never neutral. On the contrary, it only comes into existence through the activities that unfold therein. The same applies to any other social space. As Bojana Kunst points out, 'space is always formed by means of active processes of spatialisation that result from the activities, physical traits and structures of subjectivities with their social relations, fears, desires etc'.[4] Therefore, the dramaturgical conversation starts with the same words that Shakespeare also opens *Hamlet*: 'Who's there?'[5] Dramaturg Sandra Noeth elaborates on what this question comprises: '... the question of how community is created and whether we can still say "we" alongside the "I" is ... one of the fundamental questions of dramaturgy; the measuring of the distance to each respective Other'.[6] When Shakespeare's play opens we don't know what kind of Other is going to appear, a human or a ghost. When artistic collaborators enter a space to work, they come with their poetics, skills, vocabularies, ways of seeing, working methods, interests, desires, humour, and frustrations. One could say they are 'haunted' by voices and discourses that inhabit them.

Other ghosts haunt the process, too: the place, the temporality, the money, the policies, the programmers, the critics, and the audiences with their expectations, for example. Dramaturgical conversations aim to create space within this *haunted* universe, to give names to the ghosts, to clarify their agendas, and to find a way of moving and voicing among those ghosts. All interlocutors measure the field of forces they step into in order to sense what could arise.

In the working process of *Der kommende Aufstand* (*The Coming Insurrection*, 2012), initiated by the German collective andcompany&Co., we grouped collaborators from quite different artistic contexts around the issue of 'political resistance', and, more importantly, according to our approach on 'how to stage' this resistance. Dutch performers with a background in devised theatre and German actors from the Oldenburgisches Staatstheater met with andcompany&Co. One productive 'distance' we encountered during the process was the extent to which some of us would adopt a more re-presentational style of acting and others a more 'presentational' style. Whereas the actors from the Staatstheater relied more on impersonation and representation techniques, Dutch actors tended to perform in a more transparent style, meaning that they work more from their individual performative qualities. While acknowledging how entwined presentation and representation are, it was in these different types of acting that we recognized the potential to create the idiosyncratic language of the performance. By conversing and improvising together we therefore further explored how the variations in acting styles could be repurposed for this specific work. Acting in more or less 're-presentational' or 'presentational' ways tied into the question at the heart of this performance: How can one stage political resistance within the context of theatre? This was an intriguing experiment because of the tension between these two ways of approaching the question on 'how to act', which exceeds theatrical acting. From the perspective of political activism, for instance, theatre relies on representation, symbols, and abstraction, and acting can work in two ways: in the best case, it can amplify the voice of protest; in the worst case, protest acted out in theatre is nothing more than a substitute for *real* political action. Thus, one could argue that theatre that wants to address political issues and to enforce activism, should favour a concrete presentational way where the performer does not 'hide' behind a persona, but speaks what needs to be said on her own behalf.

Through our conversations in the end we realized how much the representational character of theatre is at odds with the active mode of revolt, because political issues need to be addressed directly and clearly in order to be effective. Yet, we also found historical examples of theatrical metaphors that were used in times of insurgency. The Dutch Revolt, for example, started by aristocrats and citizens dressing up as 'beggars' to reinforce their protests against tax reforms. The conversation around differences in acting style in theatre as well as in revolts produced a logic along which we could operate: we started the play as a conversation with the audience, using the 'human mic' procedure, where one performer would say something and then all the others and the audience would repeat it simultaneously. The dynamics of the play evolved then around the alternation of more discursive parts, in which the actors would employ a presentational style, and more dramatic scenes, in which a more representational style would be adopted. The moment of measuring the distance between the acting styles was followed by a movement of exercising one another's acting styles. Our research on acting through the lens of the question 'Who's there?' produced a way of playing different registers with different but specific effects. Making a play is imagining and creating another world where, as Sun Ra says in his film *Space Is the Place*, 'the music is different ... the vibrations are different, not like planet Earth'.[7] The shared endeavour between collaborators is to look away from the known, peering into the unknown. A certain will to explore one another's place, turning it into 'space as a practiced place'.[8]

The purpose of asking 'Who's there?' then in the creative process, is not so much in order to settle on whom one is dealing with. The question does not aim to 'situate' the collaborators and agents of a piece in terms of subjective states, emotions, and biographical histories that have to be part of the work. Rather than fixing positions, the aim is to set something in motion, to produce a language or explore a theme through an encounter. All agents function as 'materials' while finding out what they can vessel. Through such contagious conversations one tries to recognize the potentialities as they surface: the potentialities of strengths and idiosyncrasies, as well as the potentiality of limits, impediments, and failure.

Metaphors as Catalysts

The fact that we can ask 'Who's there?' implies that there is already 'something' that we carry along. There is some sort of linguacode one seems to develop and eventually acquire in each artistic process: vocabularies, sets of rules, a rudimentary Esperanto, that seem to be growing. However, every time a new artistic process is launched, we often face the same drama as on the Enterprise's bridge in *Star Trek*: the existing linguacode does not suffice to allow us to communicate with the 'something incredible'. It seems too primitive and fails to carry out thoughts, fails to convey what one really wants to say. We then need to slip into poetry, reaching for metaphors in order to boost our language. As Mark Johnson and George Lakoff have argued, metaphors are a matter of concepts, more than a matter of words.[9] Thought requires metaphors, and artistic processes especially seem to be fuelled by the construction of new metaphors. Metaphors initiate a movement in thinking, following the many directions their entailments point towards. They contribute to the space of reflection as they create a playing field between two concepts in which distance (difference) and nearness (similarity, sameness) between those concepts become apparent and produce new or other 'sense-making'. In this way, they open up a different dimension of conversation than the one opened up through the question 'Who's there?', that is the dimension of poetic language.

Metaphors often function as the catalyst to initiate a process of thoughts. For the performance *The Great Warmachine* (2015), for instance, my collaborators and I started off with a fascination with the phrase 'theatre of war'. In a simple metaphor like 'war is theatre' a space of truth and untruth exists between vehicle (theatre) and tenor (war) that provokes a chain of questions: To what extent does war equal theatre? Which implications are made when we envision theatre as war? What elements constitute the theatricality of contemporary warfare? Which sensations arise when thinking of theatre as war? And so on. A metaphor is like a crystal that refracts our perspectives upon things and produces a polysemic field. In a procedure of exploring the relation between the tenor (theatre) and the vehicle (war) of the metaphor, a space for rediscovery and rethinking of the metaphorical concepts that already guide our understanding of the world opens up.

In this context, I would even suggest approaching dramaturgy as a literal acting out of metaphors. By digging into conventional metaphors, or by creating new metaphors, a space is produced where the theatrical language encompasses the imperative of conveying information. Between the entailments of the metaphor, a poetic space opens up that can be explored in different directions. It resonates with each collaborator differently, thus enlarging the metamorphic complex. In extension, the audience too can enter the performance through the frame of the staged metaphor. Perceiving the metaphor is the first step in finding clues on how the multiple logics by which the work operates can be made productive.

Doing dramaturgy could therefore be considered as a conversation preparing for and infecting a coming conversation, namely with the audience. It means to uncover the metaphorical vectors along which an audience can slip into poetry. In an article on poetry and finance, Franco Berardi argues for poetry as a force to escape a language contaminated by the sphere of the market: 'Poetry is language's excess: poetry is what cannot be reduced to information in language, what is not exchangeable, what gives way to a new common ground of understanding, of shared meaning – the creation of a new world.'[10] Assuming that we indeed live by metaphors, as the title of Lakoff's and Johnson's book suggests, and that we interact with the world through conceptual metaphors, there is a poetic task at the heart of the dramaturgical conversation. Hence, working with metaphors means more than to discuss or create references to a real world that an audience may know or understand. Rather, through metaphors, we strive to displace the commonplaces, to find passages to a world where our language is carried away, 'generating effects of meaning never seen and codified before'.[11]

Queering: Out of Orbit

> If we keep on speaking the same language together, we're
> going to reproduce the same history. Begin the same
> old stories all over again. Don't you think so? Listen:
> all round us, men and women sound just the same. The
> same discussions, the same arguments, the same scenes.[12]

I consider dramaturgy as a tool to fight one's way out of the arguments, worn out questions, discussions, and metaphors we've had before. The dramaturgical conversation breaks the 'linguacode' one is raised in, dismantles dead metaphors and old conceptions, and brings together elements in a new constellation. This applies to the conversation of dramaturgy itself in the first place. Each inspiring text discussing the topic changes our conceptions of dramaturgical activity. Very often these texts are queering preconceived notions about what dramaturgy could be. One of the strongest examples is maybe André Lepecki's suggestion to see dramaturgy as a practice of erring rather than a practice driven by the desire to know.[13] In his text, Lepecki queers an idea, often heard in artistic practice, that the dramaturg is there to know, to see properly, to prevent mistakes from happening. Alongside Lepecki's insistence on the need for erring, I propose 'queering' as a necessary force for the dramaturgical conversation. Artistic processes very often suffer from an all too eager quest for clarity: we want to arrive at something. There's always a kind of authorial impatience in the face of approaching premieres and the expected (dis)approval of audiences, funders, and programmers. Facing those expectations, there is a tendency to return to the already known, to strong conventions, a habitual style, and clear positioning. Yet, whatever those well-known ingredients may be, they always disable us from seeing the potential difference, the other possibilities, the poetic proposal that the performance may hold. Hence, I would argue that fruitful dramaturgical conversation should begin with and insist on making oblique precisely those conventions, techniques, metaphors, and ingredients that we usually revert to.

Rather than solidifying the process into a product, queer-ings aim at weaving around the desire to create another world while keeping the material at hand flexible. We have a lot of con-ventions to strip, many changes of perspective to inquire. A lot of selections are needed, to make space for something unforeseen to emerge. In this regard, the strategies that feminist theorist Luce Irigaray proposes in order to be able 'to talk woman after Freud' in *This Sex Which Is Not One* can be inspiring. In her book she proposes several operations through which one may inter-vene in the phallocentric logic in order to testify to an elsewhere where the feminine exists beyond woman as the inverse of man. When Irigaray addresses how the 'theoretical machinery' should be 'jammed', she argues that to arrive 'elsewhere' and to establish a feminine language one should start by talking in disruptive excess to the existing male discursive logics in which women are already represented and subordinated in specific ways. Irigaray prioritizes 'thwarting' – I would say 'queering' – the discourse over directly challenging it. Parallel to philosophical and psychological discourse that Irigaray is especially referring to, a dramaturgical linguacode has its logics that can be found in metaphors, conventions, proper terms, styles, and recurring themes among many others. Queering them means to escape from fixation, adopting the characteristics of fluids – like 'those rubbings between two infinitely near neighbours that create a dynamics'.[14] When collaborators meet, it all depends on their readiness to rub, to scrutinize, to spoil one another's ideas and perspectives systematically. It means to unveil the fetish words, or the recurring metaphors. Only then, the distance between each Other becomes palpable, and only then a space, an 'elsewhere', for 'something incredible' to happen is disclosed.

An artistic work resembles the V'Ger, the living machine that is referred to as 'something incredible' at the beginning of *Star Trek*, and that achieves consciousness and accumulates astronomic amounts of power by nourishing itself with the 'friendship messages' it finds on its path through space. However, as the story goes, V'Ger desires merging with its creator to complete its mission. I would say that it is exactly this fusion of creator and machine that prevents perfection and in fact makes the living machine evolve into a new life form.

1 Livingston, *Star Trek: The Motion Picture*, www.dailyscript.com/scripts/startrek01.html.
2 Here I am referring to devised theatre processes of performance works that I have initiated or that I have participated in, which were conceived by other artists such as Sarah Moeremans, Dood Paard, and andcompany&Co.
3 Noeth, 'Protocols of Encounter', p. 254.
4 Kunst, *Artist at Work*, p. 57.
5 Shakespeare, *Hamlet*, p. 1.668.
6 Noeth, 'Protocols of Encounter', p. 254.
7 Sun Ra. *Space Is the Place*, www.youtube.com/watch?v=qvbXEYninTo.
8 De Certeau, *The Practice of Everyday Life*, p. 117.
9 Lakoff and Johnson, *Metaphors We Live By*, p. 244.
10 Berardi, 'Emancipation of the Sign', www.e-flux.com/journal/emancipation-of-the-sign-poetry-and-finance-during-the-twentieth-century.
11 Ibid.
12 Irigaray, *This Sex Which Is Not One*, p. 205.
13 Lepecki, 'We're Not Ready for the Dramaturge', pp. 181–97.
14 Irigaray, *This Sex Which Is Not One*, p. 79.

— Berardi, Franco. 'Emancipation of the Sign: Poetry and Finance During the Twentieth Century'. *e-flux*, 2012. www.e-flux.com/journal/emancipation-of-the-sign-poetry-and-finance-during-the-twentieth-century (accessed 21 November 2015).
— Cvejić, Bojana. 'The Ignorant Dramaturg'. *Maska 16*, nos. 131–132 (Summer 2010), pp. 40–53. www.sarma.be (accessed 21 November 2015).
— De Certeau, Michel. *The Practice of Everyday Life*. Berkeley: University of California Press, 1984.
— Irigaray, Luce. *This Sex Which Is Not One*. New York: Cornell University Press, 1985.
— Kunst, Bojana. *Artist at Work: Proximity of Art and Capitalism*. Alresford, Hants: Zero Books, 2015.
— Lakoff, George and Mark Johnson. *Metaphors We Live By*. London: University of Chicago Press, 2003.
— Lepecki, André. 'We're Not Ready for the Dramaturge: Some Notes for Dance Dramaturgy'. In *Rethinking Dramaturgy: Errancy and Transformation*, ed. by Manuel Bellisco, María José Cifuentes and Amparo Écija, pp. 181–97. Madrid: Centro Párraga, Centro de Documentación y Estudios Avanzados de Arte Contemporáneo, 2011.
— Livingston, Harold. *Star Trek: The Motion Picture*. Film Script. 1978. www.dailyscript.com/scripts/startrek01.html (accessed 18 October 2015).
— Noeth, Sandra. 'Protocols of Encounter: On Dance Dramaturgy'. In *Emerging Bodies: The Performance of Worldmaking in Dance and Choreography*, ed. by Gabriele Klein and Sandra Noeth, pp. 247–56. Bielefeld: Transcript Verlag, 2012.
— Shakespeare, William. *Hamlet*. In *The Norton Shakespeare*, ed. by Walter Cohen, Jean E. Howard and Katherine Eisaman Maus, pp. 1.659–1.759. New York and London: Norton & Company, 1997.
— Sun Ra. *Space Is the Place*. Film. YouTube. 1972. www.youtube.com/watch?v=qvbXEYninTo (accessed 21 November 2015).

Dramaturgy, What a Queer Thing to Do!

Jasna Jasna Žmak

There were six of us: a singer-songwriter, two activists, two dramaturgs, and a forensic anthropologist. All of us, more or less, queer. We spent a week together in an abandoned town somewhere along the coast, wondering what our chances of survival would be in case of an apocalypse. (Not too high, we estimated... but it was still fun to imagine ourselves as part of an end-of-the-world scenario.)

Then, one day, D, the forensic anthropologist, asked: 'But, guys, what is it that you dramaturgs really do?'

I don't think there exists such a heterogeneous practice as dramaturgy today, but I am quite sure that the one thing all dramaturgs have in common is the fact that they regularly get asked that same question.

Milan (Marković Matthis), the other dramaturg in the group, went on to explain that everything that lasts for any period of time has a dramaturgy, from relationships to TV shows, from history to music records... which means that dramaturgy is basically the art of dealing with time, a means to decide on how different elements of a given subject interplay mutually over a given period of time. And, of course, since every human activity has a temporal dimension, as Bojana (Kunst) claims in her text on projective temporality, this means that dramaturgy, too, can be found everywhere, which doesn't help a lot when it comes to attempts at defining it, I know...

That's why I just smiled and got a bit anxious, as I do every time someone asks this question. Then I remembered that I would soon have to write a text on the topic, so I told D I would send him this text, and maybe it would help him get a clearer picture about what it is that we dramaturgs really do.

On second thought, though, I realized that I could just write a letter *to* D, than write yet another text on the subject.

So, D, here is my letter to you, about what it is that we dramaturgs really do.

Dear D,

I remember being twenty and studying dramaturgy and not knowing what it was.

I remember being twenty-five and doing dramaturgy and thinking the same thing.

I remember being thirty and teaching dramaturgy and still not knowing what it was.

As you can see, I have a lot of memories of myself and dramaturgy and the unknown... but none of them helps when it comes to giving a straightforward answer to your question.

Recently though I realized that this is exactly what dramaturgy can be for me — handling complexities. Especially since the emergence of postdramatic theatre, which is not exclusively or primarily based on text, dramaturgy can be seen as the structuring of a multitude of different elements that are complex enough in themselves and which become so much more complex once they become intertwined. Before there was *just* a story, a plot, some characters, and that was it (yes, I am being deliberately over-simplistic!), but now there is an explosion of material that comes in, and all of it more frequently fragmented then logically structured.

Notice the verb I used above, *can*, not *is*, as I see dramaturgy as a field of endless potentialities. That's exactly why it is so hard to put a clear end on it, that's why it is more suitable to put a question mark at the end of its definitions, or maybe even an ellipsis, rather than a straightforward full stop. Yes, just like you and me, it is a very queer thing — it can be this, it can be that, a boy and a girl at the same time, but most of the time actually something in between and around, because it never stops to say, 'I am this' or 'I am that'... because it is well aware that, as D. W. Winnicott once said, those two words, *I am*, are the most aggressive, and therefore the most dangerous words in the languages of the world.

I know what you're probably thinking right now: 'This is just another pile of postmodern bullshit.' And, yes, I hereby admit: dramaturgy can be that as well.

Just, please, notice the verb I use. *Can*, not *is*.

I am sitting in a Belgrade café as I'm writing this. It's Monday morning. I just arrived here yesterday. It's not raining, but for the sake of this letter we're going to pretend it is. It's raining

heavily. This pleases me as I've got work to do and rain agrees with work.

My computer is open in front of me. Next to me is Maja (Pelević), a dramaturg, across the table from me Olga (Dimitrijević), another one, both of them with their computers open. (I don't know if you've ever met any of them, but I hope one day you'll have the chance to do so, as they are really wonderful people.)

We are all working, we are all working dramaturgs, dramaturgs at work.

I am writing a letter to you, this letter, which is actually a text on dramaturgy undercover (dramaturgy often operates that way, undercover and *incognito*; it is, just like a political agenda, for example, not necessarily visible, but always there, always present). Maja is exchanging emails about a program on philosophy and theatre that she is organizing at the National Theatre in Belgrade. Olga is working on an adaptation of some nineteenth-century novel for the National Theatre in Užice.

Working dramaturgs, dramaturgs at work.

And there are some others in town as we speak: Nina (Gojić) is also here. We both arrived yesterday from Zagreb. She had a premiere at the Belgrade International Theatre Festival (BITEF) last night, as did Rok (Vevar), who arrived a week ago from Slovenia to attend rehearsals of the same piece.

Olga was also part of the dramaturgs' team, and Ana (Vilenica), too, who is not here, and who is not usually a dramaturg, but was one on this occasion. You don't have to be a dramaturg to do dramaturgy, you see, that's the wonderful thing about it!

Minja (Bogavac) is also around somewhere, probably preparing for one of the roundtable discussions she is moderating during BITEF. Goran (Ferčec) is in town, too, reading at home.

Again, notice the verbs I'm using. Notice the verbs since there can be no dramaturgy without verbs... after all, a verb is a word used to describe an action, and *drama* is the ancient Greek word for action. So, to understand what we do as dramaturgs, notice the verbs. And then add a few more of them, and this is what you'll get:

We are watching dramaturgs, dramaturgs at watch.

> Listening dramaturgs, dramaturgs lending an ear.
> Dramaturgs asking questions, questioning dramaturgs,
> dramaturgs with question marks.
> Dramaturgs reading, editing, adapting.
> Writing dramaturgs and dramaturgs being written.
> Dramaturgs being talked to and dramaturgs talking.
> Dramaturgs at rehearsals, rehearsing dramaturgs.

But let's go a few steps back... linear narration is so passé these days, anyway. Let me be conservative for a moment and say that for me dramaturgy was always first and foremost about words.

> Yes, words.

I know you won't be the one to think I am conservative for saying that; you will probably be relieved. Words! Yes, words! Finally, something more graspable than all that po-mo nonsense. But my colleagues, dramaturgs, will probably think differently; they'll presume I'm on my way to becoming some kind of reactionary playwright... Words, what an old-fashioned thing to say.

I also believe it is a very old-fashioned thing to say, and although I couldn't exactly set a date for when it became old-fashioned, I am sure it falls somewhere in the previous century, somewhere around the time words stopped being synonymous with text, or rather, ever since text became much more than words... Once we started taking for granted that images, too, can be read, just like words, once we understood the same goes for sound, and movement, and film, words lost their privileged position, their magic aura.

So nowadays dramaturgy is about so many things, so many types of texts, that words easily fall behind. But I believe dramaturgy actually emerges the moment when one starts translating texts into words. Translating, another verb, yes. Translating images, sound, movement, film, in other words: translating texts, from one type of language to another, so that they could speak more easily to one another.

An analogy may help: we do with texts, what you, as a forensic anthropologist, do with bones. The only difference is, what you have in your hands is pretty solid, whereas what we have in our hands is constantly crumbling. We articulate them, give them a new meaning. You dig up bones, examine them,

find their connections and implications, create their context. We dig up texts, wonder about their identities, interpret them. And for that, we both need words.

We bring different types of texts back into words so we can understand them better.

> I hope you're not getting bored, D?
> I hope things are a bit clearer?

Just let me know if I am rushing too much, it is something I often do. I know it happens because I have a problem with time; I always try to squeeze as many things as possible into as little time as possible, so that later I will have more time on my hands.

If Milan is right, and I think he is, if dramaturgy can also be about dealing with time, I guess that makes me a bad dramaturg. Or maybe not necessarily bad, but neoliberal for sure. Trying to save time in a world in which time equals, well, money.

But you know what is wonderful about dramaturgy?

It never ceases to amaze you. It's like a game you can play with yourself. Yes, as a person, too, you can decide whether you want to be linear, predictable, or maybe opt for an open end or some kind of rhizomatic structure instead. I am not sure whether it is true that every man is the architect of his own fortune, but I am pretty sure you can at least be the dramaturg of your own actions!

What do I mean?

Here, I just decided I am going to stop rushing, I am going to break this bad habit of worrying about time and, for a change, I am going to pretend I have all of the time in the world.

So, I am going to fall silent, in a minute or so. And I am going to ask you to do the same. I am going to ask you to just sit in silence and observe that very silence. I think dramaturgy can be a great vehicle to remind us about the importance of being silent. I told you before, there is dramaturgy in everything, and this goes for silence as well... Yes, you can use dramaturgy in such a way to direct one's attention towards things one would normally (although I really don't believe there is such a thing as normal, but, as you know, I love contradictions!) not pay attention to.

Because you know what they say... maybe time is money, but silence is golden.

So, D, in a minute or so I am going to ask you to close your eyes and keep them closed for a while.

You may do whatever you wish with this silence. You may try to figure out the stuff that silence is made of, since silence, too, can be quite queer, if you know what I mean. You may want to estimate what your chances of survival would be in case of an apocalypse. You may want to think about what you're going to have for dinner, about whether it will ever stop raining, or about what John (Cage) would think of this. You can decide whether you want to stop or continue breathing. You can decide to open your windows beforehand, turn on your radio for some background noise, or put in earplugs. You can lie down or start jumping. You can smile or be dead serious. You can keep your eyes closed for as long as you want. It can be just a couple of seconds. It can be a few minutes. It can be several hours. The decision is all yours ... as I invite you to be the sole dramaturg of this silence you are going to create.

| There is just one thing I will ask of you.

After opening your eyes, I want you to remember something Tomislav (Gotovac) once said: 'As soon as I open my eyes, I see a film.' That is another thing dramaturgy can be for me – a blurring of the distinction between fiction and reality. Theatre always had problems with its own realness, and maybe even more with its own fakeness, the postdramatic kind even more so... and dramaturgy can engage with this distinction beautifully. Dramaturgy can be used in such a way that distinctions transcend their own binarity. When you finally do open your eyes, D, you will have to decide for yourself what it is that you are going to see, whether it is a film or theatre or something real.

And, along the way, I hope, you may understand a bit better what it is that we as dramaturgs do, since every decision you will make on how to use this silence will be an act of dramaturgy: by choosing *this* instead of *that*, by doing *this* instead of *that*, you will be shaping a moment of time according to what you believe is important...

Bibliography

— Kunst, Bojana. 'The Project Horizon:
  On the Temporality of Making'. *Le
  Journal des Laboratoires September*–
  December 2011. www.leslaboratoires.
  org/en/article/project-horizon/
  suivre-capturer-le-temps-dans-
  la-performance-contemporaine
  (accessed 24 February 2016).

A Brief Flight with Dramaturgical Thrusters
A Performance of Dramaturgy at Work

Nicola Conibere

A version of this brief text was originally presented at a round-table discussion in London as part of the project 'Dramaturgy at Work'. Embedded in the writing are three questions that were offered by the editors of this book as prompts for the discussion's participants. While preparing for the public dialogue I understood that the invitation I had received did not demand I reply to all, or any, of those questions. However, I soon found myself beginning to respond to each of them through a desire to find something like a complete answer to just one. It's tempting to name this a strategy of inefficiency because the only thing it could guarantee were fragments of what would be, presumably, more full and proper thoughts. Sure enough the words that emerged, and that were spoken live, claim some proximity to uncertainty, interference, and misdirection. In these pages I revisit their exploration of dramaturgy as term and practice through which to answer those questions.

> **Question 1**
> What types of actions are involved in your work? And, if we conceive of dramaturgy as 'working on actions', then what is the relationship of your practice to dramaturgy, from whichever perspective you work (maker, dramaturg, writer, curator, theorist, and so forth)?

The question is about my work. The work I choose to focus on is my choreographic work. There are multiple strands to this work and not all of them relate to the practice of choreography. I have chosen to separate these strands into two main categories:

1. Actions towards and of the *presentation* of a piece of choreography
2. Actions towards and of the choreography

In having identified these categories I don't wish to deny the other webs of thought through which I could have come to identify actions. For example, I could have considered all actions of my work through the frame of career advancement or through the filter of poetics. To that degree, the very idea of actions strikes me as a relatively arbitrary one, because it incurs categorization, and categorization is something we can mess around with if we choose. On that basis, noting a degree of arbitrariness seems quite productive.

Here are the lists I came up with:

Actions towards and of the presentation *of a piece of choreography:*

Gathering people
— To talk-think
— To make the piece
— To perform the piece

Securing resources/Entering systems (variable)
— To acquire funding
— To have money to live
— To have somewhere to work
— To have time to work

She realizes this list is potentially limitless, because everything in her life could find a way into it, and because its categories overlap endlessly. So, she stops having hardly begun.

You might notice that she has begun to refer to herself with the third-person pronoun. We may consider this as a form of dramaturgical interference. She wonders if calling on a third person means a first and second are already present somehow, perhaps residing in 'we'. She wonders if their bodies also haunt this text. She considers that her movement from first to third is one that invokes a change in perception of distance between subject and object, or object and person, or person and body, and so on. For now, her main concern is finding escape from the potentially boundless content of this initial inventory of actions.

Next she shares her list of:

Actions towards and of the choreography:

Thinking in her head but which does not deny her body:
— Conceiving
— Questioning
— Proposing
(these are immaterial acts)

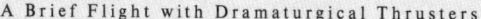

Thinking through practical explorations that will:
- Create relationships between materials
  or materialities (human bodies, space of
  performance, time of performance, other objects
  all can be experienced as tangible in different
  conditions)
- Create fields of sensorial relations (that may
  include: sense of time, sense of emotion, sense
  of thought — could be called atmosphere)
- Create situations in which thinking, feeling, and
  relating will occur, that is, in which people will
  affect and be affected through their bodies
- Propose ways for people to be with one another
- Propose ways that people may appear with and
  to one another

Presenting the piece:
- Making a social gesture (of exchange or encounter)
- Inviting people to exercise attention, or shifts
  in attention (possibly away from dominant
  discourses)

She is struck that if she were to reduce the actions on this list — this list of actions towards and of choreography — into one single action, then it would be: to socialize, or, to explore what it is to be social.

She decides to return to the question. If dramaturgy is working with these actions as the actions involved in her practice, then dramaturgy creates the nature of the proposal of a given piece. She considers that she also calls this choreography. She is not claiming that choreography and dramaturgy are the same craft, nor that choreographers and dramaturgs do the same thing, simply that this journey, of answering a question about actions, has produced that statement.

He wonders where, within the terms provided here, some distinctions may arise between choreography and dramaturgy. He considers that choreography may be experienced as emergent from within a choreographic event, or that choreography's reach may encompass the quality of encounter for its spectators. So, then, does choreography partly exist in the socializing, whereas dramaturgy hangs mostly with structures? But choreography is structural, too. He's thinking of structures as organizing forces. He asks himself if dramaturgy is inherently antisocial, but this seems unlikely, because it so often works with people.

> *As you can see, he has changed his gender pronoun. This is probably connected to that whole idea about categorization being arbitrary and something we can play with. Given that this is his second pronoun movement in this short text, he wonders if the establishment of a pattern undoes a claim to interference. He thinks this might be a matter of duration – that the effects of a particular style of formal distraction depend on its iterations and accumulation over time. He thinks about thinking – that in these sections of narrative he 'considers' and 'wonders' and 'asks', and that these terms do not offer a definitive claim to a subject. They are not expressions of conclusion.*

He reads 'Question 2' but does not want to answer – its references seem daunting.

Question 2
What kind of conditions, contexts, frames, and institutions do you set up in order to trigger actions that support experimentation, research, and, potentially, knowledge production?

He thinks about what it would be to reimagine institutions, including conceiving their forms as organic, as unfixed. He lives in a society in which institutions are built on foundations of patriarchy and discrimination against certain types of bodies, and in which institutional racism is common, so he wonders what potentials an institution of unstable or changing form may offer for challenging these concerns. He thinks that choreography, in part, offers the risk of a social encounter whose nature is no different from that of meeting people on the street. That it can propose ethics for what people may generate together. That we can imagine forms of institutions as proposals for how people can be with one another just as choreography does.

But he doesn't set these things up, which is what the question asks. His words are divergent.

He realizes that he is refusing, or failing, to answer the query and yet moves on to the third and final question, which is:

Question 3
How may dramaturgical actions that are indirect or inefficient, ambiguous, interfering, or even sabotaging, enable a continuous dialogue between discourse and practice, or lead to further artistic and social imaginings?

Records indicate that they would not answer this question for a number of reasons:

1. They remained uncertain about what constituted a dramaturgical action.

2. There was an end reference in the question, about continuing dialogue and imaginings. They realized that if actions could generate those outcomes as desirable, then they would no longer be inefficient or interfering (but perhaps they could still be ambiguous).

3. They realized that this question had become a form of interference for the stratifications that may locate them in time and in space and in their bodies.

Desperately confused, but finding solace in their decision, they fired up the engines.

'Specimen 115,' it said. 'Let us render the subject useless that it may find new fields of being.'

'Yes,' said it. 'The potentials of the body is not in its deeds, but in its capacities for affect.'

At the point of leaving Earth's atmosphere the amorphous mass fell about a bit. The cause of its movement is unknown.

Dramaturgy or Not: Shaking the Grounds

Unworking Dramaturgy

Simon Bayly

We worked on actions. Without funding or gigs lined up, we simply met and played around. We found a pub landlord happy to lend us his upstairs room for no money for as long as we liked. We worked elsewhere: in hospitals, sandwich bars, hotels, and budget restaurants. Or we did not work at all. We eyed up and sometimes conversed with our peers in London's ICA bar, incongruously located a few hundred metres from Buckingham Palace, after performances we'd seen listed in *City Limits* magazine (now long defunct). We went round to people's houses just to see if they were in. We marched against the poll tax, ran away from the police horses that charged at us across Trafalgar Square, and went home to watch the riots on the television news. Cars and buildings were burning in central London.

Above the pub, we generated tasks, routines, movement sequences, bits of scenes, and sections of dialogue. But the real problem was always how to get from one bit to the next bit — and why. Everything always got lumpy, congealed, constipated. We worried enviously about shows made by other artists that we hadn't seen, shows that really went for it, that doubled down on 'shitting and fucking their way across the stage', as we enviously called it. We struggled with the 'through line', motivation, and emotional arcs, and all the rest of the dramaturgical baggage we thought we could leave behind. What did it all add up to? We were anxious. One show followed the next but not in a way that made sense. Things didn't feel quite right. John Major took over from Thatcher as leader of the Conservative party and then implausibly won the 1992 election. What were we anxious about? We were anxious about how an action ought to imply and lead forward into the action that followed it and necessarily arose from the one before. We were anxious about what to do when the inner logic of a theatrical — or political — sequence didn't follow a logic we could recognize, a logic that wasn't part of the plan, even if the plan was not to have a plan. We were anxious about *dramaturgy* or, more precisely, about the absence of a dramaturgy, which, we considered, ought to look after itself.

At the tail end of the 1980s, we were happy enough with the label 'experimental theatre'. But through the intervening years the labels that named an uncertain centre of attention in the ecologies of the European performing arts scene were often taken as less than satisfactory, from performance art and Live Art through to physical theatre, dance-theatre, postmodern performance, postdramatic theatre, and on to conceptual dance, the metamodern and the altermodern. During this sequence, as drama and the theatre itself were dialectically interrogated as objects of concern for many theatre makers and theorists, the dramaturg emerged from the darkness of a seat in the stalls of the theatre institution to take her place in the ensemble of performance professionals at work in the well-lit studio. Among the many identities and roles attributed to the dramaturg in the performance-making process, one particular figuration recurs: the dramaturg enters the scene of creativity as, above all, the harbinger of anxiety.

More Anxious Dramaturgy

The title of Myriam Van Imschoot's well-known essay 'Anxious Dramaturgy' introduces what may seem a merely accidental leitmotif in the construction of the character of the contemporary dramaturg: 'the discourse on the new dramaturgy (be it theatre or dance related) is mostly structured around a couple of tropes, or to put it another way, anxieties'.[1] The shift here from tropes to anxieties seems studiously casual, as if tropes always come freighted with anxiety. While the title is ambiguous as to who is actually anxious – is it the dramaturg herself? – the body of the article is clear that a certain configuration of the dramaturg is the object of anxiety experienced by the artist. With a view to generating an alternative version of an un-anxious dramaturgy that has no need of a dramaturg, Van Imschoot is interested in a 'counter narrative that brings a different emphasis and tilts the tropes'.[2] In the multiple articulations of this counter narrative that propose a dramaturgy without a dramaturg that follow on from Van Imschoot's initial provocation, anxiety demonstrates its powerfully recursive ability to reproduce itself, generating not just more anxiety, but also anxiety about being anxious. This is clearly in evidence in Pil Hansen's introduction to the 2015 collection of essays, *Dance Dramaturgy*, which attempts to finally have done with the apparently inescapable aspect of anxiety provoked by the dramaturg:

> Tropes of anxiety have dominated discussions of dance dramaturgy since they were first effectively articulated by ... Van Imschoot in her article 'Anxious Dramaturgy' in 2003... . When I too begin my discussion with these

tropes, it is done as a step towards fresh proposals that are embedded in practices from different contexts and times than those for which Imschoot wrote. ... Surely now, this figure is ready to leave anxieties behind and formulate new tropes of dramaturgy to draw from, discuss, critique, and evolve.[3]

But why *does* anxiety so persistently attach itself to the figure of the dramaturg? It is hard to think of another affect that cleaves so closely to any other type of artistic identity, despite its widespread circulation within a broader turn towards emotion and feeling within cultural theory over the last two decades. In his contribution to Hansen's collection of essays, André Lepecki provides a striking restatement of dramaturgically induced anxiety:

His or her arrival (whether early or late) reveals a constitutive anxiety at the core of our current economy of authorship.... The dramaturge personifies a function that generates anxiety at the level of readiness, and readiness for what? Readiness for knowing what the piece is (about).[4]

For Lepecki, the dance dramaturg embodies a crisis of 'knowing and owning' within the distributed labour of contemporary performance making, 'putting into question the authorial stability of those who are supposed to know the work to come'.[5] In outlining this chimerical identity, Lepecki makes use of the Lacanian concept of the-subject-supposed-to-know, characterizing the dramaturg as a kind of stand-in for the analyst within the psychoanalytic dyad: the figure into which the analysand (or artist) must necessarily project the knowledge about the source of his or her own suffering (or lack of knowledge) in order to mobilize the transference that is the motor of the analytic (or creative) process. The role of the dramaturg-as-analyst then becomes the dissemination of this projected figure of knowledge among the ensemble of performance makers. As a consequence, the dramaturg, alongside her colleagues, is thus released into 'pure work' so that all may wonder, wander, and err in negotiating with the logic of the '*work-to-come that owns its own authorial force*'.[6] While we may have become somewhat comfortable with the language of knowledge, ownership, and work as terms of value within artistic practice within wider contexts of the so-called 'knowledge', 'experience', or 'sharing' economies, their presence within discourses of making performance is disarming. 'Pure work', along with 'the sovereign force of the work, of the need for all to work for the work' are themselves unusual, anxiety-provoking turns of phrase.[7] This is especially the case within cultures in which artistic subjectivity is increasingly characterized as the iconic form of existence for all subjects labouring under what gets called neoliberalism or late capitalism. What happened to, say, *play* rather than work, or *intuition* rather than knowledge, terms that were given priority in artists' own understanding of their activities not so very long ago? Not-knowing, navigating the unknown, wandering, erring, and similar phrases have, in the intervening period, become the standard descriptions of the artistic (non-)method required to justify itself in the struggle against the authority of knowing better. While this shift may indeed mark a 'dismantling of a certain (theological) image of creation' that valued the signature, the auteur, and an individualized mode of authorship — a job that remains as incomplete as ever — what today is more theological than the unassailable value assigned to *work*?[8] And what happens when the errancy of not-knowing itself becomes a heavily worked object of knowledge, for inclusion in measures of research excellence, collaborative funding bids, and self-evaluation documents, no doubt involving the further work of dramaturgs? There is no straightforward response to the hysterical form of these questions, which bring with them their own kind of creeping anxiety. Later in this essay, I return to notions of work, dramaturgy, and agency within the wider context of political transformation. But here, I want to draw out more precisely just what is so anxious about dramaturgy.

In several anecdotes about dramaturgy, the dramaturg is often figured as an uninvited or accidental guest. In this sense, the dramaturg enters the scene as a figure of fantasy from the outset, since presumably in most actual situations, dramaturgs are actively solicited for their contributions. Van Imschoot tells what I presume has become almost a founding parable of the politics of contemporary dramaturgy: a story from the early 1990s of how the Belgian Klapstuk festival requested that the Portuguese choreographer Vera Mantero work with 'a dramaturge of the North'.[9] In her telling, it's not clear that such a request was either agreed or worked through, but that does not seem to be the issue, since the demand itself is the problem. Similarly, trying to find professional placements for students in his experimental dramaturgy course, Lepecki finds New York's dance and theatre companies curiously resistant to his enquiries. Nobody is ready for a dramaturg right now, but maybe next year. Lepecki ends his second strewn note on dance dramaturgy with a Brechtian poem-fable:

> Who is ever ready for the dramaturge?
> When is one ever ready for the dramaturge?
> Why is one rarely ready for the dramaturge?[10]

Lepecki reminds us that the anxiety induced by the dramaturg arrives not through the abstraction of a knowledge that is lacking in the rehearsal studio but in the very physical presence of the dramaturg's body. This accords with the psychoanalytic understanding that anxiety does not arise from the absence of an object but from its excessive presence. At the most basic level, anxiety results from the intrusion of the always excessive enjoyment (*jouissance*) of the other, be that the other whose music plays too loudly in their headphones, talks too much on their mobile phone in the train, smells too much, spits in the wrong place, says the wrong thing, or arrives – as does the dramaturg – with the knowledge of the power of non-knowledge that no one else realized that they didn't have. Within the fragile ecologies of non-industrialized forms of creativity, non-knowledge is typically held to be common knowledge. We all forgot how to carry on quite a while ago: the drugs of method, technique, or system don't work, that much we *do* know. Everyone knows that we don't know and so we don't need to talk about it. That's how we, minimally and anxiously, enjoy. If and when the dramaturg arrives, even from among ourselves, she arrives as a 'plus one', the one whose arrival reveals a sense that there is something missing that no-one knew was missing, some kind of creative juice or other libidinal, sense-making stuff, the stuff of dramaturgy. The arrival of the dramaturg thus indicates the irruption of the absence of an object – non-knowledge as a stand-in or placebo for knowledge – but one that was always lost. Not-knowing was never ours, neither was knowing. But we didn't know *that* until the arrival of the dramaturg, who brings the gift of something she doesn't have, for those who don't want it because they don't know that they didn't have it in the first place. This is properly *enervating*, in the sense of being in the presence of something vital and potent that drains one's own vitality and potency while simultaneously attempting to animate it. And what is the gift of dramaturgy, its promise? As Lepecki has it: 'aesthetic consistency, solidity, and coherence (even if the desired coherence is to be incoherent)', the balm for every artistic anxiety.[11] In what form does this gift arrive? Words, mostly words: the intimacy and proximity of talk or conversation, the promise of dialogue.

But aren't words, like other people, exactly what gives us trouble, what provoke our anxiety? Words, like thoughts and bodies, are what confront us, what we have to cope with. If there is a word, it arises out of something that requires our attention, like the arrival of the other, something that we cannot ignore. This strange kind of trouble is what we *enjoy without knowing,* since we cannot get on the far side of our enjoyment to examine it. And so what I ultimately enjoy is not my enjoyment, but yours, in a play of mutual disturbance, which neither of us *know* about. The dramaturg brings the thoroughly ambivalent gift of words and a body that is revealed – in a dance situation perhaps more than any other – as strictly surplus to the requirements of pure work. *What are you doing here?* A question that could be repeated, the repetitions giving each word a special emphasis that would generate another question that requires its own answer: *What* are you doing here? What are *you* doing here? What are you doing *here*...?

In this sense, the dramaturg arrives already dressed up in a cloak of theatricality, somehow appearing as both an equal member of a collaborative community operating under an ethics of mutual support *and* an alien presence commanded by a mysterious higher power whose intentions may well be malevolent. This added complication provokes yet more anxiety, since enjoyment reveals its deceptive inconsistency when we sense its manifestation as a simulation, as a performance put on for show. We understand that the performance of not-knowing is proper to the role: the dramaturg will profess her ignorance, tell us that she knows that she doesn't know. But isn't it precisely because of this performance that we invest in our belief that the dramaturg does actually hold a special kind of secret knowledge in reserve, a knowledge that is brought to the threshold of the room but not quite inside it? (I know very well that you don't know, but all the same ...). Furthermore, it remains unclear in whose interests this secret knowledge may be put to use. The dramaturg's errant performance of not-knowing avows there is no enjoyment to be had in knowing, that her hands really are empty. Yet this very avowal seems to carry its own residual kernel of enjoyment — something *must be* up a sleeve somewhere — which is provocatively maddening.

If dramaturgy as the art of knowing how to produce 'aesthetic consistency, solidity and coherence' belongs to everyone — yet no-one feels like *they* 'have' it — and if it can only be immanent in the fantasy that is the work-to-come, then it becomes a fantasy without a subject, a project without a 'prime mover'. Which may well be how it is, but no less anxiety-provoking at the level of experience for being so. This is why the fantasies of dramaturgy without a dramaturg actually have so much to say about the dramaturg as an actual person, dealing in stories and confessions of what she does or does not do, the feelings she generates, the difficulties of her position.

The disturbing physical presence of the dramaturg (or even the anticipation of such a presence), apart from and to one side of her words of non-knowledge, mobilizes a deceptive sense that a lost originary drive towards coherence and consistency may be recovered through her 'hands-on' capacities. In that sense, the dramaturg is used to fill the void left by the dismantling of former figures of authority and agency. But this is a role she cannot fulfil. Thus at the same time, this fantasy facilitates an anxiety-producing encounter with the impossibility of the dramaturg functioning as an effective stand-in, which demonstrates a flaw in the habitual symbolic structures of authorship, knowledge, and belief: here is the dramaturg who comes with the news that she has, in effect, no actual dramaturgy. Indeed, within the dramaturgy of this fantasy, the notion of agency itself falls into an instant obsolescence, leaving behind a de-dramatized disarray of a knowing not-knowingness. Put simply, the presence of the dramaturg, whether in the rehearsal studio or in the production credits of the programme handed to an audience, sets in motion this process of disorder when it comes to making sense of what happens and who is responsible for it.

Dramaturgy in the Expanded Field: Working on Actions
As hinted at in my opening evocation of a minor personal artistic crisis of dramaturgy taking place within a much larger context of the altered dramaturgy of British politics in the 1990s, we can connect the crisis of agency effected by the dramaturg

in the rehearsal studio to broader questions about who or what is responsible for the dramaturgy of *political* transformation. These questions arise as consequence of a widespread loss of faith across the spectrum of leftist thinking about the potential of any agent whatsoever to bring about a 'consistency, solidity and coherence' that may bring a post-capitalist horizon into view. What has to be confronted in this situation is the public loss of a privileged object. In relation to the politics of dramaturgy and the dramaturgy of politics, that lost object is, at its most basic level, a prearranged set of dramaturgical roles and responsibilities in the initiation and sustenance of a political sequence. The question of how to mourn the loss of that object and move on from what Wendy Brown diagnosed as the contemporary version of Walter Benjamin's notion of 'left melancholy' has provoked a set of antagonistic responses, ranging from a micro-politics of local communitarianism, to Michael Hardt and Antonio Negri's horizontal conception of a global multitude that is allergic to all forms of institution, from Alain Badiou's philosophy of the event to Slavoj Žižek's call for a return to Leninist formulations of hierarchical organization and party, all further complicated by the messy, ongoing realities of the Arab Spring, Occupy, and the tactics of occupations in urban centres from Madrid to Istanbul to Hong Kong.[12]

Another, more oblique response to this situation is contained in the brief from the editors of this volume for the roundtable discussion that prompted this essay.[13] There, the phrase 'working on actions' was used to describe an unspecified kind of practical activity that related to questions of dramaturgy, which I took as an invitation to think about the relevance of dramaturgy outside the confines of not just the rehearsal studio but of artistic practice itself. As the start of this essay suggests, my thinking snagged on the elegant awkwardness of the phrase: actions, to act, work, to work, yes — but 'working on actions'? What did that imply that may be different from either acting or working? And working on actions *where*? In the rehearsal studio or the urban occupation — or both? And what would be the connection between the two spaces? These kinds of questions bring their own anxiety in relation to the ways in which artistic discourse has internalized an impossible demand to become the sole agent of a response to the contemporary political impasse. The extent to which such a demand has become relatively unproblematic is demonstrated, for example, by the fact that

Boris Groys is able to assert, apparently without irony, that 'in our contemporary world, only art indicates the possibility of revolution as a radical change beyond the horizon of our present desires and expectations'.[14] Yet at the same time, other articulations diagnose new forms of artistic subjectivity as entrepreneurial, autonomous, collaborative, risk-taking, flexible, nomadic, and operating in close proximity with the latest phase of neoliberalism expansionism, where Joseph Beuys' notion that 'everyone is an artist' has mutated into the demand to continually strive to invest in and maximize one's social capital.[15]

'Working on actions' appears to allude to activist language for the preparation of a direct action, which aims to prevent or obstruct another organization from carrying out a particular action to which activists are opposed. As the phrase implies, a direct action entails a material intervention into other spheres of life beyond the context of its conception and preparation, which may or may not involve violence and destruction. Several of the questions in the brief alluded to above asked explicitly about how dramaturgy may be thought with regard to cross-overs between art and activism, concluding with the following: 'Can we talk of "effective" political actions today? What would those be?' With these questions, with a jump straight from the studio to the street, dramaturgy is once again put into intense and perhaps unbearable proximity with politics. Once *again*, because, as most of the recent debate on dramaturgy within postdramatic theatre and dance appears to keep at more than arm's length, dramaturgy as a concept has a fraught relationship with the political, dating back to (and far beyond) the dramaturgical sociology of Kenneth Burke and Erving Goffman in the 1940s and 1950s, Victor Turner's notion of social drama and Raymond Williams' concept of the dramatized society from the seventies, and the subsequent consolidation of Performance Studies as an academic field of enquiry. The deployment of dramaturgy in relation to politics was a cause of anxiety from the start. In 1959, Goffman had already put it plainly: 'All the world is not, of course, a stage but the crucial ways in which it isn't are not easy to specify.'[16] Even Judith Butler, from whose understanding of the performative many have tried to extract the possibility of effective political actions, remained awkwardly resistant to any straightforward move to political efficacy in a 1999 interview:

> But a politics, you want me to move to a politics... (*Police car siren sound*)... there's politics... a state of emergency... I actually believe that politics has a character of contingency and context to it that cannot be predicted at the level of theory.[17]

But the political appeal of the dramaturgical is equally difficult to dismiss. In another interview that touches on recent politics and practices of occupation, Butler asks a question that is essentially dramaturgical:

> perhaps we can ask more precisely how to make sense of bodies that assemble on the street, or that occupy buildings, or that find themselves gathering in public squares or along the routes that line the center of cities?[18]

Rather than simply a question of making sense of such assemblages from the point of view of a disinterested spectator (what does all this add up to? what does it mean? what can one make of it?), I take this question to be one about sense-making as composition – what can we make *from* it? How do we compose, connect, and articulate these assemblages with other ones? And not just those that appear similar but also those that do not resemble them, but nevertheless share some kind of essential orientation. This would seem to be the essence of dramaturgical work. Indeed, contemporary activism and philosophies of multitude or insurrection do seem to share, along with the arts of performance, choreography, and dramaturgy, an affinity for the bringing together of bodies in physical space. In these figurations of the embodied collective, what commands attention are the sensory qualities of encounter and the production of pleasurable intesities in the reinvention of everyday life. The inclination towards the affectively charged atmosphere of mutual aid seems particularly active in the practice of occupation and its commitment to persistence, duration, and self-organization over and against acts of temporary insurgency, however playful, imaginative, or inspiring. The critique of the aestheticization of politics as being essentially the politics of fascism has been entirely rerouted – the city square occupations of 2008 to 2011 have been repeatedly made sense of as transient acts of self-organized, collective, aesthetic compositions of the social that put centre stage the discursive practice of free citizens interested in the organization and running of the *polis*. Hence the significance accorded to the 'general assembly' in these occupations and analogue theatrical fetish of something like the 'human mic'.

But for many of the earlier theorists of social and political dramaturgy, this reification of the apparatus of performance within delimited spaces of appearance would point to its restricted mode of operation: spectacle met with more spectacle and then the predictable spectacle of its repression. With the proliferation and near-naturalization of the performance paradigm over the last two decades, Goffman's problem about the ways in which the world is *not* a stage has only become more acute. If we admit that Jon McKenzie's assertion that the universal *dispositif* of capital endures as the pumped-up demand to 'perform or else', then an activist or anti-capitalist dramaturgy surely has to ask what remains unperformed and unperformable today.[19] What, in social or political life, is *not* subject to the logic of dramaturgy, choreography, or performativity?

In the contexts of politics beyond the theatre or dance studio, what contemporary activist and neoliberal modes of subjectification share today is obviously the demand to act continuously: that we don't just sit there, but *do* something, get busy producing and marketing (or creating and actualizing) intimate subjectivities in public. As no-one needs to be reminded, anxiety is the overriding emotional experience in the attempt to bolster a perpetually failing identity in the face of a generalized fetish for the full performance of enjoyment. Hence the theoretical energy recently devoted towards demonstrating that just sitting there — for example, as a spectator — may in fact function as an alternate mode of being that complicates straightforward notions of activity and passivity. Put crudely, since the ideal subject is now condemned to a life of permanent action called work, spectatorship can be redeemed from its status as the paradigmatic activity of false consciousness, as it was — and in some cases remains — in several versions of the dramaturgical sociology outlined above.

But the latent sense of dramaturgy in 'working on actions' seems as distant from the renewed emancipatory possibilities of spectatorship as it is from those of activism. Working on actions speaks of a certain kind of intentionally myopic preoccupation rather than the far-sighted preparation of events that deploy effective and creative ingenuity towards forms of intervention in the public sphere. Working on actions places some kind of distance between the preparation of an act and its realization. In fact, it places an activity called 'work' between the preparation and realization, an *impure* or self-sabotaging work that is also a deferral of that for which it prepares. When someone in a meeting asks about, say, an action point that you may be responsible for, which you have perhaps failed to complete or even start, you say: 'I'm working on it.' But it's common knowledge that this does not mean that you are *actually* working on it, but that other things — perhaps not work-related — have deflected you from your otherwise good intentions. Or perhaps this refrain is a contemporary version of Bartleby's 'I'd prefer not to...', a way of permanently deflecting and deferring the demand to take an undesirable action or decision but without an outright refusal. In this familiar language game, to be working on something is *not* to be working on it. So what am I actually doing when I am 'working on actions'? Am I preparing for something or putting it off? Working on actions thus seems beholden to imperatives different from those that emanate from the work-to-come. These imperatives are connected to more chronic and dissipative kinds of existence than the futural demand of work: distraction, delay, waiting, fatigue, boredom, depression, and despair among them. These are aspects of the affective *terrains vagues* that constitute the new landscape of contemporary cultural theory, which attempts to map

> a present which is increasingly felt as stuck, strung out between a truncated or foreshortened future and a past increasingly conceptualized through the rubric of trauma, seemingly unable to proceed or unfold in ways that were once associated with the progressive projects of modernity.[20]

Rather than being released into a total commitment to the sovereignty of work, how may dramaturgy — wherever it manifests itself — make room for what interferes with the work-to-come in the mode of these kinds of going-on-being? And not simply within its representational economy through performed tropes of, for example, exhaustion or collapse, but within the social complexities of its actual production? What may be entailed in a less wilful (or less workful) letting be that opens the work to its outside, to what cannot be choreographed, dramatized, or otherwise structured through the immanent inner logics of whatever performance?[21] If the political promise of performance remains as ambiguous as ever, in what ways may a recovery of the *dramaturgical* and its accompanying anxieties mark itself out from the demand of the performative, the demand for the elision of the expression of an act and its execution? How may a *dramaturgy without dramaturgy* be articulated, one that is not purely the consequence of a faith in either the immanent spontaneity of the work-to-come or a decisionist politics or aesthetics of prescriptive action? 'Working on actions' seems to me to be a name for the kind of non-dramaturgy that wants to address such questions without — as it must — knowing how to proceed. Yet it may still find its improvisatory method not by seeking to leave its anxieties behind but by making them the object of its own enquiry.

Notes

Bibliography

1 Van Imschoot, 'Anxious Dramaturgy',
   p. 58.
2 Ibid.
3 Hansen, 'Introduction', p. 16.
4 Lepecki, 'Errancy as Work', p. 57.
5 Ibid., p. 53.
6 Ibid., p. 60, italics given in the
   original.
7 Ibid.
8 Ibid., p. 56.
9 Van Imschoot, 'Anxious Dramaturgy',
   p. 60.
10 Lepecki, 'Errancy as Work', p. 57.
11 Ibid., p. 65.
12 See Brown, 'Resisting Left
   Melancholy' and a challenging
   response in Dean, *The Communist
   Horizon*, 157ff; Hardt and Negri,
   Multitude; Žižek, 'Afterword: Lenin's
   Choice', pp. 165ff.
13 This essay is a response to an
   invitation that arose from a
   presentation given at the seminar
   'Dramaturgy at Work' (26 February
   2015, University of Roehampton)
   organized by the editors of this
   volume.
14 Groys, 'On Art Activism', n.p.
15 This perspective has been recently set
   out at length in Kunst, *Artist at Work*.
16 Goffman, *The Presentation of Self in
   Everyday Life*, p. 72.
17 Bell and Butler, 'On Speech, Race and
   Melancholia', p. 172.
18 Butler and Athanasiou, *Dispossession*,
   p. 192.
19 McKenzie, *Perform or Else*.
20 Baraitser, *Enduring Time*. A list
   of this exponentially expanding
   literature may include, for example,
   Berlant, *Cruel Optimism*; Cvetkovich,
   Depression; Southwood, *Non-Stop-
   Inertia*; Sharma, *In the Meantime*;
   Fisher, *Ghosts of My Life*; Žižek, *Living
   in the End Times*; Povinelli, *Economies
   of Abandonment*.
21 By way of example, some fascinating
   responses to this question can be
   found in the work of Sora Han,
   Fred Moten, and others, who have
   recently begun to press nuanced
   understandings of 'blackness as nonperformance' out of legal histories and
   theories of slavery. See Han, 'Slavery
   as Contract' and Moten, 'Blackness
   and Nonperformance'.

— Baraitser, Lisa. *Enduring Time*.
   London: Bloomsbury, 2016.
— Bell, Vikki and Judith Butler. 'On
   Speech, Race and Melancholia'.
   Theory, Culture & Society 16, no. 2
   (1999), pp. 163–74.
— Berlant, Lauren, *Cruel Optimism*.
   Durham, NC: Duke University Press,
   2011.
— Brown, Wendy. 'Resisting Left
   Melancholy'. *Boundary 2* 26, no. 3
   (1999), pp. 19–27.
— Butler, Judith and Athena
   Athanasiou. *Dispossession: The
   Performative in the Political.*
   Cambridge and Malden: Polity, 2013.
— Cvetkovich, Ann. *Depression: A
   Public Feeling.* Durham, NC: Duke
   University Press, 2012.
— Dean, Jodi. *The Communist Horizon.*
   London: Verso, 2012.
— Fisher, Mark. *Ghosts of My Life*:
   *Writings on Depression, Hauntology
   and Lost Futures.* Alresford, Hants:
   Zero Books, 2014.
— Goffman, Erving. *The Presentation
   of Self in Everyday Life.* Edinburgh:
   Anchor, 1959.
— Groys, Boris. 'On Art Activism'.
   e-flux 56, June 2014. www.e-flux.com/
   journal/on-art-activism (accessed 14
   January 2016).
— Han, Sora. 'Slavery as Contract:
   Betty's Case and the Question of
   Freedom'. *Law & Literature* 27, no. 3
   (2015), pp. 395–416.
— Hansen, Pil. 'Introduction'. In *Dance
   Dramaturgy: Modes of Awareness,
   Agency and Engagement*, ed. by Pil
   Hansen and Darcey Callison, pp.
   1-27. Basingstoke: Palgrave, 2015.
— Hardt, Michael and Antonio Negri.
   *Multitude: War and Democracy in the
   Age of Empire.* New York: Penguin,
   2004.
— Kunst, Bojana. *Artist at Work:
   Proximity of Art and Capitalism.*
   Alresford, Hants: Zero Books, 2015.
— Lepecki, André. 'Errancy as Work:
   Seven Strewn Notes on Dance
   Dramaturgy'. In *Dance Dramaturgy:
   Modes of Awareness, Agency and
   Engagement*, ed. by Pil Hansen
   and Darcey Callison, pp. 51-66.
   Basingstoke: Palgrave, 2015.

— McKenzie, Jon. *Perform or Else: From Discipline to Performance*. London and New York: Routledge, 2001.
— Moten, Fred. 'Blackness and Nonperformance.' YouTube. www.youtube.com/watch?v=G2leiFByIIg (accessed 17 February 2016).
— Povinelli, Elizabeth. *Economies of Abandonment*. Durham, NC: Duke University Press, 2011.
— Sharma, Sarah. *In the Meantime: Temporality and Cultural Politics*. Durham, NC: Duke University Press, 2014.
— Southwood, Ivor. *Non-Stop-Inertia*. Alresford, Hants: Zero Books, 2011.
— Van Imschoot, Myriam. 'Anxious Dramaturgy'. *Women & Performance: A Journal of Feminist Theory*, 13, no. 2 (2003), pp. 57–68.
— Žižek, Slavoj. 'Afterword: Lenin's Choice'. In *Revolution at the Gates: A Selection of Writings from February to October 1917 by V.I. Lenin*. London and New York: Verso, 2002.
— Žižek, Slavoj. *Living in the End Times*. London: Verso, 2010.

The Dramaturgical Adventures of a Theorist

Betina Panagiotara

Reading Instructions
- Stay alone in the room
- Stand up
- Breathe in and out three times in a row, trying to slow your pace down
- Hold the text in your hands
- Read steadily, slow and loud
- Repeat with audience

* Works better in the afternoon

Welcome Note
Meet Dramaturgy
Dramaturgy is
a 'monster-phantasmal'[1]
a movement and a process
a web and a practice

Instead of an Introduction
To begin this text by framing dramaturgy as a 'monster-phantasmal' is to already point out that dramaturgy is elusive and hard to define as a notion and a practice. So from the very beginning I declare my ignorance and difficulty, and then I go on to tell you how I met dramaturgy and why I write about it.

I am a PhD researcher, a performance theorist, a journalist, and a writer, faithful to all clichés and habits attached to those professions that have to do with words on paper. That is, I like to drink lots of coffee, I wear glasses, and my home office is full of books and scattered papers. Just like in the movies, I am all alone with my dog, standing in front of my home computer screen, staring at nowhere just before I start writing, hoping that I can make my daily deadlines. Given these facts, if one would ask me some time ago where I belong — with practitioners or theorists — I would have vowed that it would have been with theorists. Well, ask again.

The starting point for that mighty change in my own head occurred when, full of doubts, I entered the workshop 'Contemporary Dramaturgy: Conditions of Working and Social Imaginaries'.[2] As already said, dramaturgy is not an easy term to define. Describing it as a 'monster-phantasmal', Sandra Noeth makes it look like a magical creature stepping out of a Harry Potter novel.[3]

Such views are quite telling about the way dramaturgy acts as a shifting site that needs to be revisited and redefined depending on contexts, people, and intentions.[4] Adrian Heathfield has even argued that '[d]ramaturgy, no longer belongs to the theatre, nor to dance-theatre, it is a practice spanning diverse disciplines and cultural sites'.[5] This is one of the reasons why I joined the abovementioned workshop on dramaturgy, and also why I found myself writing a text about it, given that I am not an artist but rather interested in those intersections between dramaturgy and other fields.

Instead of Content

The popular proverb has it that 'curiosity killed the cat'. If that were true, though, most of us who do research on the arts would be long gone by now. My point is that I primarily joined a dramaturgy workshop out of sheer curiosity towards what dramaturgy is, what my relation to it is, and how it works not as a theoretical approach but rather in practice, in a studio with artists. This latter aspect, however, partly also became my concern, given that I am not an artist, but rather a theorist and a writer. What is a theorist doing in a dramaturgy workshop for *practitioners*? Despite such concerns, I decided to hold on to the open call that reached out to artists and theorists alike, linking dramaturgical modes of working to socio-political contexts, and thus making the workshop's focus very relevant to my own research. In particular, my PhD research looks at artistic practices and production modes — such as collectivity and collaboration — during a period of socio-political crisis, focusing on and discussing the contemporary dance scene in Greece. Thus, the workshop's emphasis on the interplay between socio-political conditions and artistic working modes was key and the pretext for my participation.

One of the things that I had to deal with from the very start of the workshop was that I found no reply there to the initial, ontological question any beginner has about what dramaturgy *is*. Our first discussions in the workshop, after introducing ourselves to one another, had to do with different understandings of dramaturgy that derived from our own practices and experiences. Although this can act both as an obstacle and as liberation, in my case it came as an invitation to meet dramaturgy as an open process, a practice of many practices. In other words, I took this process as an invitation to us to step in, share our practice

with others, and make our own affiliations to what a dramaturgical approach may be. Later, participants were asked to read certain articles on dramaturgy and create their own dramaturgical manifestos in groups of three. One of the groups went for a well-defined map of 'what is'/'what is not' dramaturgy, another one for a poetic approach that featured dramaturgy as a web that keeps changing, and the third one for dramaturgy as part of an artistic creation of micro-utopias. I was part of the group that approached dramaturgy as a shifting site, a web of relations that brings together different agents, spaces, and materials, and opens up the field to a variety of practices but also to understandings of what dramaturgy may be, or become in every single practice. That is where my ontological question found something of an answer, inviting me at the same time to think of my own writing as a practice of doing and a process of relating that has common denominators with dramaturgy. In my case, it may be that I work in a room surrounded by papers, but that does not mean that I am all alone as the movie-clichés would have it, or as I described at the opening of my text. What is of utter significance for me as a human being, a theorist, or a writer is my ability and desire to relate. In my research, I write for and I relate to dance artists in Greece and their practices during the socio-political crisis. They are my co-writers in this adventure and it is along with them that we form part of the dance community and its several micro-dramaturgies. That said, I just gave a first response to my question about how I relate to dramaturgy as a practice.

During the workshop, we were also invited to stage and share part of our work with other participants. It is at this point that the question occurred to me: How on earth can I stage a theoretical PhD? 'This is definitively not for writers', was my first thought, and then I decided to accept the challenge, step out of the image I have of myself and share my writing habits on stage. From sitting and writing in front of a screen, to performing in front of others, this was a major shift of perception in regards to my own practice. It created a shift from framing myself as a theorist to being a practitioner, which is actually quite a loophole. 'I always write with my hair up because it makes me feel safe', is what I said in my short presentation. It was trivial as information but indicative nonetheless of the way I work and how I react to the untidiness of my mind. As a first feedback response towards my presentation I asked everyone to share with me on a note their compulsions when working. One of the participants ignored the rule and gave me a note written with red capital letters on a white A4 page saying: 'Betina, write with your hair loose.' That note is now hanging on the wall next to my desk. It is an important dramaturgical apparatus that works as a challenge prompting me to step out of my comfort zone. I have tried several times to leave the control freak with the tidy hair behind me, and even if liberating, it only lasts for a while. However, what that note whispers to me is to let go of certainties and habits or, as Lepecki proposes, to move towards a dramaturgy that calls out for a removal of the clichés so that 'something could start to build'.[6] Stepping out of established patterns of thought and action, even as simple as letting one's hair loose, proves refreshing if only as a mechanism to breathe and reboot.

After the workshop, 'dramaturgy' turned out to be 'dramaturgies', a 'theorist' turned out to be a 'practitioner', and 'writing' turned out to need some dramaturgical input in order to turn into 'being written'. And those were my dramaturgical adventures.

Instead of an Epilogue

The curiosity that works as a motivation force, the stepping out of habits that opens up space for experimentation is sometimes misunderstood as a hunt for something new. However, it could be that this new is not always innovative and looking at the future but coming from the past, in the form of a shared experience or knowledge. 'Betina, write with your hair loose', written in red ink, is a sign from the past that acts as a dramaturgical apparatus interrupting my present moment, and inviting me to keep on trying in different ways. In my view, dramaturgy does not need to invent the wheel but to make it work. In this sense, my suggestion would be for a dramaturgy that disengages from the fascination with the new and takes a look at what is left behind — for it could be that the past is full of treasures. I am thinking here of the famous film *Casablanca*, dating back to 1942, and of the moment when Rick says to Ilsa: 'We will always have Paris.' He refers to a past moment, a shared experience between two people that forms a lost utopia, becoming a motivating force for the present time. What are the utopias that we — as society, communities of artists, minorities — have left behind? Can we return? How can dramaturgy then relocate lost meanings, re-appropriate forgotten words, and (re-)make ends meet between Paris and the future?

Please let me be a researcher with no answers. By the same token, let dramaturgy blind you to what you already know. Let it craft encounters. Let it generate doubts that make one shiver about one's practices, intervene, and mess up one's notebook and thoughts as it did mine.

And let me remain ignorant yet faithful to a dramaturgy and a writing practice that favours encounters, tickles curiosity, builds pathways, bridges territories, and provokes dialogue, creating doubts in an overwhelming rational approach to things and mode of engaging with others. Dramaturgy may be elusive as words can sometimes be, but that does not mean it is not there. It is there as a ghost with many tales.

Notes

Bibliography

1 Noeth, 'Protocols of Encounter', p. 255.
2 The workshop 'Contemporary
   Dramaturgy: Conditions of Working
   and Social Imaginaries' was held
   in Thessaloniki, Greece in May
   2015 as part of the research project
   'Dramaturgy at Work'.
3 Noeth, 'Protocols of Encounter', p. 255.
4 Cvejić, 'The Ignorant Dramaturg',
   www.sarma.be/docs/2864.
5 Heathfield, 'Dramaturgy without a
   Dramaturge', p. 117.
6 Lepecki, 'We're Not Ready for the
   Dramaturge', p. 197.

– Cvejić, Bojana. 'The Ignorant
  Dramaturg'. *Maska* XVI, nos.
  131-132 (2010), pp. 40-53.
  www.sarma.be/docs/2864 (accessed
  10 January 2016).
– Janša, Janez. 'From Dramaturgy to
  Dramaturgical'. *Maska* XVI, nos.
  131-132 (2010), pp. 55-61.
– Lehmann, Hans-Thies and Patrick
  Primavesi. 'Dramaturgy on Shifting
  Grounds'. *Performance Research* 14,
  no. 3 (2009), pp. 3-6.
– Lepecki, André. 'We're Not
  Ready for the Dramaturge: Some
  Notes for Dance Dramaturgy'. In
  *Rethinking Dramaturgy: Errancy
  and Transformation*, ed. by Manuel
  Bellisco, María José Cifuentes
  and Amparo Écija, pp. 181-97.
  Madrid: Centro Párraga, Centro de
  Documentación y Estudios Avanzados
  de Arte Contemporáneo, 2011.
– Noeth, Sandra. 'Protocols of
  Encounter: On Dance Dramaturgy'.
  In *Emerging Bodies: The Performance
  of Worldmaking in Dance and
  Choreography*, ed. by Gabriele Klein
  and Sandra Noeth, pp. 247-56.
  Bielefeld: Transcript Verlag, 2011.
– Van Kerkhoven, Marianne.
  'European Dramaturgy in the 21st
  Century'. *Performance Research* 14,
  no. 3 (2009), pp. 7-11.

Impersonal Sociability and the Function of Dramaturgy

Una Bauer

Contemporary dramaturgy, I argue in this article, is a practice of creative *systemic* thinking. It is engaged both with creating new systems, and criteria for evaluation of those systems. As dramaturgy moved on from attempts at creating universally acclaimed perfection, it got better at handling jagged lines, irregular patterns, strange and twisted shapes, twists and turns, holes and gaps. Its ability to handle complexity and brokenness, its ability to think beyond particularities can be mobilized in social struggles and in building fair social systems.

The so-called social turn in the arts,[1] however, has perversely reduced art's ability to think socially, that is, systemically, because it has allowed for the focus to be placed on the particularities of various marginal groups and on disconnected projects. Hijacked by capitalist tactics, art has ended up emphasizing the importance of individual and, essentially, private care for the self and those one is close to, trying to replace, both materially and ideologically, systemically organized social care and other affordances of the welfare state. It is thus crucial to explore one of dramaturgy's main strengths, which is in my view the ability to think systemically and to work with jagged lines and irregular patterns, in order to connect seemingly disparate activities into new arrangements of social relations across the entire social space.

The 'social turn' in the arts is indivisible from interdisciplinary art practices that include performative elements, that are embodied, durational, spatial, and inter-dependent, and that actualize combined or overlapping understandings of aesthetics and politics. Even if that does not include the entirety of the 'theatre and performance field', a lot of these experimental practices are dependent on the combination of movement, sound, space, image, and text, all of which we find in performance. The propensity towards the 'totality' of performative and theatre practices, their reliance on numerous senses, stimuli, and life rhythms coincides to a great extent with the 'totality' of social relations, to the all-encompassing way in which social relations are produced, by rationality, emotionality, imagination, proximity, and second guessing, sound and touch and sight — a smile, a nervous tick, a way of pronouncing a word, a game of hide and reveal, easily expressed and violently disregarded.

It may therefore seem that the function of dramaturgy can be closely related to the sociability inherent in theatre and performance practices. This sociability is to a great extent 'private sociability' or 'micro-sociability' of people whom you know — those you work with, those who are in the same field, those you made performances with, participated in actions and protests with, and those you ended up caring about. Yet, it could be argued that this inherent sociality of theatre practices, although by no means unimportant, is not enough to make the function of dramaturgy especially important in helping the creation of 'new dreams for the twenty-first century'[2] or in imagining different social realities. It needs to be combined with something else.

Namely, one of the fundamental functions of dramaturgy is to create structures and systems, to organize relationships among various dynamic factors, having in mind relevant contexts. If dramaturgy deals with putting things (such as objects, performers, affects, lines of thought, flights of fancy, ways of reasoning, concepts, ideas, imagery, and situations) together under a distinguishable yet dynamic arrangement in time and space, then its function is to make these relations produce an interconnected system that would account for more than the sum of its parts. Thus, the function of dramaturgy is a crucial one insofar as dramaturgy is primarily involved in systemic thinking, in structuring various performative operations, in considering how systems appear, in seeing 'the bigger picture', in articulating the discrepancies between the situation as it is and the 'freedom from want'.[3]

Paradoxical as it may sound, the more we understand contemporary dramaturgy as an expanded practice, the more its tendency towards *systemness* becomes clear. It doesn't matter what kinds of things dramaturgy is dealing with, or what combination of things it engages with in every particular manifestation of its practice, as long as what is created is a complex logic of worthwhile interactions. Yet, this *systemness* is not a robust and straightforward monolith, nor are its 'faults' or 'failures' permanently *fixable*.

Systems tend towards invisibility, not unlike the phantom role of dramaturgy. That is, they are invisible until they break or up to the point when it becomes clear that their inner logic is flawed or has gone awry. When functioning, they are hard to see, quite like 'good' dramaturgy. An inefficient social or health system is, unfortunately, very visible, and the same goes for road works, non-functioning street lights, detours on the road, and other issues. Breaks in the expected functioning of systems cause a high level of stress, anxiety, and discomfort in everyday life and the misery they bring is so visceral and palpable that it becomes difficult to remember that these are exceptional circumstances. One moment at which the system failed will have a far stronger impact in terms of how we remember things, than all those countless instances when it was working just fine. And the better it was working, paradoxically, the stronger its failure resonates.

It seems to me that in artistic practice, the creation of systems, conceiving the abstraction of how the work operates, which I identify primarily as the work's dramaturgical function, is a necessary and crucial activity. And because each creation of a system is relatively unbound, there are no fixed laws of behaviour that we can rest upon. To a certain extent, every production also produces its own methodology of production. This situation is inherent to the function of dramaturgy, which is why this function carries a responsibility towards imagining systems, inside and outside the art field.

Yet unlike 'traditional' drama with its firm and functioning structure and obsession with universal solutions, which are always on the lookout for eternity and truth, contemporary dramaturgy, in the words of Janez Janša,

> has the structure of a broken line, the structure of a broken arc. These broken lines don't mean that the structure will fall apart. We see that there are holes, that there are breaks in between, but somehow the structure still holds. The question is: what here is actually holding this structure together? And this is the first point at which we can somehow start to think about dramaturgy in contemporary performance. These empty spaces or broken elements in the structure of performance are actually places of invitation.[4]

In other words, this *systemness* of contemporary dramaturgy consists of *brokenness*. Or rather, *brokenness* is inherent to the way that contemporary dramaturgy envisages itself. As such, contemporary dramaturgy has a lot to contribute to the thinking with and thinking through of the inevitable *brokenness* of social systems. It thus needs to work on those feeble moments of widely accepted failures and intensive attempts at living with the inherent 'brokenness' of every system, and the inevitability of imagining 'better', 'more fair' systems.

There are particular ways of thinking that could contribute to the conceptualizing of *brokenness* and one of them is to insist on (re)-linking the idea of 'impersonal sociability' to the idea of a fair life, through the inherently *broken systemness* that contemporary dramaturgy operates with.

Let me first try to articulate what I understand as the importance of 'impersonal sociability' via an example.

'It was June 29, 1896, and Charlotte Smith was beside herself with concern for the young women of the United States.' This is the opening sentence of the chapter 'The Devil's Advance Agent' in Sue Macy's *Wheels of Change: How Women Rode the Bicycle to Freedom (With a Few Flat Tires Along the Way).*[5] In her thirties, Catholic businesswoman Charlotte Smith (1840–1917), born Odlum, owner of a hugely successful dry goods store, became sensitive to the struggle of the poor and the disadvantaged, women in particular. She called for equal pay for equal work for women. Particularly focusing on the plight of prostitutes and women inventors, she was very successful as a lobbyist, passing more than fifty bills through Congress. The list of her activities is fascinating, including: running Civil War blockades with medicine and food, founding the union of female federal clerks Women's National Industrial League, pushing for a form of workers' compensation and unemployment insurance, proposing an early form of the Center for Disease Control, doing undercover research into working conditions for women and girls, being the only female delegate at labour conventions, founding the periodicals *Working Woman* and *Woman Inventor*, fighting for the role of women in the great World's Columbian Exposition of 1892–1893, and fighting for the recognition of women inventors.

It may seem that the opening sentence quoted above had to do with Smith's struggle for better working conditions for young women, but Macy alludes to the fact that this extraordinary and brave woman was particularly obsessed with the moral danger of cycling for women. In a strange plot twist, Smith claimed that the 'bicycle is the devil's advance agent morally and physically in thousands of instances'[6] and that it was responsible for 'the alarming increase of immorality among young women in the United States'[7] as 'it has a tendency to lure young girls into paths that lead directly to sin'.[8]

To argue against women learning how to ride bicycles while at the same time fighting for their rights as workers seems like a bizarre logical inconsistency, which one may simply dismiss given Smith's idiosyncrasy and a particular historical understanding of morally appropriate conduct.[9] But I argue that it is more than that. It sounds as if Smith wasn't thinking through the dramaturgy of her political activism, through the interconnectedness of her political performance. Her thinking on how to improve conditions for women was muddled with bourgeois propriety, strangely obstructing her efforts. Smith wasn't imagining her political project as a systemic dramaturgical creation – a web of connections and conditionings in which a link between public exercises and sin was contributing to the oppression of women. She was producing simplicity out of complexity, not as a dramaturgical strategy of her life-work, but as an obvious and simple mistake, a failure in producing meaningful connections between different systems of thought.

Another rather more dangerous *non-sequitur* of hers and a deeply flawed understanding of what constitutes socially responsible behaviour seems to have caught on with fervour in the twentieth century. This was the case not only among the prominent politicians of the right such as Margaret Thatcher, who reduced understanding of society to the support of those we personally know, and argued that this is the only conceivable kind of 'social' support.[10] Namely, Charlotte Smith was lobbying to introduce laws that would prevent primarily men, but also women, from remaining single. It is her reasoning on why these laws should be introduced that is relevant in this context: Smith was arguing that in order for the person *not to be* a burden to society in her old age, she is required to reproduce and create a workforce that would take care of her. Smith understood social responsibility primarily as 'private' responsibility or 'individual' responsibility for one's own reproductive abilities – a means of providing for yourself by relying on the workforce that will directly come from your womb, without any understanding or sympathy for imagining 'interdependent connection spatially and temporally to humans who will, for the most part, remain strangers to us'.[11]

Smith was trying to work on a systemic level, through changing the laws. But her demands were undermining the extraordinary possibilities of human social systems – that they can imagine and work with the social beyond existential proximity, through what we may call imaginary interdependence.

I argue that this is crucial for the understanding of what the function of dramaturgy is — the tendency to abstract from, and yet keep the concrete dedication to the particularities of individual practices that makes it crucial for the construction of social systems. With the help of dramaturgical work, the work of imagining links, we can work towards the articulation of those systemic dependencies that seem too abstract, not close enough, not *warm* enough. Dramaturgy may enable us to find ways of promoting and arguing for 'impersonal sociality', a concept whose articulation needs strengthening today.

We may relate the breakdown of the concept of 'impersonal sociality' already to the 'fall of the public man', Richard Sennett's abstraction of the eighteenth-century social performance of spontaneous interaction of human masks.[12] Yet through that genealogy it was actually (among other things such as industrial capitalism and state interventionism) the universal right to vote and social issues that brought down the ideal of the public sphere. Its abstract impersonality was actually rather personal — a fake neutrality of white bourgeois men of no necessity. Other social groups wanted their share of 'neutrality' and 'impersonality'. And the only way to reach them was through what was later on understood as identity politics. The breakdown of social utopias of the twentieth century thus was not only the result of the conservative right promoting family values and extreme individual responsibility to the point of their own caricature.[13] It was, in a way, already included in their initial social demands that were those of particular social groups who wanted their rights to be recognized as 'particular social groups'. Thus, it seems less contradictory that it was also, for instance, New Labour (and other nominally social-democratic parties in Europe) complying to organized business that contributed greatly to the disintegration of understanding why collective protection is important, what is the necessity of 'freedom from want', and what constitutes good life. All this severely endangered prolonged efforts of movements for labour rights and other popular movements of the twentieth century. We have been witnessing the devastating growth in inequality, the breakdown of the welfare state, and systematic destruction of those ideas, actions, and institutions that fought hard in order to create and sustain a vision of a fair life. Social rights, such as workers' rights, free healthcare, and free education, as well as unemployment benefits, support for persons with disabilities and for other vulnerable social groups (that we may become members of at any time, if we are not already) that were a part of a long struggle of humanity for a decent life (of, not just some, and not simply an arbitrarily chosen few, but all of its members) are exceedingly coming under serious threat.

I argue that the function of dramaturgy, earlier described as a practice of imagining systemic relations, is to work towards the creation of the fabric of imaginary interdependencies, to make connections where there were none before, but also to make meta-connections, to interlink connections with connections, in search of larger structures.

Contemporary art has contributed significantly, paradoxically partially through its 'social turn', to the unmaking of some vital impersonal and indirect social connections. Art theorist Claire Bishop has pointed towards a certain tragic and ironic correspondence between, on the one hand, the disintegration of the welfare state and, on the other, the 'social turn' in contemporary art. In the context of Great Britain under New Labour, and in line with European Cultural Politics, the social turn in the arts was fuelled by the promotion of works that engage with forms of 'soft social engineering'.[14] Differently put, the agenda gradually shifted towards using arts and funding for the arts in order to: a) relieve the state of those duties and obligations that it was forced to recognize as their own for much of the twentieth century via pressure from labour movements; b) indirectly increase profits for the business sector; and c) promote the idea of the artist as an ideal citizen, with her entrepreneurial skills, propensity to embrace risk, and ability to generate her own employment and career development opportunities. Thus, the effects of the arts are, as now seems to be widely accepted, supposed to be clearly and immediately measurable along the lines of bolstering the employment rate, lowering the crime rate, helping people feel less isolated and saving them from poor living conditions, raising the price of private property through gentrification, encouraging individual responsibility, and so forth.

Hidden behind the language of social inclusion, at the issue's core is the promotion of the idea that one needs to take care of oneself and that one is solely responsible for one's own well-being, and exceedingly so, as social services are disappearing in the generate climate of austerity. As Bishop has noted, the idea that social problems are, in fact, individual problems has been heavily promoted and 'biographic solutions [have been perceived as answers] to systemic contradictions'.[15] To be socially responsible, as in Charlotte Smith's late-nineteenth-century understanding, means *making sure that you are not a burden to the society* even though the arbitrariness of life means that there may be instances where there is little that one can do in this regard.

While the general understanding of the arts as a critically and socially crucial activity was directed towards re-establishing broken social links that capitalist production of exploitation and self-interest was responsible for, it seems that, in the 'social turn', 'business' found another outlet for the promotion of its values, and another domain where it can practice its language of efficiency and cost-effectiveness.

What has happened as a result is a paradox. That is, by using the word 'art' in order to describe different social practices, a sad side-effect seems to have occurred: instead of enlarging funding for the arts — as would be logical for an advanced state of human society— we are confronted with a reduction. At the same time art is unapologetically expected to provide direct financial benefits and a return on investment.

Things are, of course, not completely straightforward. The idea of public funding does imply the logic of accountability or of being responsible with and for spending tax payers' money. It also means being able to justify your expenditure in language that is not solely that of autonomous artistic language of experimentation. And it is hard to imagine how this accountability would look without some level of bureaucratization, and without strong emphasis on the rhetoric of aims, goals, objectives, audience development, reports, and so forth. A certain tolerance for the procedural rhetoric of argumentation and justification will necessarily follow any spending of public money. However, what we need to be mindful of is the encouragement of argumentation solely along the lines of heteronomous effects of the art field.

The function of dramaturgy already implies as one of its internal strong points precisely the organization of systems that would not only work towards alleviating the consequences of capitalistic social destruction. In practical terms, quite concretely, this means that we need more unions, more organized movements, and more unmasking and imagining of interdependencies.

Yet this is not enough. While the arts and culture field has always been committed to providing a corrective to the systemic

violence of the state, it also correspondingly contributed to the 'public disdain over the concept of public government'.[16] And it becomes very hard to imagine sustainable social institutions, social systems such as urban planning, labour, sanitation, and other forms of interdependent support without some level of trust in the concept of public government. In the growing climate of state-supported racism, xenophobia, and right-wing conservatism, it may seem difficult to think of the state as a cornerstone of social interdependence awareness. Yet we mustn't forget that state mechanisms, with their thorough reach and interconnectedness, are still the most infrastructurally organized ones. We need to find ways of using this already existing infrastructure, these already organized systems and steer them towards emphasizing their own *systemness*. We are now in a good position to do that in fact as various social movements, through their particular fights, contributed to the expansion of the idea of the universal in the twentieth century, so that it doesn't any longer rest on bracketing out specifics of our identities. It is precisely because of that that we are able to conceive of 'impersonal sociability' on different grounds, through particularities, rather than through supposedly disregarding them. Yet we also need another impersonal glue that will hold us together. And that impersonal glue is work. We are workers; we work to stay alive, whether we are paid for it or not. That is the lowest common denominator; that is the basis of our 'impersonal sociality'. However, this is only a basis for an act of dramaturgical imagining of how to proceed, how to create the space for understanding of the necessity of distant relations, and the interconnectedness of social operations.

Despite her insistence on individual responsibility, Smith's care and protection of poor working girls and her fight for women's rights as such also implies some form of 'impersonal sociality'. Those girls and women were neither her daughters nor members of her family. The trouble with her approach is that it resembled too much the arbitrariness of philanthropy. Although philanthropy means a 'love of humanity' it is always: a) a privately directed and motivated 'love of humanity'; and b) love for a particular 'part' of humanity, to whom the philanthropist chooses to give his money, because in his view this particular part of humanity is the most deserving of his money. There is also another paradox hidden within the very concept of philanthropy. As Michael Edwards asks in his *Just Another Emperor*, when discussing the

Mexican 'philanthrocapitalist' Carlos Slim who donated fifty million dollars to purchase cheap computers for children in Mexico and throughout Central America, 'Would you rather rely on the generosity of the world's richest man or have the wherewithal to buy one for yourself as a result of the changes in the economic system?' He then continues, quoting Slim, 'Wealth is like an orchard. You have to distribute the fruit, not the branch', which he explains by adding: 'presumably because the branch, tree and forest all belong to him'.[17] In other words, while arguing for individual and personal responsibility, 'philanthrocapitalism' really promotes reliance on whims of fortune, on being at the mercy of someone's willingness to give. And while fortune is a necessary component of the logic of being alive, when it comes to matters of fair life, the arbitrariness of it should be fought on a systemic level. Because I work at being alive, I have the right to protection from the whims of fortune through the fabric of social relations. But these relations need to be imagined and created, in a continuous fashion, as creative projects, rather than taken for granted as preexisting and repetitive elements of a purely social world. Rather than relying on the operation of existing social mechanisms, we need to conceive and create new ones, always creating meaningful connections between seemingly unrelated things, and disentangling links that pose a danger to a fairer future. However well meaning or capable Smith was, left entirely to her own devices, she was harvesting some odd and harmful ideas, such as that rubbing one's clitoris on the bicycle saddle will make women more promiscuous, a fear shared by extremely few people of her time. Most of us are not unlike Smith when it comes to necessary and conventional irrationalities, although our irrationalities are probably very different. Through the emphasis on communal and collaborative practices, organizing nets of interdependencies across various sectors, through deliberately fighting struggles that are *not yours* as a general strategy, imagining alternative forms of relationality, thinking through human agency and how that agency gets constructed through the care for the unknown other, through ways of inducing collective corporeal sensations, stimulating the interests of the unfamiliar and unexpected... there are many ways in which we can negotiate how to be together while we are distant. It is my claim that dramaturgy as a concrete practice of, and at the same time, an abstraction from, practice, can contribute to organizing systems that could confront the negative consequences of the arbitrariness of life.

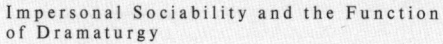

Notes

1   Art theorist Claire Bishop coined the term in her essay 'The Social Turn' and it has since been used by many theoreticians and writers both positively and negatively, reluctantly and eagerly, to mark how contemporary art adopts various forms of social life, as its own formless form.

2   Dunne and Raby, *Speculative Everything*, p. 2. This reference was specifically used by the editors of the book in the description of the workshop that took place in Zagreb, Croatia, in October 2015.

3   From US President Franklin Roosevelt's 1941 *Four Freedoms Speech*. The freedom from want served as an inspiration for the inclusion of the right to an adequate standard of living in the Universal Declaration of Human Rights (UDHR).

4   Janša, 'From Dramaturgy to Dramaturgical', pp. 54–61.

5   Macy, *Wheels of Change*.

6   Quoted in Macy, *Wheels of Change*, p. 28.

7   Ibid., p. 36.

8   Ibid., p. 32.

9   In fact, very few of her compatriots agreed with her on that matter and she was ridiculed for her stance on women and biking, so we can't really argue that such attitudes were common at the end of nineteenth century.

10 Margaret Thatcher, talking to *Women's Only* magazine in 1987: '[T]here is no such thing as society. There are individual men and women, and there are families. And no government can do anything except through people, and people must look to themselves first. It's our duty to look after ourselves and then, also to look after our neighbour.'

11 As Shannon Jackson describes Richard Sennett's anticipation of the diminishing capacity of humanity to imagine a non-personal sociality in *The Fall of Public Man*. In Jackson, *Social Works*, pp. 27–28.

12 Richard Sennett, *The Fall of Public Man*.

13 To insist on the complete and utter independence of self-governing individuals who are completely in control of every single aspect of their lives not only in the cases of obesity and smoking habits, but also in terms of genetically inherited cancer, auto-immune diseases, heart failures, accidents, floods, earthquakes, and all other imaginable situations that may leave one unable to, for instance, work, cover her medical bills, or find a place to live, seems to me to be an example of caricatural reasoning.

14 See Bishop, *Artificial Hells*.

15 Urlich Beck, quoted in Bishop, *Artificial Hells*, p. 14.

16 Jackson, *Social Works*.

17 Edwards, *Just Another Emperor*, pp. 59-60.

— Bishop, Claire. 'The Social Turn: Collaboration and Its Discontents'. *Artforum* 44, no. 6 (February 2006), pp. 178–83.
— Bishop, Claire. *Artificial Hells: Participatory Art and the Politics of Spectatorship.* London and New York: Verso Books, 2012.
— Dunne, Anthony and Fiona Raby. *Speculative Everything: Design, Fiction, and Social Dreaming.* London: MIT Press, 2013.
— Edwards, Michael. *Just Another Emperor.* New York: Demos and The Young Foundation, 2008.
— Jackson, Shannon. *Social Works.* Oxon and New York: Routledge, 2011.
— Janša, Janez. 'From Dramaturgy to Dramaturgical: Self-interview'. *Maska* XVI, 131–132 (2010), pp. 54–61. See also: http://sarma.be/docs/2871 (accessed 22 April 2016).
— Macy, Sue. *Wheels of Change: How Women Rode the Bicycle to Freedom (With a Few Flat Tires along the Way).* Washington, D.C.: The National Geographic Society, 2011.
— Roosevelt, Franklin. *Four Freedoms Speech.* 1941. www.americanrhetoric.com/speeches/fdrthefourfreedoms.htm (accessed 20 June 2016).
— Sennett, Richard. *The Fall of Public Man.* London: Penguin, 2003.
— Thatcher, Margaret, talking to *Women's Only* magazine in 1987.

Dramaturgy and Sabotage

Arabella Stanger

Dramaturgy, suggests Eugenio Barba in the context of theatre art, is 'the "work of the actions" in the performance'.[1] Embedded in this definition is the prospect of sabotage. The work of the actions in an artistic performance is always work enacted by some(one), for some(one), on some(one), and these categories do slip over and into one another. The people involved in such work — its enactors, beneficiaries, and those whom it affects — may be performers, choreographers, composers, directors, writers, dramaturgs, designers, technical crew, producers, administrators, back-stage and front-of-house personnel, audiences, and critics (the list goes on). Once the interests of any of these groups misalign, sabotage emerges as a possible mode by which the work of the performance may be undertaken and by which the performance itself may be transformed into a protest. Sabotage resides, generally speaking, in acts that disrupt production or slow it down and specifically in acts that turn the mechanism of a way of working against itself. What would be revealed about the entwinement of work, action, and protest in artistic performance if the dramaturgical mode of performance were to become one of sabotage? The present discussion is motivated by such a question. Moving from Barba's incipient definition of dramaturgy, I think about dramaturgies of sabotage as particular 'weavings' of action that *emerge from* but *work against* artistic productions and that are initiated from within productions by any one of their makers (including those who come to the production at or after the point of its performance).[2] By shifting dramaturgy into this resistive mode, the saboteur may interrogate the social and economic contracts that exist between the people involved in the making of a performance, expose those contracts and so position them, as in acts of public protest, as the very subject of the performance. Sabotage, I contend, is a dramaturgical mode through which a reconfiguration of aesthetic action may both reveal and transform the social relationships woven through the making of performance.

Antonio Negri characterizes sabotage as a

> force that destructures the system of power and
> dislocates its components, overturning them,
> appropriating them and gathering them up as offensive
> weapons into the new body of the socialized proletariat.[3]

Four points embedded in this statement will illuminate the possibility of sabotage in artistic performance, Negri's focus on the revolutionary action of a labouring underclass in capitalist forms of production notwithstanding: 1) sabotage is an act of some kind; 2) it is an act that disrupts a system of which the saboteur is part, but of which they do not have primary control; 3) it disrupts by turning the mechanism of that system somehow against itself; and 4) it does all this in the name of upending a power relationship. This final point speaks of the relationships between the groups named above as those involved in the work that makes a performance. The saboteur in this case is one who sets out to destructure the system of power into and through which these relationships are organized.

The following pages think through disruptive actions of industrial protest as a basis from which to examine a historic act of artistic sabotage: the New York Philharmonic's 1964 performance of John Cage's *Atlas Eclipticalis* (1961–1962). This performance lives in legend as an event in which musicians sabotaged both the work they were employed to play and that work's composer. Cage is a suitable figure with whom to explore the dramaturgical mode of sabotage because he is an artist not only whose practice has elicited protests from those on whom it works but also who built so much of his career on a departure from forms of compositional control, while remaining absolutely committed in certain ways to the personal control of his own work in performance. The issue of control is pertinent to the social imaginings brought about in Cage's art, especially given his tendency to align his practice with anarchism as a political outlook and model for societal organization.[4] In light of Cage's self-alignment with anarchism, then, it is worth first of all attending to the historical bases of sabotage as theorized in strands of anarcho-syndicalism. The notion of dramaturgy as the work of the actions of a performance opens a line of association between acts of sabotage in artistic contexts and the sabotage enacted by workers involved in revolutionary unionist struggles.

Sabotage

While the precise etymology is contested, we can be clear that the word 'sabotage' is derived from the French word '*sabot*', which is the name of a kind of wooden shoe.[5] After that, different stories take over, one being that in protest against poor pay or labour conditions, industrial workers used to take off their sabots and throw them into the machines they were operating.[6] Another and apparently more likely story, is that the word sabotage has something to do with slowness. Because sabots are cumbersome shoes, those who wear them move slowly. The act of deliberately slowing down production and breaking labour efficiency came to be called sabotage because it was an act that mimicked the slowness of sabot-wearers. This theory gathers inspiration from the older Scottish practice of *ca'canny*, which means to 'go slow' as a disruptive protest at work.[7] The derivation of sabotage as the practice of inefficiency, be it through mechanical blockage or bodily slowness, is summed up by Rudolf Rocker in his *Anarcho-Syndicalism: Theory and Practice* (1938): 'The whole import of sabotage is actually exhausted in the motto: for bad wages, bad work.'[8] Sabotage, in these accounts, emerged historically out of the capitalist system of wage labour and was practised as a tactic around which workers could organize their collective resistance to exploitative processes of production.

The formalization of sabotage as a tactic of resistance in continental labour movements took place in the late nineteenth century. In 1897 the French writer and activist Émile Pouget presented his report 'Boycotting and Sabotage' to the Confédération Générale du Travail (General Confederation of Labour) (CGF), an organization oriented towards anarcho-syndicalism and so committed to the overthrow of the bourgeois state via industrial unionism and the direct action of workers. Pouget proposed sabotage as one such method of direct action with the hope that it would be formally endorsed by the CGF, as it was eventually in 1900.[9] Sabotage, according to Pouget, was to be a means by which workers both could become 'no more a heap of nerveless flesh to be trampled upon with impunity' and 'whereby they can affirm their own virility and prove to their oppressors that even the toilers are men [*sic*]'.[10] The notion that sabotage performatively brings about the realization of its enactors' coordinated social agency aligns with Negri's later assertion, made from the point of view of 1970s Italian autonomism, that sabotage is 'the antagonistic, subversive force of the project of workers' self-valorization'.[11] That both Pouget and Negri use plural nouns (toilers, workers, men) is not insignificant.[12] The instantaneous transformation of the saboteur from passive, individuated cog-in-machine to active ensemble performer of a set of collective interests is enshrined as an ideal in the communitarian underpinnings of this strand of anarchism.

Given the provenance of sabotage in communitarian thought and practice, a set of questions emerge around the position and interests of the individual in such acts. These are questions to which I will return shortly in relation to Cage's brush with sabotage in art. But first, an example of an act of the union-led sabotage theorized by Pouget. This example presents its own kind of dramaturgy that will come to chime with the performer-led sabotage enacted on Cage in 1964, foregrounding especially the ways in which the historic emergence of sabotage as an anarcho-syndicalist tactic for *collective* world-making can be taken as a ground from which to call into question the so-called anarchism of Cage's experiments in music performance.

Pouget recalls the following account, given at the CGF Congress of 1898 by a delegate of the Cooks' Federation:

> The cooks of a great Parisian cafe, having some unsettled grievances with their employers, remained the whole day at their places before the red hot stoves – but in the rush hours when clients were swarming the dining rooms, nothing was found in the pots but stones that had been boiling for hours, together with the restaurant clock.[13]

The example models a carefully planned performance of unproductivity in which a weave of actions (woven through techniques of duration, rhythm, proxemics, harnessing of props, treatment of audience) activates our four principles elaborated earlier from Negri's definition into a dramaturgy of sabotage. Efficiency – a quality of work that is signalled, secured, even threatened in the ticking of the workplace clock – was disposed of, its commanding object destroyed by the very act it was intended to regulate.

In light of the actions of the Cooks' Federation, it is clear that the sabotage performed in the context of unionist struggles always has a dramaturgy in the simple sense that sabotage is brought about in the work of a set of actions. Reciprocally, the claim that industrial resistance has its own dramaturgy is helpful because it demands that we pause to consider the shifting meaning of 'work' in this context. Barba's preliminary remarks on the nature of dramaturgy not only permit us to think about dramaturgy outside of strictly artistic situations but also specify *work* as a property of *action*. The word 'work' is used here not to describe a thing — that 'curious unity' produced by artists — but to refer to the transformations affected by actions.[14] To continue with Barba's definition, we could say that the full scope of those transformations amounts to the dramaturgy of the performance. In the case of the kind of resistive action performed against the system of wage labour, the work referred to in Barba's definition of dramaturgy needs to be cleaved into two categories. Let us return to the cooks.

Before (or without) the act of sabotage, the work of the actions performed by the cooks in their employers' kitchens is that which is sold as a commodity. Their work, in other words, becomes waged labour. The day-to-day action that takes place is enacted by the cooks-as-labourers but *works for* their employers who own the means of production as well as the profits generated by it. However, once the action is woven into a dramaturgy of sabotage the tables are turned. During that protest day's resistive action, the cooks continued to perform the same acts they had typically performed as labourers (cooking in front of the 'red hot stoves'). However, because they reconfigured certain elements of this action (the replacement of food with stones) the work done by these actions was instead that of transforming the relationships dictated by the conditions of wage labour. On that day, the workplace actions *worked against* the employers (who no doubt lost money through the unproductive service) and so *worked on behalf of* the cooks, who were now performing as a unionized group of saboteurs. To put it another way, the dramaturgical mode of the workplace performance was shifted to one of sabotage, and so too shifted the power relations of those involved in the day's work. That the work of sabotage is to transform the relational agency of those involved is an issue pertinent to artistic acts of sabotage, too, and one that looms large in the infamous case of the orchestra that rebelled against Cage.

The New York Philharmonic Sabotages John Cage
To place Cage in the same category as the cooks' employers — as a victim of a kind of action that seeks to destructure a system of power — is at first glance a paradoxical idea given Cage's own commitments to power-destructuring through art. Branden W. Joseph explains such commitments as follows:

For Cage, the traditional, determinate passages from composer to score, score to performer, and performer to listener were understood in terms of power relations. Thus, to disarticulate them as necessary, bi-univocal relations meant that neither performer nor audience had to be subservient to the will of another; they could instead work from their own centers, not by doing whatever they want, but nonetheless without being 'pushed' as Cage put it, in any one direction.[15]

The social relationships imagined in this disarticulation of the composer-score-performer-audience hierarchy permitted Cage to align his work with anarchism, meaning here that each person could be a centre in themselves with no one obstructing the will or action of any other. Obstruction, in Cage's work, was to take place instead at the level of the passage of information between those involved in the performance. Aleatory methods were employed in the obstruction of this semantic passage so that composer and performer could be liberated from the tyranny of their instincts and so that audience members could be liberated from the tyranny of the artists' communicative vision. Sounds, after this process, were divorced from their expressive capacity in order to become simply, sounds. However, what if the obstruction of determinacy held at the heart of Cage's work came to be employed *against* the determinative purpose of his 'purposeful purposelessness'?[16] In other words, what if this obstructive way of working through chance was turned against itself?

The story is well known. On 9 February 1964, the New York Philharmonic prepared to perform Cage's *Atlas Eclipticalis* at Lincoln Center. Leonard Bernstein introduced the evening's programme – part of a series titled The Avant-Garde – to an audience made up largely of subscription holders. The orchestra was to be conducted by a large mechanical clock and the seventeen musicians were equipped with contact mics that would feed signals to a mixing desk in the auditorium at which Cage would control the volume levels of each instrument. The score itself was difficult and, according to the sheet music, many of the musicians would have nothing to play for minutes on end. There are conflicting reports of what happened once the performance began, but by all accounts the orchestra staged a kind of sabotage.[17] Some or all of the following may have taken place: when not playing their instruments the musicians coughed, giggled, and talked together; during the performance the musicians began to play music of their own devising, not stipulated on the score, which included some of Cage's least favourite determinate groupings of sound (melodies and scales); some musicians messed about with the contact mics, fiddling with, removing, and stamping on them, causing screeching noise — not controllable by Cage at his desk — to emanate from the speakers of the auditorium; the orchestra booed and hissed at Cage during his curtain call.[18]

Cage was furious and had this to say:

> They are a group of gangsters... They do everything wrong
> on purpose, not to make fun of something, but to ruin
> it. They get in mind criminal ideas, artistically criminal
> ideas. They are vandals. The moment they can ruin a
> piece, they are delighted... They also have tenure; you can't
> throw them out. Their job is secure. Therefore, they can
> act any way they like. They're not like children; the
> L. A. Orchestra is like children. The New York orchestra is
> like grownups who intend to be bad. They are criminals.[19]

The reason for Cage's indignation, I would suggest, is that the orchestra created a surprise dramaturgy that broke with — indeed it broke — the way of working he had been cultivating since the 1950s. His utilization of chance techniques for composition and pre-planned indeterminacy in performance, although self-described as anarchic, was not meant to set up a free for all. The faithful execution of the score — a plan that already disarticulated the habits and structures of classical music — was, for Cage, the action necessary for the enactment of a liberatory politics. By introducing further elements (unplanned and mischievous) to the performance, the orchestra broke the set of social contracts set up for it by Cage-the-composer. Here the musicians disrupted a system of which they were not the authors but of which they were part by their employment as performers. They did so by turning the mechanism of this system — the privileging of indeterminacy — against itself. The musicians heightened their staging of sabotage by behaving like the Parisian cooks: they rebelled against the timepiece (the mechanical conductor-clock) and destroyed the instruments (the contact mics) by which their performance was to be regulated. As with the cooks, the orchestra metabolized the system of temporal control that had been set in place by an external authority. The irony here of course was that Cage had set up that system as a way of liberating the performers from the instinctive timekeeping of a human conductor.

As an account of sabotage, the story is full of paradoxes. The destructuring of a power system (to be enacted in Cage's eyes by the faithful embrace of his aleatory methods) created a new power system (the subjection of the orchestra to these methods), which was in turn destructured by the ensemble as they worked in performance. Taking into account both Cage's outrage at the shifted dramaturgical mode and aspects of that performance over which Cage had planned to exert complete control (the work at the mixing desk, for instance), Benjamin Piekut dismisses claims that Cage's work was anarchic and instead aligns his way of working with the politics of liberalism. 'The 1964 performance of *Atlas*', argues Piekut, 'offers up another of its paradoxical lessons: it is both a model of anarchism and a mirror of liberalism. To imagine the former, Cagean indeterminacy enacts the latter.'[20] By understanding the dramaturgical mode of this performance as one of sabotage, Piekut's critique of Cage's politics can be supported in two ways.

First, if we are to take Cage at his word, then the composer positions himself as the controller of the means of production of *Atlas*: if the piece really were something that could be vandalized then it is also a form of property. He then positions the members of the orchestra as a workforce obliged to comply with the means of production, lamenting their status as tenured employees who are protected from dismissal by union laws. Such a scenario maps a social space not so much of anarchism but more precisely of the kind of workplace encountered in the cooks episode: one structured around the capitalist system of wage labour. The social space imagined in this performance only became properly anarchic once that workforce took matters into its own hands. The dramaturgical mode of performance enacted by the orchestra can rightly be called sabotage, in this case because it was designed to destructure a set of social relationships inherent to the workplaces of 'liberal capitalist democracy', that of empowered boss and obedient labourers.[21] The performance is more precisely one of sabotage when viewed through Cage's own commentary because it represents what Negri describes as an 'antagonistic, subversive force of the project of workers' self-valorization'.

In their disobedience, the musicians performatively brought about their coordinated agency as performing artists and as unionized workers. They did so by obstructing (and in some cases materially destroying) that which they perceived to be the unsatisfactory means of production as determined by Cage.

Piekut's charge of liberalism can be further supported if we continue to think through the anarcho-syndicalist theory of sabotage and the way in which it pitches collective interests above those of the individual. Cage had in mind an ideal weave of action for the performance that evening. Piekut has characterized Cage's vision of the ideal performing orchestra as 'a disinterested collection of ... individuals who pay no attention to the people around them and concentrate solely on the execution of their own narrowly defined tasks'.[22] With this vision, Piekut argues, Cage had set up for the orchestra an opposition not between enslavement and freedom (in which aleatory methods would presumably liberate the performer from the tyranny of the composer and conductor) but 'between enslavement and atomism'.[23] Had they followed Cage's instructions, in other words, the members of the orchestra would have receded into individuated action, activating Cage's ideal of multiple centres by performing their work as an atomized group.

Given the historic motivations of sabotage as a mode of direct action taken against the capitalist mode of production, an association may be drawn between Cage's atomized orchestra and a workforce of labourers alienated from their work as from one another, and who, according to Negri, may restore their very sociality by uniting in syndicalist action. Through the lens of both Pouget's and Negri's theories, which foreground the communitarian force of anarchic action, sabotage had previously been defined in this text as the instantaneous transformation of the saboteur from passive, individuated cog-in-machine to active ensemble performer of a set of collective interests. The New York Philharmonic performed just this kind of transformation in its sabotage of Cage's work. By bringing about the elevation of their collective interests above those of the individual composer, but more precisely because of their mutual destruction of the atomized performance environment in which Cage would have them work, the musicians of the orchestra magnified in their sabotage the liberal, and even libertarian, values carried in Cage's tendency to aestheticize the autonomy of the individual.[24]

Dramaturgies of Sabotage

What do these stories of sabotage reveal about dramaturgy itself? I would like to propose three short answers. The first is that there is a certain kind of dramaturgy that lives at once and at one with a performance. This idea is made evident in the event of artistic sabotage. Clearly, the type of performance that unfolded when the New York Philharmonic played *Atlas Eclipticalis* in 1964 was not the type of performance Cage had in mind. Indeed, the performance held a surprise dramaturgy, as did the weave of actions enacted in 1898 by the cooks of Pouget's Parisian café. In both of these cases it is apparent that dramaturgy comes to exist in and through performance. This is because in each case, the dramaturgical plans for the performance as it was imagined and prepared for by those who held authority over the production, were not carried out. From this we can conclude that each performance carries its own *in situ* dramaturgy, whether pre-planned or surprise, obedient or disobedient, faithful or unfaithful to whatever dramaturgical plans have been put in place (by a specialist dramaturg or anyone else) in the period of preparation that precedes a performance. To put it another way, dramaturgy does not need to be thought of as something that originates, determines, or even that prepares for a performance but as something that can emerge with a performance. For this reason, there is in each performance the possibility of doing 'differently' the weave of the actions.

To be clear, in making this point I do wish to erase from discussions of dramaturgy the work of the dramaturg or the dramaturgical work that goes on in the making process that leads to any artistic performance. Rather I hope to propose a distinction between what André Lepecki calls *'dramaturging'*[25] (a practice wedded to the temporality of the making process) and that which has been discussed throughout this text as 'dramaturgy'. The latter is not so much a practice of making as a property of performance, wedded to the immediate time and place of the performance and that can be resolved to the idea of the work of the actions of that performance. The distinction may be mapped as follows. Lepecki is concerned with exploring and unravelling the work of the dramaturg and so trains his discussion largely to the temporality of dramaturging, a practice that 'derives from accepting how all elements (personal, corporeal, objectal, textual, atmospheric may already be creating events)' and that 'is a question of understanding their modulation, of picking up adequate or inadequate qualities for the piece to come'.[26] Because of this focus on the practices of attention and transformation that precede a future performance, Lepecki's object of interest is different to my own. Where he is concerned with the making of 'the piece to come' (dramaturging), I have been concerned in these stories of sabotage-in-performance, with the dramaturgical nature of the piece once it is happening. If, as Barba has it, dramaturgy is the work of the actions of the performance, then I would like to identify one species of dramaturgy and describe it as *the scope of transformations affected by the enactment of a performance.* This kind of dramaturgy belongs to the here and now: it has a spatio-temporality bound with the location and the moment in which performance takes place. And where does sabotage fit into this definition? To continue with our linguistic distinction, sabotage is a dramaturgical mode that can be shifted into at any moment in the life of a production, at the point of dramaturging or of dramaturgy, in rehearsal or in performance (or indeed beyond, although the idea of post-performance sabotage would require a theorization of its own). In instances of artistic sabotage-in-performance (the cooks and the orchestra), the dramaturgy of the performance may be designed to derail the vision of those involved in the dramaturging of the work.

This leads to a second point about the nature of dramaturgy, this time concerning ideas about work. Lepecki again provides a helpful starting point when he offers another way of understanding dramaturgy, stating that it 'is the name one gives to a work's overall aesthetic consistency, solidity, and coherence (even if the desired coherence is to be incoherent)'.[27] These words both clarify Cage's purposeful purposelessness as a dramaturgical structure and suggest that dramaturgy can refer to the overall aesthetic weave of *a work*. However, if dramaturgy is also *the work of* the actions of the performance (in keeping with Barba), then the aforementioned events created by the performance elements must be thought of not only as aesthetic events but also as social ones. The expansion of the concept of dramaturgy to include the social (by virtue of its inclusion of the aesthetic) is explained in the way that the term 'work' is used differently by Lepecki and Barba. In Lepecki's usage, work refers to an aesthetic entity that has been produced and that is made of a number of elements *active* in creating its overall consistency. In Barba's usage, and this has been noted earlier in my discussion of the cooks' protest, work refers to the transformations brought about by those active elements. These transformations are always social because they are worked by, worked for, and worked on the people involved in the making of performance. If Barba's definition of dramaturgy is to be taken seriously, the category of the aesthetic offered by Lepecki must be enlarged to include the social relationships that are produced in any weave of aesthetic action.

A last thing is then revealed about the nature of dramaturgy, namely that it may be thought of as a primary site in which the politics of a given performance are nestled. In being a weave of aesthetic action, dramaturgy is also the weave of social relationships produced between those who undertake the work involved in bringing that action to life. In the case of the New York Philharmonic's sabotage of Cage, the dramaturgy of the performance lies in the work done by the orchestra to disrupt the Cagean aesthetic: a way of working (and system of power) imposed upon the musicians from without. Given this example, it is possible to imagine dramaturgies of sabotage that are initiated in artistic performance by any of the groups involved in its making: crew-led sabotage, audience-led sabotage, usher-led sabotage, and so on. In each of these potential cases, the affective field of the performance should be thought of as expanding to include the disruptive or inefficient action introduced by the saboteur/s, and the dramaturgy of that performance thought of as the means of describing how that affective field (of action that is at once aesthetic and social) is woven.

While sabotage is a dramaturgical mode designed to interrogate, expose, and reorganize the social and economic contracts between those involved in the making of a performance, those contracts do not, of course, drop away in the absence of sabotage, although they may remain unexamined. An artistic performance is always the product of action undertaken by people who work together. As the scope of that work, the dramaturgy of a performance — regardless of its mode — may be used as an optic through which to view the social life of the production. Dramaturgy is a primary site in which the politics of a given performance are nestled because it is structured by structures, and so can be used to destructure the relationships between the people who together make a performance work.

Notes

1   Barba, 'The Nature of Dramaturgy', p. 75.
2   Ibid.
3   Negri, 'Preface to the Italian Edition', p. xlvii.
4   Cage, 'Where Are We Going?', p. 237; Joseph, *Beyond the Dream Syndicate*, p. 81.
5   Pouget, *Sabotage*, p. 14; Rocker, *Anarcho-Syndicalism*, p. 85; Dray, *There is Power in a Union*, p. 364.
6   Dray, *There is Power in a Union*, p. 364.
7   Pouget, *Sabotage*, p. 15.
8   Rocker, *Anarcho-Syndicalism*, p. 85.
9   Pouget, *Sabotage*, p. 21.
10   Pouget's 1897 report to the CGF, cited in Pouget, *Sabotage*, p. 19.
11   Negri, 'Domination and Sabotage', p. 268.
12   That both Pouget and Negri also conceptualize the proletariat either through ideas of masculinity or as a homogenous group of (presumably white, male) waged labourers who experience exploitation in undifferentiated ways exposes the blind spots of strands of leftist theory and activism. For a feminist, postcolonial corrective to such views, as expressed through the prism of a Marxian political economy, see Federici, *Caliban and the Witch*, especially pp. 61–131 and 219–42.
13   Pouget, *Sabotage*, p. 20.
14   Turner and Behrndt (*Dramaturgy and Performance*, p. 18) borrow the phrase 'curious unity' from Foucault who introduces it in 'What is an Author?', p. 198.
15   Joseph, *Beyond the Dream Syndicate*, p. 81.
16   Cage, 'Experimental Music', p. 12.
17   Many of these accounts are gathered in Benjamin Piekut's suitably titled 'When Orchestras Attack! John Cage Meets the New York Philharmonic' (2011).
18   Ibid.
19   Cage cited in Piekut, 'When Orchestras Attack!', p. 22.
20   Piekut, 'When Orchestras Attack!', p. 64.
21   Ibid., p. 63.
22   Ibid., p. 62.
23   Ibid.
24   For a discussion of Cage's commitment to anarchism in relation to strands of North American liberalism, see: Cardew, 'John Cage' and Pace, "The Best Form of Government...".
25   Lepecki, 'Errancy as Work', p. 56, emphasis given in the original.
26   Ibid., p. 58.
27   Ibid., p. 56.

Bibliography

- Barba, Eugenio. 'The Nature of Dramaturgy: Describing Actions at Work'. *New Theatre Quarterly* 1, no. 1 (February 1985), pp. 75-78.
- Cage, John. 'Experimental Music'. In *Silence: Lectures and Writings*, pp. 7-12. London: Marion Boyars, 2006 [1961].
- Cage, John. 'Where Are We Going? and What Are We Doing?' In *Silence: Lectures and Writings*, pp. 194-259. London: Marion Boyars, 2006 [1961].
- Cardew, Cornelius. 'John Cage: Ghost or Monster?' In *Stockhausen Serves Imperialism*, pp. 34-39. London: Latimer New Dimensions, 2004 [1974]. www.ubu.com/historical/cardew/cardew_stockhausen.pdf (accessed 21 March 2016).
- Dray, Philip. *There is Power in a Union: The Epic Story of Labor in America*. New York: Doubleday, 2010.
- Federici, Silvia. *Caliban and the Witch: Women, the Body and Primitive Accumulation*. New York: Autonomedia, 2004.
- Foucault, Michel. 'What is an Author?' In *Modern Criticism and Theory: A Reader*, ed. by David Lodge. London and New York: Longman, 1988.
- Joseph, Brandon W. *Beyond the Dream Syndicate: Tony Conrad and the Arts after Cage*. New York: Zone Books, 2011.
- Lepecki, André. 'Errancy as Work: Seven Strewn Notes for Dance Dramaturgy'. In *Dance Dramaturgy: Modes of Agency, Awareness and Engagement*, ed. by Pil Hansen and Darcey Callison, pp. 51-66. Basingstoke and New York: Palgrave, 2015.
- Negri, Antonio. 'Domination and Sabotage: On the Marxist Method of Social Transformation'. In *Books for Burning: Between Civil War and Democracy in 1970s Italy*, pp. 231-90. London and New York: Verso, 2003 [1977].
- Negri, Antonio. 'Preface to the Italian Edition: 1997 — Twenty Years Later'. In *Books for Burning: Between Civil War and Democracy in 1970s Italy*, pp. xxxviii-xliix. London and New York: Verso, 2003.
- Pace, Ian. '"The Best Form of Government...": Cage's Laissez-Faire Anarchism and Capitalism'. *The Open Space Magazine* 8, no. 9 (2007), pp. 91-115.
- Piekut, Benjamin. 'When Orchestras Attack! John Cage Meets the New York Philharmonic'. In *Experimentalism Otherwise: The New York Avant-Garde and its Limits*, pp. 20-64. Berkeley and Los Angeles: University of California Press, 2011.
- Pouget, Émile. *Sabotage*, trans. Arturo M. Giovannitti [from French]. Chicago: Charles H. Kerr & Company, 1913 [1911]. http://theanarchistlibrary.org/library/emile-pouget-sabotage.pdf (accessed 21 March 2016).
- Rocker, Rudolf. *Anarcho-Syndicalism: Theory and Practice*, Edinburgh, London and Oakland, CA: AK Press, 2004 [1938].
- Turner, Cathy and Synne K. Behrndt. *Dramaturgy and Performance*. Basingstoke: Palgrave MacMillan, 2008.

Out of This World: Rescaling Dramaturgy

Undoing What We Know
Dramaturgy as Cosmology-in-the-Making

Andrea Božić and
Julia Willms

1. Undoing What We Know
Andrea Božić and Julia Willms

Hello, welcome to *Undoing What We Know.*

> *Undoing What We Know* is an exercise in attention.
> It is an exercise in looking.
> We would like to invite you to take part and, to do so,
> you can simply stay where you are.
> The exercise is a proposal for a practice. You can do it
> wherever you are at any time of day or night, here or in
> the future.
> We meet one another here within the space of this book.
> The space we share.
> What is space?

For the next fifteen minutes, we propose that space is not something that we are *in*, but space is something that we *are*. There is no such thing as empty space; space is always full.

Right here, there is the architectural space we are sitting in: we in ours as we write and you in yours as you read. Perhaps there are people in the space, objects, tables, chairs. There is the conceptual space of the thoughts that are shared through this text. There is the space of the emotions that are felt, the light, the sounds that we hear, the vibrations, the sensations... And then we are already in the arena of the other senses: the vibrations of air in the room, the sensations felt on the skin or in the body, the warmth, the cold, the taste in your mouth. But also, the vibrations produced by all the relations we are part of right now. Perhaps we know one another, or we have not met (yet); there are others involved in the book who know one another and that we may want to meet. And further into the invisible but present here, we have been brought together here by individual efforts of people involved in several institutions, from several different countries, by an investment of public and private funding for cultural and educational activities, part of the policies of the parties currently in power. We are paid to be here and you may be paying to be here. It is day, or perhaps it is night. The sun is shining behind the clouds. The space is full. It is not empty.

> How to attend to all of these different spaces? Is this
> space one field or is it a bunch of fragments?

I look. I look and I see that this is a book, that this is a text, and that this is an idea. How can I really see something if I already know what it is?

How can I look without knowing but allow myself to enter this space of not having to know yet?

We propose an exercise to suspend the knowing in order to see: *Undoing What We Know.*

The exercise consists of two parts: Looking In-between and Divided Attention. In order to be able to do this exercise while reading, look for a comfortable rhythm of shifts between reading the instructions and doing them.

Looking In-between

We are not separate islands in space but we are always in relationship to something else. If I look at a person or an object, I probably already have a word to define them: a man, a woman, white, a book, a chair, and so forth. But if I look at the space between two objects, I have no words to define the 'negative' space between them, so I can allow a different kind of looking to take place.

— Look at the space between two objects in the room you are in. You will see both the space between them, and the two of them as part of this field. They are not separated from one another but connected; they inform one another.

— And as they move in space, regardless of how far they go from one another, they will always stay connected through the space between them. It is a dynamic field.

— Now, shift your attention to two other objects and the space between them. Look at them as part of this field between them.

— And now, the space between two people (perhaps outside of the window).

— And now, the space between a person and an object.

— And now, between the book you are reading and your thoughts about it.

— And shift back to the first two objects.

— As you are looking at them, you are not separated from them either; you are part of this dynamic field: you are forming a triangle. There is space between you.

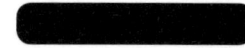

Divided Attention

Divided Attention means: you look at something and at the same time you are aware of yourself looking. Looking is not only with your eyes. At this moment, you are reading these words and at the same time you are aware of yourself reading. Perhaps you are agreeing, or disagreeing with what we are saying, or you have questions about it, or maybe you are thinking about something else — so there are thoughts coming up. Perhaps you like, or dislike the exercise; perhaps you feel resistance or you are curious about it — there is a slight emotion. In this way, you are not a separate object in space, but you are connected to us; there is movement going on between us. There is no strict division between what we feel as internal and what we feel as external. I am always in a responding relationship to something going on outside of myself. In this way, I can never be outside of the space. Can you keep reading this and keep attending to yourself reading at the same time? It is not about multitasking or switching between the two, or reflecting on the act of reading. You divide your attention so that one part of it is on reading and another on yourself observing yourself reading. You look, and you look that you are looking at the same time.

— And now, allow the whole visual field to enter your view. See everything as one ongoing image. Pay attention all the way to the periphery of what you see and then let the total field emerge.
— We have been trained to single out one thing, to focus on one object at a time and ignore the rest of the environment most of the time. You can now allow the whole field to emerge into view. Is this a familiar sensation?
— Keep attending to the visual field and keep the attention to yourself looking at the same time.
— Focus on one object again. And shift back to the whole visual field. Where is this object within the total visual field? Keep attending to yourself looking at the same time.
— Now, listen to all the sounds that you can hear as one ongoing field.
— Keep attending to yourself listening at the same time.
— Are there sounds inside you?
— Keep attending to the sound and combine it with everything that comes into your visual field. The total audio and

the total visual field at the same time.
— Notice the parts of your own body that you see. You are also part of this field yourself. You are touching the space. Your body makes contact with the chair at several points.
— Keep attending to where your body touches something, the visual field and the sound field at the same time. And keep attending to yourself looking, too.
— Notice the movement going on inside you. Is there something emerging?

Try to sustain this total field for a while, and yourself in it.

We invite you to continue the divided attention exercise for the rest of the day and if you like it, to take it further with you.

Thank you for your attention.[1]

2. Dramaturgy as Cosmology-in-the-Making
Andrea Božić

'Undoing What We Know' is part of *Spectra*, a long-term project developed by Julia Willms and myself that operates as the basic principle of our entire practice. *Spectra* engages with the space it appears in as a living organism, embedded in a larger environment. It works with the whole space as part of the work and everything that is in and related to it is treated in that way. There is no position outside. We create installed environments that incorporate the architectural and organic structure of the space the work is presented in and the audience's attention and movement through it as part of the work.

By reorganizing the logic of how the space functions and decentralizing where the event takes place, we are interested in creating a space of a particular attention. It operates as a trajectory of spaces where the inside is outside is inside. It becomes a space of poetic logic: it embraces the experience of the paradox as part of its dynamics. It is a space where we do not know yet where we are, so we attend to what is there, and encounter one another, with a curious and open gaze. This internal movement of attention produces a sense of suspended presence in the space that becomes affective.

The reorganization of the space and one's presence in it through what I call 'a choreography of gaze' becomes a reconfiguration of what is felt or perceived as internal and what is felt or perceived as external. A coexistence of elements emerges, a porosity of borders between organic and inorganic, natural and artificial, internal and external, political and personal, individual and social.

A World within the World

With *Spectra*, we create a world-within-the-world we operate in. This world-within-the-world can be seen as a training ground: it is Henri Lefebvre's space of parenthesis,[1] a break from the habitual or 'normal' order, a space where we do not know yet where, what, or how we are, a space to imagine and exercise other possible realities. Art can reconnect us with the spaces we have forgotten and the ways of being that we have not even imagined yet.

The first step in this process is to distance oneself from the world one is conditioned into and to allow a different one to emerge and to be experienced. One needs to pursue this with all their faculties and all the time, and cannot be satisfied with less, be discouraged by the forces working against them, or distracted by the praise they receive for doing it. What matters is the practice, continuous work through all of the activities one is involved in. That is the actual artwork and the products that emerge from this process need to always be considered as part of that process.

As artists, we play with the position of the outsider but the problem is that we are not really outside. We do not embrace this position of being outside fully. Instead, we waste precious energy constantly trying to get inside. Embracing the position of the outsider can be a consciousness-altering moment from which new realities, models of coexistence and cohabitation, as well as new experiences of presence and reality are possible. Hannah Arendt's proposal to embrace the position of a refugee,[2] the person without a country, without trying to assimilate into a new one, as a paradigm for new historical consciousness, should be embraced by artists. As artists, we should not create new countries, claim new territories, or produce new ideas. We should create conditions for new worlds to emerge – not by abandoning this one, but by opening up new realities within it.

Attention.

Internally, all of our work is based on divided attention. Practising divided attention works in a double movement. On the one hand, it makes visible and felt the regimes that hijack and guide our attention to select segments of the world that need to be owned, consumed, or won over, and to exclude the rest. The practice is about undoing attachment to those regimes, about recognizing the existence of these regimes, and one's own place within their production. It proposes expanded attention, attention to the whole field, and to oneself within it. It proposes training attention in new and surprising ways, which reconnect with the world. It is a way to reclaim our own agency over attention. Divided attention includes strategies such as looking in-between, zooming in and out at the same time, drawing in and distancing, and immersion and interruption at the same time.

A process of world creation starts within a specific artistic interest in a studio and needs to be separated from the outside at first. One creates a world in the studio and as one creates it, one begins to grasp the force that is guiding this world's creation and in the next step allows it to be an active agent within the work. One follows the work, what the work wants to be and, through that process, one learns about how it operates. One does not create a world, in this case, from a position of a *demiurge*, someone with omnipotent knowledge and power given beforehand, someone somehow outside of the work; rather, one is always within the work, in the 'ecstasy of attentiveness'[3] that creates it.

This sense of being fully immersed in an object one is creating, of being outside of oneself and in that object, implies the inevitable moment of separation, the moment one sees the object they have created as something outside of themselves, where one is divorced from the process of creating it. In our work, we sustain the process, where one stays within the object of creation and steps out of it at the same time. One practices this process until the object becomes part of oneself. In this sense, one cannot separate from it anymore but can let the object become an active agent within the world outside of the studio and let oneself be guided by it.

Cosmology-in-the-Making

Dramaturgy plays an important role in this process and is an integral part of our artistic practice, as it facilitates artistic strategies becoming operative within the larger world as one ongoing and interwoven field, rather than bubbles separated by the studio or theatre door.

There are three levels of dramaturgy here: (1) within the individual works; (2) in the way the individual works create larger constellations and in how we form collaborations; and (3) in the way that the works engage with the larger context they operate within and with the world, becoming a cosmology-in-the-making.

1. The first level of dramaturgy, that of the individual works, is based on the (re)organization of the space and the corresponding internal movement of attention. We use the words 'set-up' and 'generator' to describe this process: there is a paradoxical set-up at the base of each work, which produces movement, as it cannot be resolved. This movement is what we call a generator, which informs how this paradoxical set-up develops in time. The word 'generator' is borrowed from mechanics, where it describes a device that converts mechanical into electrical energy. In our works, a similar conversion or transformation takes place over time, where generator is a mode in which dramaturgy operates.

2. The second level is the dramaturgy of constellations. It is based on the same principles and strategies as the first level, but here constellations inform how the individual works relate to one another and how we form collaborations. We are not a collective, but three individual artists that make their own work and at the same time collaborate in various constellations. Each of our works is a world of its own and is at the same time part of a larger constellation, which informs each work from a different perspective. In this way, the works made in the past are informed by the more recent ones and transformed by them. This informs also how elements of other people's works appear in ours, how we link to other people's works, and how we create a wider context or a responding relationship.

3. The third level of dramaturgy has to do with how the artistic works engage with the larger context they are presented in and how the principles and strategies developed in the artistic practice become operative in the dramaturgies of 'real' life processes 'outside' of the artistic work. By this we mean the way we engage with the infrastructures we are embedded in and the way in which

artistic work informs and becomes operative in our individual (personal) and communal (political) life and relations. In this way, life is not only a generator of art but art is a generator of life. This is a two-way process, so that the three levels of dramaturgy are interconnected in a feedback loop.

In this process, the three levels of dramaturgy become a cosmology-in-the-making. It is a cosmology because it is a study of space. Our approach to studying is not scientific or religious but artistic. It is not an approach from outside, from a given framework but from within the questions, experiences, and insights generated within the artistic practice. It is a cosmology-in-the-making because we are learning how to learn along the way. This process of learning becomes the process of creating the space and ourselves within it.

Notes

1 Lefebvre, *Toward an Architecture of Enjoyment*.
2 Arendt, *We Refugees*, pp. 111–19.
3 Sloterdijk, *Bubbles*, p. 18.

Bibliography

— Arendt, Hannah. *We Refugees, Altogether Elsewhere: Writers on Exile*. Boston and London: Faber and Faber, 1943.
— Lefebvre, Henri. *Toward an Architecture of Enjoyment*. Minneapolis and London: University of Minnesota Press, 2014.
— Sloterdijk, Peter. *Bubbles*. Los Angeles: Semiotext(e), 2011.

The Rock, the Butterfly, the Moon and the Cloud
Notes on Dramaturgy in an Ecological Age

Augusto Corrieri

> We are not just with the earth, with the stars, with ground, with blood, with skin. In advance, and without our even being informed, everything is already ordered-classed according to a scale which gives primacy to one element over another. And power to one thing, or to one being over another. All the time. And in an unfounded manner.
>
> *Hélène Cixous*[1]

In his 1968 book *The Empty Space*, director Peter Brook famously declared that one person watching another walk across a bare stage 'is all that is needed for an act of theatre to be engaged'.[2]

In a 2001 interview with Jérôme Bel, when asked, 'What is a show for you?' the choreographer answered simply: 'It is live people in the dark who watch other living ones in the light.'[3]

And in their 2007 book, dramaturgs and performance scholars Cathy Turner and Synne Behrndt wrote: 'Dramaturgy is ... produced through a dialogue between the play and a particular community of people in a particular time and place.'[4]

Whenever we speak of theatre and performance, we speak of relations between particular humans — 'living ones' — observing or in dialogue with other humans.

So far, the picture is rather clear and familiar.

However, in her 1994 State of the Union address, dramaturg Marianne Van Kerkhoven distinguished between two kinds of dramaturgy, a minor and a major. The first type refers to the theatrical production and its audiences, 'those things that can be grasped on a human scale', while beyond it, in ever-expanding orbits, we find the major dramaturgy: 'around the production lies the theatre and around the theatre lies the city and around the city, as far as we can see, lies the whole world and even the sky and all its stars'. In her address Van Kerkhoven urges that it is now necessary, 'awfully necessary', that we turn our attention to the major dramaturgy.[5]

But what kind of theatre would this be, to engage the whole world 'and even the sky and all its stars'? If followed to the letter, Van Kerkhoven's proposition would entail an exceptional shift in scale; this impossibly 'expanded' dramaturgy would require a radical reconfiguration of theatre itself, as well as the entire conceptual apparatus by which we construct and apprehend acts, human or not. If we were to genuinely include sky and stars as dramaturgical elements (not just as 'props' or painted backgrounds), then we would have to start writing manifestos for a theatre based on cosmic interelations, featuring subatomic matter and non-matter, as well as entities, scales, and temporalities that escape human understanding altogether. In short, we would need to declare as woefully obsolete the humanist tradition that still underpins Western theatre and its all-too-human dramaturgies.

As unrealistic as all this may sound, such a radical act of reorientation is in fact already underway. Courtesy of ecological catastrophe and anthropogenic climate change, the Heideggerian idea of humans as sole 'world-makers' is no longer tenable, as we witness just how much of the world is alive, vibrant, and in motion, where it had once been declared dead, inert, or at best an exploitable resource (according to the humanist fairy tale). Cary Wolfe, a theorist in post-human and animal studies, goes one step further by referring to our current epoch as a 'new reality', given that 'the human occupies *a new place in the universe*, a universe now populated by what I am prepared to call non-human what I am prepared to call non-human subjects': non human beings, animals, and other biotic and abiotic entities, which are typically cast in the background, have now appeared centre stage in our awareness.[6] For Wolfe, such a new reality calls for 'an increase in the vigilance, responsibility, and humility that accompany living in a world so newly, and differently, inhabited'.[7] Welcome to the Ecological Age, or (conversely) the Anthropocene, a term coined to highlight the extent to which human industry has geologically altered the planet: we are witnessing a sixth extinction, the

> certainty of a long and slow demise of our ecosystems, brought about by decades of overexploitation of the planet's resources in the name of progress and human emancipation from 'Nature'.[8]

In the context of a discussion on dramaturgy, the question becomes: given the 'new reality' of the Anthropocene, what do we find when we zoom back to consider theatrical questions and concepts? A first speculative answer could be this: what we find is that the small-scale focus no longer works so well, for the major dramaturgy now inhabits the minor (to use Van Kerkhoven's terms), blurring the boundaries between living/non-living, human/non-human, and dissolving theatre's 'here and now' into an infinity of sites and extended temporalities. Non-human subjects, both cosmic and earthly, have gatecrashed the party, and they are here to stay. In this unprecedented situation it seems increasingly strange for theatre to follow ordinary coordinates, as though 'the human' weren't in the process of losing its centre-stage position. If there is a twenty-first century avant-garde, it is not human-led.

Let's pause a moment to define a couple of historical terms. It is not a coincidence that the Western theatre (the art form as well as the building) was re-invented in the Italian Renaissance, in other words precisely as a certain idea of 'Man' was being crafted. Leonardo da Vinci famously drew the 'Vitruvian Man', arms and legs stretched to a perfect squared circle, in an ordered cosmography of the microcosm; unsurprisingly da Vinci also sketched the first proscenium arch theatre, effectively outlining the apparatus that has largely defined and housed live performance ever since. This Humanist Renaissance inheritance is arguably the main paradigm for live theatre, whose dramaturgies are structurally anthropocentric. The history of much performance, especially from the historical avant-gardes onwards, could be seen as a series of varied attempts at dethroning, decentring, and denaturalizing such a construction: whether questioning the primacy of the theatrical text, aiming for a democracy of scenic elements, challenging the virtuous dancing body, or recognizing the complex agency of spectators, performance has variously challenged the Humanist inheritance embodied in da Vinci's drawing. The Anthropocene, however, presents a new paradigm, proposing to erase the figure of man like 'a face drawn in sand at the edge of the sea' (as Michel Foucault famously anticipated),[9] and alerting us to previously under-recognized non-human species, scales, and temporalities. The question, therefore, is whether we can now imagine a non-anthropocentric theatre – and if this sounds like a contradiction in terms, then it is precisely a matter of refiguring the terms themselves.

Somewhat irresolutely and indirectly, courting neither hope nor despair, this text is spurred by a set of open-ended questions: if we turn our attention away from the Human, and towards a major dramaturgy of sky and stars, air and water, quarks and neutrinos, metal and carbon and plants and insects, do we then need to abandon theatre altogether? If so, may such an act of abandonment be thought of as artistically continuative (as a challenge to/within the theatre)? And how may we locate practical-conceptual ways of engaging a dramaturgy of sky and stars from *within* the apparatus, reorienting performance in order to challenge the dogma that dictates that humans should occupy the leading role?[10]

In place of tackling these questions head on, in the following pages I take an indirect route, by focusing on works from different disciplines: a 1970s video work, a recent book of photographs of dilapidated auditoria, a 1960s music composition, a visual artist's work, and a live performance. All except one, these are deliberately not what we might call 'theatre' or live arts, and the hope is that it is precisely by looking elsewhere, towards other durations and forms of making present, that we may then return to and reflect back on the limits and potentials of theatre's dramaturgy. Since 'the "copresence" of living beings within the "here and now" of space and time remains *the* truism of theatre', looking to other art forms helps to defamiliarize such a seemingly familiar theatrical apparatus.[11]

1. The Rock

In his book *Reasons for Knocking at an Empty House*, video artist Bill Viola describes a simple work in which, by his own account, he was able to show the movements of an unmoving rock. All that was required was the substitution of the background for the foreground, and the use of slow motion. In the video we see a large rock, and some people walking past in the background. At one point the video slows down, as is made obvious by the slow-motion walk of the human bodies. But since the main subject of the video is the rock, and people are only shown up to their waist, we understand what Viola's proposition is: that we are now watching the rock slowing down. Unseen yet clearly foregrounded, here are the slow unfolding movements of inanimate stone, occurring no differently than the slow unfolding movements of familiar bipedal animals, only imperceptibly and over a more extensive duration.

It is a question of shifting between different scales, not unlike certain passages in *Alice in Wonderland*. Viola is first of all asking us to consider that the familiar human scale is always only one possibility among countless non-human others and, second, inviting us to tune in to the slower speed of the rock: to become rock-like in our perception and thoughts. This is not something that can be easily practised or grasped in our everyday lives, at least not firmly enough to produce a genuine shift in perspective, yet through the video work, as described by Viola, it becomes possible to engage with geological scale and duration, perceptually, imaginatively, critically if we wish. There are always other kinds of spatio-temporal worlds and phenomena alongside those we consciously notice and acknowledge; there is always a geocentrism alongside our anthropocentrism, and with that the potential to practice swapping the background for the foreground. As in the elegant conundrum posed by nature writer Annie Dillard: 'What if *I* fell in a forest: would a tree hear?'[12]

Through this kind of reversal, Viola is rehearsing what we may call a dramaturgy of the background: a form of reorientation where stone and rock, typically considered inert and lacking any degree of animation, are shown to move in the same circles usually reserved for plants and animals. French poet Francis Ponge remarks how stone, due to it not procreating like other beings, cannot be made into a symbol of longevity and passivity, for 'it is truly the only thing in nature which is constantly dying'.[13] Whereas 'plant life, animals, gases and liquids revolve quite rapidly in their cycles of dying and returning to life', pebbles and stones are bound to a slow and 'continual disintegration'.[14]

Through the example of Bill Viola's video let's turn to consider a typical theatre auditorium. Seemingly as dead and inert 'as a stone', a traditional theatre also moves and unfolds slowly, regardless of whether humans are present or not: the stage floor has its own motion and speed, the walls have their own motion and speed, as do the curtains, the seats, the balconies, and so on. To this we may then add the activity of air, moisture, dust, insect life, plant life, and animal life, both human and not.

In her book *Stages of Decay*, photographer Julia Solis offers captivating images of abandoned theatres across the US and Germany, temporally dislocated predictions of what lies in wait for the climate change generation. By the artist's own admission, the photographs are 'meant as a celebration of these ruins, as the theatres are slowly turning into the playgrounds of their own demise'.[15] The book is, truly, an uncritical and romantic celebration of decay, and could be dismissed as yet another example of 'ruin porn', given the way these lavish images of architectural destruction are disconnected from their political and social contexts. Despite these reservations, Solis' work draws attention to the animations of the inanimate, for example in her striking description of the process of dissolution of a typical auditorium:

With their abandonment, a whole new drama begins to unfold. It starts slowly at first, with a few open windows letting in the wind and rain, the snow and the spores for the first patches of moss to take hold ... the top layer of paint begins to crack, often in a sharp, continuous stroke that sounds like a clawed animal scurrying across the wall. Plaster ornaments dissolve right on the wiring until they can no longer support themselves... Horsehair, once used to hold together plaster decorations, begins to stick out between structural elements like strange, insect-like antennae... The seats burst ... The stage curtain drops as its fireproof backing splits and bubbles into the mouldy fabric, combining with the deteriorating floor of the stage into a fantastical fungal landscape.[16]

Such a spectacle of dissolution remains unperceived when we go 'to the theatre'. The material capacities of the building and décor are typically concealed or arrested by the demands of functionality and social usage: in order for the building to remain 'open', it needs to be 'maintained', which means, essentially, that its physical properties need to be tightly policed to conform to certain values and modes of inhabitation. Auditoria around the world are treated as expressions of humanist grandeur or civic pride, never as lively and chaotic assemblies of entropic processes.

Solis' photographs of abandoned theatres are powerful reminders of how non-human subjects act and interact, for example as slow-forming fungal events, or as the dynamic weathering of artefacts. Here, as elsewhere, entities that we typically refer to as the background come to the fore and compose particular eventful alliances. Wouldn't the next step be to see how human *and* non-human agents may assemble, co-choreograph, and flourish in such a space?

2. The Butterfly

Some years ago now I read about a musical composition by La Monte Young. The piece begins when a butterfly (in my memory, always a yellow one) is released into the auditorium; it finishes when the winged insect, having flown around the space for an indeterminate length of time, finally exits through an open window.[17]

The butterfly is the protagonist, and the invitation — for one minute, one hour, one evening, or longer — is to attend to its presence in the auditorium: its aerial trajectories, its pauses, and its possible or eventual exit. More importantly, since this is a piece of music, Young's composition is asking us to carry out an impossible task, which is to *listen* to the butterfly. As its wings beat the air, the auditorium is filled with vibrations and sounds, no differently from those at a traditional concert; yet unlike a trombone's or a flute's, these vibrations are too subtle to be picked up by humans. Unless the winged insect should happen to fly a couple of centimetres past one's ears, the audience cannot properly perform its role: if we cannot hear, we cannot be an audience (etymologically, from *audire*, to hear).

We may wish to quickly label the piece (and somewhat close off its potential) as 'conceptual': its motor is the ideation itself, while the sonorous and sensuous aspects are inaccessible or irrelevant. If we try to resist this labelling, however, we may notice that something else is at stake here. Perhaps unwittingly the piece is staging a paradox and a challenge for our times: how to be present to an event that does not address us. What La Monte Young's composition places centre stage is not just an insect but, crucially, the question of how to engage with it, if at all possible: how can we attend to events and phenomena that lay beyond the senses, such as insects' *insensible* sonorities? Can we form relations predicated upon a kind of non-relationality? As audience members who can no longer play the role of those who listen to sounds, we must radically reorient ourselves, readjusting our expectations and desires, and give up a little of our sovereignty: in an auditorium that is host to indiscernible non-human phenomena (that is to say, each and every auditorium), we can no longer rehearse our ideal of 'presence' in the here and now. Young's work is a reminder of that complex unfolding of sonorous energy that is, simply put, not 'for us', yet forms a great part of shared sonic environments. Casting a line across the ordinary human limits of perception and audibility, the composition asks us to dwell in that limit zone where nothing is happening, yet so much always is.

We may speculate what kind of dramaturgical model this piece offers, in which the main act is neither 'expressive' (of human intention, will, mastery, and so forth) nor does it become matter for perception – a situation no longer defined by the opposite poles of production and reception, and in which the roles of artist and spectator are suspended ... but in favour of what exactly?

I have never attended a presentation of Young's piece, but I am often reminded of it when, sitting in a theatre watching a performance, I catch sight of a moth or a fly on the lit stage, usually circling above the performer's heads.[18] Generally speaking these insect appearances are either entirely ignored or at most treated as negligible interruptions, far too irrelevant to upstage the human performers. Unlike dogs or donkeys, whose stage appearance may engender cross-species empathy and reflections on the role of animals in theatre, insects are too 'lowly' for us to project human dramas on to: their bodies are too small and frail, their appearance too alien, their lives too unimportant (I have never killed a rodent or a bird, but plenty of ants, mosquitoes, and flies). We tend to regard insects as pieces of moving dirt, and it is fitting that for centuries it was thought that flies generated spontaneously from dirt and dust.[19] Yet we are vastly outnumbered by smaller life forms, as Annie Dillard reminds us: 'The average size of all living animals, including man, is almost that of a housefly.'[20] Our scales are dramatically in need of recalibration.

Whenever I see a fly buzz around the stage during a dance performance, I think to myself, perhaps naïvely and hippy-ishly: how can that insect be given the same level of attention as the dancer? More critically, I am reminded of how the theatrical apparatus configures modes of attention and attendance that exclude 'less-than-human' lives, and how each time we buy an admission ticket and take our seats, that exclusion is reaffirmed and naturalized.

On reflection, La Monte Young's piece, as reframed by current ecological concerns, seeks not so much to give the butterfly the 'same' level of attention as human-produced music, but rather to intervene in the very apparatus of the auditorium itself, skewing our anthropocentric listening habits, in order to make room for other scales of sense and sensibility. The piece's dramaturgical direction may read: the interruption is here to stay.

3. The Moon and the Theatre

Artist Katie Paterson has been liaising with cosmic entities for some time, producing a kind of neo-romantic-conceptual body of work that features dead stars, black holes, and meteorites, as well as earthlier performing matter, such as melting glaciers, lightning storms, and specks of desert sand.

One of Paterson's recurring strategies consists of playfully aligning human and planetary activities, often through iconic works of music. Her piece *As the World Turns* features a turntable rotating in time with Earth, 'one revolution every 24 hours, playing Vivaldi's *Four Seasons*'.[21] Lasting four years if played in total, the record's movements are too slow to be perceived by the naked eye. Paterson is taking a human artefact, Vivaldi's record, and slowing it down to match the speed of our host planet's revolutions: the composition's avowed content (the passage of the seasons) is thus subjected to an operation that silences or backgrounds the music, foregrounding the planetary motion that Vivaldi was originally referring to; something is no doubt lost, but much is gained. As in Viola's invisible rock movements, and Young's inaudible composition, here the human senses are denied traditional cultural consumption, in favour of what political theorist Jane Bennett describes as 'an aesthetic-affective openness to material vitality'.[22]

Earth's moon has featured in a number of Paterson's works, most notably through a form of radio transmission called E.M.E. (Earth–Moon–Earth). This allows for sound to travel from our planet outwards for approximately 800,000 miles, after which it is reflected off the moon's surface and returned to Earth two and a half seconds later; the sound effectively bounces from one 'body' to another. Paterson first made use of E.M.E. transmission by sending four minutes and thirty-three seconds of recorded silence to the moon and back, thus reframing Cage's *4'33"* as an interplanetary activity. In a later piece, the artist transmitted Beethoven's *Moonlight Sonata*, and because the moon's surface only reflected part of the content (some is always lost in the moon's shadows), what returned to Earth was a slightly broken up version of Beethoven's composition. Visitors to the gallery could hear this 'moon-altered' edition performed live on a self-playing grand piano.[23]

As though taking dramaturg Van Kerkhoven's proposition to the letter (although admittedly not dealing with 'theatre'), Paterson's E.M.E. works connect the minor to the major dramaturgy, tracing orbits of interconnection in a yearned for affinity between cosmic and human acts. Paterson's moon works replay the Romantic unfathomable, this time casting the artwork as merely a privileged moment – for example, the visit to the gallery – within ungraspable processes involving prodigious bodies, distances, and timescales.

How may theatre similarly shift out of its orbit, given its inbuilt reliance on the here and now, the visible and graspable, in other words the minor dramaturgy we started out with? How may the theatre apparatus — that aesthetic, perceptual, and architectural construct that we're always inside of when in proximity to performance — engender antidotes to its own humanism, and enact a radical reorientation towards non-human subjects? If this seems too much to ask of theatre and performance (this remains an open question), we may speak of this shift as though it were already underway. For instance, on the day before the Brussels workshop 'Unfolding Dramaturgies' organized by the book's editors, we attend a performance of *Prelude* by Ula Sickle, Yann Leguay, and Stine Janvin Motland, presented in the Kaaitheater's main space.[24] In a memorable sequence, the lone performer (vocalist Stine Janvin Motland) sits at the edge of the bare stage telling the audience a captivating story, and then suddenly presses a button to release a large cloud of white smoke. The performer continues her narration as though nothing happened, while the wisps of white cloud slowly take over the large cavernous space of the Kaai, swirling and expanding upwards in an intricate 'dance', visually overwhelming the increasingly smaller human body. The performer telling her engaging story, the cloud unfurling upwards ... both things happening, differently yet equally matter for perception, and myself struggling with where and how to place my attention. I turn my head repeatedly away from the performer's narration and towards the cloud, and then back to the performer, unable to decide, to settle on either one: which rhythm to follow? Which event to give my attention to? Although not quite travelling to the moon and back, in this example the theatre is reconfigured as a place in which to witness different scales, 'lives', and modes of existence; it is an opportunity to get caught in the undecidable rift between semantics and material, flesh and cloud, the here and the elsewhere.

We might describe this, once again, as another example of a dramaturgy of the background: what is being tested out, within the deeply anthropocentric theatrical apparatus, is precisely an alternative to such human-centredness. And why is such an alternative necessary? Because, courtesy of ecological catastrophe and anthropogenic climate change, an irrevocable shift in perspective has suddenly imposed itself: the outside has burst inside the auditorium; or rather, we are only now realizing that *the outside has always been inside*. As Jane Bennett notes: 'There was never a time when human agency was anything other than an interfolding network of humanity and nonhumanity; today this mingling has become harder to ignore.'[25]

The good news is that, despite our best efforts at concealment, the theatre has always been a place and a time for the mingling of human and non-human events. More than that privileged moment in which humans observe and dialogue exclusively with other humans, today we can acknowledge that performance is a manifestation of ecological relations, an opportunity for attending to the ever-present 'interfolding network of humanity and nonhumanity'. The invitation here is to remodel our understanding of events and phenomena, in line with Steven Shaviro's radical suggestion that in 'the vast interconnections of the universe, *everything* both perceives and is perceived'.[26]

In practical terms, I am not referring to environmental shows about global warming, presented in theatres that run on solar power, nor am I referring to works that feature animals and objects, if this means simply making a little room for them on the human stage, for the duration of an evening. It is rather about recognizing the transformation of the very category of the human, and how this transformation needs to be practised in the domain of performance, yielding dramaturgies as yet undreamt.

For too long performance has been caught up in tropes like presence, liveness, and ephemerality, in other words the here-and-now trap, which necessarily ignores non-human subjects. What forms may performance take when we recognize that it is *always* enmeshed in non-human spatial and temporal scales and durations? Why not loosen, or even risk losing, the human two-way traffic of theatre, to see what kinds of impossible dramaturgies may emerge?

It is not a question of 'staging' or 'representing' the Anthropocene, but rather of understanding, experimentally and provisionally, how this epoch and its emergent paradigms are changing representation for good, just like the outburst of a river bends and reconfigures a bridge, a dam, or a street. The challenge and the call to performance is to outplay its anthropocentric bias, again and again, and to reorient towards ecological relations (and non-relations), at the risk of having to abandon concepts and practices we hold dear.

Notes

1 Cixous, *Rootprints*, p. 11.
2 Brook, *The Empty Space*, p. 7.
3 Bel, 'Interview with Fabienne Arvers', www.82.238.77.78/jeromebel/eng/jeromebel.asp?m=4&t=1.
4 Turner and Behrndt, *Dramaturgy and Performance*, p. 36.
5 Van Kerkhoven, 'State of the Union Address', www.kaaitheater.be/marianne.
6 Wolfe, *What is Posthumanism?*, p. 47, italics given are mine.
7 Ibid., p. 47.
8 Florêncio, 'Enmeshed Bodies, Impossible Touch', p. 53.
9 Foucault, *The Order of Things*, p. 422.
10 This sentence is taken from a question posed by film director Michelangelo Frammartino, whose work *Le Quattro Volte* (2010) strongly inspired the thoughts in this text. Frammartino's question reads: 'Can cinema free itself of the dogma which dictates that human beings should occupy the leading role?' See Frammartino, *Le Quattro Volte Press Book*, www.kinolorber.com/data/presskit/lqv_pressbook.pdf.
11 Fischer-Lichte in Schneider, 'New Materialism and Performance Studies', p. 9.
12 Dillard, *Pilgrim at Tinker's Creek*, p. 93.
13 Ponge, 'The Pebble', p. 64.
14 Ibid., p. 64.
15 Solis, in Pow, 'Final Curtain', www.dailymail.co.uk/news/article-2314483.
16 Solis, *Stages of Decay*, p. 19.
17 The piece in question is La Monte Young's *Composition # 5 1960*, which I first read about in 2006. In fact, the score is slightly less precise than my memory of it: any number of butterflies may be released in the space, and their potential window exit is to be staged only if an unlimited amount of time is available. See Potter, *Four Musical Minimalists*, p. 50.
18 Regarding small animals in theatres, I have dedicated a lecture-work and essay on the appearance of a swallow inside Vicenza's Teatro Olimpico. See Corrieri, *In Place of a Show*. Also Nicholas Ridout's 'The Animal on Stage' begins with an account of a mouse scuttling across the floor during a West End production: 'so small, so accidental', the mouse may 'prove too fragile a frame on which to build a theory of theatrical labour'. See Ridout, *Stage Fright, Animals, and Other Theatrical Problems*, p. 101.
19 See Connor, 'Making Flies Mean Something', p. 9.
20 Dillard, *Pilgrim at Tinker's Creek*, p. 129.
21 Paterson, 'As The World Turns', www.katiepaterson.org/worldturns.
22 Bennett, *Vibrant Matter*, p. x.
23 An extract can be listened to on Paterson's website. See Paterson, 'Earth–Moon–Earth'. www.katiepaterson.org/eme.
24 Advertising information on 'Prelude' can be found at Van Kerkhoven, www. kaaitheater.be/en/e1468/prelude.
25 Bennett, *Vibrant Matter*, p. 31.
26 Shaviro, 'Deleuze's Encounter with Whitehead', p. 9.

Bibliography

- Bel, Jérôme. 'Interview with Fabienne Arvers', 2001. www.jeromebel.fr (accessed 11 April 2013).
- Bennett, Jane. *Vibrant Matter: A Political Ecology of Things*. London: Duke University Press, 2010.
- Brook, Peter. *The Empty Space*. New York: Touchstone, 1994.
- Cixous, Hélène. *Rootprints: Memory and Life Writing*. London: Routledge, 1994.
- Connor, Steven. 'Making Flies Mean Something', 2009, www.steven connor.com/flymean/flymean.pdf (accessed 21 March 2016).
- Corrieri, Augusto. *In Place of a Show: What Happens Inside Theatres When Nothing is Happening*. London: Bloomsbury Methuen Drama, 2016.
- Dillard, Annie. *Pilgrim at Tinker's Creek*. New York: Harper Collins, 2007.
- Florêncio, João. 'Enmeshed Bodies, Impossible Touch: The Object-oriented World of Pina Bausch's *Café Müller*'. *Performance Research* 20, no. 2 (2015), pp. 53–59.
- Foucault, Michel. *The Order of Things: An Archeology of the Human Sciences*. London: Routledge, 2002.
- Frammartino, Michelangeo. *Le Quattro Volte Press Book*, 2010. www.kinolorber. com/data/presskit/lqv_pressbook.pdf (accessed 21 March 2016).
- Paterson, Katie. www.katiepaterson. org, undated (accessed 21 March 2016).
- Paterson, Katie. 'As The World Turns', undated. www.katiepaterson.org/ worldturns (accessed 21 March 2016).
- Paterson, Katie. 'Earth-Moon-Earth', undated. www.katiepaterson. org/eme (accessed 21 March 2016).
- Ponge, Francis. 'The Pebble'. In *The Nature of Things*, trans. Lee Fahnestock, pp. 48–51. New York: Red Dust, 2011.
- Potter, Keith. *Four Musical Minimalists: La Monte Young, Terry Riley, Steve Reich, Philip Glass*. Cambridge, MA: Cambridge University Press, 2000.
- Pow, Helen. 'Final Curtain: America's Once Enchanting Theaters That Have Been Abandoned and Left to Crumble'. *The Daily Mail*, 25 April 2013. www. dailymail.co.uk/news/article-2314483 (accessed: 11 March 2015).
- Ridout, Nicholas. *Stage Fright, Animals, and Other Theatrical Problems*. Cambridge, MA: Cambridge University Press, 2006.
- Schneider, Rebecca. 'New Materialism and Performance Studies'. *TDR: The Drama Review* 59, no. 4 (2015), pp. 7–17.
- Shaviro, Steven. 'Deleuze's Encounter with Whitehead', undated, p. 9. www. stevenshaviro.com/Othertexts/articles. html (accessed 11 March 2015).
- Solis, Julia. *Stages of Decay*. Munich: Prestel, 2013.
- Turner, Cathy and Synne Behrndt. *Dramaturgy and Performance*. Hampshire: Palgrave MacMillan, 2008.
- Van Kerkhoven, Marianne. 'State of the Union Address', 1994. www. kaaitheater.be/marianne/ (accessed 21 March 2016).
- Van Kerkhoven, Marianne. 'Prelude', 2014. www. kaaitheater.be/en/e1468/ prelude (accessed 21 March 2016).
- Viola, Bill. *Reasons for Knocking at an Empty House: Writings 1973-1994*. Cambridge, MA: MIT Press with London: Anthony d'Offay Gallery, 1995.
- Wolfe, Cary. *What is Posthumanism?* Minneapolis: University of Minnesota Press, 2010.

Epilogue
Konstantina Georgelou
Efrosini Protopapa
Danae Theodoridou

In Conversation

The final text that follows is a staged conversation among us (the editors). Here we seek to practice a dramaturgy of co-authoring through which the individual views, dynamics, and antagonisms between us can emerge. We do that by posing questions or discussion points to one another, related to issues that may have been overlooked or not mentioned until now in the book, or that occurred to each one of us individually in the process of writing and have not been addressed explicitly elsewhere. This echoes and puts into practice, in some way, the conversational aspect of dramaturgy that has also been explored by some guest authors' texts (for example, Guy Cools', as well as Jonas Rutgeerts' and Ivana Müller's). What this process triggers, it is hoped, is a written debate on dramaturgy, on our proposed notion of 'working on actions', and the catalytic principles that we have outlined on artistic research and on infrastructures. In this written conversation, our questions and responses have acted namely as catalysts, setting in motion a type of co-authoring that is very different from the one in the Introduction and Part I of the book, where the three of us have co-written as 'one voice'.

> **Danae Theodoridou** — I would like to return to our point that, coming from different backgrounds (theatre making, choreography, theory), our meeting ground as far as artistic creation is concerned is the field of dramaturgy. This seems to suggest that dramaturgy is what is 'common', a shared concern among the different agents beyond the particularities of their distinct roles in a creative process (be it different performance qualities for the performers, composition and production issues for the makers, and so forth). Given the fact that, also, at different points, one or more of us has claimed their indifference towards the term as such, I was wondering if our suggestion ends up blurring 'dramaturgy' even more than it is already blurred as a term, making it appear as interchangeable with terms and phrases such as 'collaboration', 'ethics', and 'modes of production'. Or, to put it differently: on my side, I recognize my explicit research interest in the term since 2008, when I started my PhD on dramaturgy, but what is it that interests you, now maybe, after the workshops and the book have been completed, in dramaturgy?

Konstantina Georgelou — My first encounter with dramaturgy as a term and as a practice was when I started working with a choreographer in Greece in 2003,[1] which is to say that initially I got curious and interested in it as a peculiar 'mode of doing' (that included try-outs, failures, experiments, various types of research, and articulated processes of decision making) as integral parts of choreographic practice. It was during this time that dramaturgy became for me a very productive area from which to pose questions and to form viewpoints on various other practices and subject matters, such as choreography, performativity, relationality, modes of production, perspective, address, and ethics. I would even say that I have so far 'made use of' dramaturgy for addressing concerns and topics that do not have to do with investigating dramaturgy per se (in the sense of studying the history of the discipline, its applications, its developments, and more). In our collaborative work for this project, I believe we followed a similar path. We realized that dramaturgy constitutes for us a shared point of view, which does not have to be articulated by means of binaries (for instance, dramaturgy versus artistic practice), but can still be considered and studied as a distinct area of 'work', which points to a 'working on actions', as we have claimed. My overall approach to dramaturgy has not really changed after this project, therefore. However, the research we undertook together and the book we have co-edited have greatly influenced my understanding of how dramaturgy can be considered and practised within educational, artistic, and research environments. More concretely, in the fields of artistic research and education I have started thinking of and organizing very differently the sessions and seminars on dramaturgy that I am asked to teach or facilitate, by specifically trying to work towards the devising of tasks and of procedures that can 'set into motion' dramaturgical processes for and with others, rather than only identify, situate, and explain existing dramaturgical operations. I try working in this way both in sessions with artists-researchers, which have to do with the development of their artistic work, as well as in sessions that explore analytical and theoretical approaches to performance, by devising ways to work with this material that are exploratory, rather than explanatory, and task-based.

Efrosini Protopapa — I think it is telling of our journey how we are identifying here a potential link (if not blurring) of the notion of dramaturgy not necessarily with other fields of artistic practice, such as choreography or performance making, but with terms and phrases like 'collaboration', 'ethics', and 'modes of production'. This is already a shift in the way we have discussed the interchangeability of terms in the past and in fact speaks to where I find myself now in terms of my interest in dramaturgy.

The truth is that throughout this research project I have never felt particularly attached to the term 'dramaturgy'; I have considered it more as a vehicle (an excuse, perhaps) through which to get to a number of issues that relate to working modes in performance, questions of ethics within and beyond creative processes, the relationship between research and artistic practice.

About a year ago, I would have been keen to discuss the boundaries or differences between dramaturgy and choreography — since this is the practice I mostly associate myself with; at the end of the project, I find myself much more intrigued by the ways in which our research, which we have located within the field of dramaturgy, has allowed me to reconsider other areas of concern that I have, especially by furthering my understanding and practice of choreography in an expanded sense. I am referring here to the proposition of artists and theorists, such as Xavier Le Roy, Bojana Cvejić, and Mårten Spångberg, that choreography has transformed to involve the engineering of 'situations, organization, social choreography and movements', but has also expanded 'towards cinematic strategies, documentary and documentation' and is 'rethinking publication, exhibition, display, mediatization, production and post-production'; it has therefore been claimed that choreography 'is gaining momentum on a political level as it is placed in the middle of a society to a large degree organized around movement, subjectivity and immaterial exchange', becoming 'a practice that in and of itself is political'.[2] Although excited by this idea or prospect for dance and choreography, my question has been how or why choreography could or would take on new expressions, as Spångberg has proposed,[3] that is, what would facilitate or prompt such a development, and why would that even be desirable? In other words, I don't see myself as a choreographer thinking, 'Oh, I'd like to practice choreography in an expanded sense', and then wondering how I may do that, and yet, I do feel that there is a larger scope of concerns I want to address as a choreographer that perhaps a more traditional practice of choreography does not allow me to.

This is where dramaturgy as 'working on actions' comes in. I find that this concept as we have discussed it in the book releases new potentials for choreography, in two ways: first, it offers concrete proposals on how I may work with a choreographic concept, with bodies, movement, and situations in the studio. I am referring here to principles like the three that we have proposed, which promote interference, disruption, estrangement, and difference; I am particularly drawn to these operations because I usually work with tasks and the qualities of such operations are key to imagining tasks that do not complete or exhaust themselves instantly, but are productive and generate a situation for performers to investigate. Second, and more crucially, these same principles can be applied to how I conceive a choreographic project more broadly, in terms of its relation to modes of production and conditions of working, to institutions and markets, to time, money, and so forth. It is here that expanded choreography meets working on actions for me, where I can start considering the overall set-up in which I do choreography, so that it potentially interferes with particular systems of producing, touring, and marketing, triggering new relations to such systems and demanding their reconfiguration along the way.[4] This determines not only the work itself, but also how I am as an artist 'in the world'. Now, whether I consider these operations as dramaturgical or not, I don't really care — although it is significant, of course, that we have arrived at such propositions by returning to the etymology of none other than 'drama-turgy'.

DT — I find these observations quite useful for what we are trying to suggest here. Although I recognize the great value of the discussion on the relation between art and its context, especially when the context keeps shifting continuously, becoming more and more oppressive as is the case today, given the fact that this relation has already been addressed in several ways since the 1990s through what has been called the 'conceptual turn' in art and choreography in particular, my interest in what you say now lies more in two other aspects. The first one relates to dramaturgical discourses, whereas the second to research in general. I find it indeed necessary (given also the many discussions we had with workshop participants on the way they think of the role and function of dramaturgy and the dramaturg) to stress again the practice of dramaturgy as a working mode that includes a certain attentiveness to ethics, encounters, and modes of production, rather than a 'job' or something one does in order to gain specific outcomes or profits. At the same time, I am also particularly interested in the suggestion of research on a term (in this case 'dramaturgy') not in order to understand *it* but in order to shed more light on other terms/practices. This creates a more complex movement of actions that does not proceed via one-to-one relations of cause and effect or linear connections between things and their meaning. Having said that, however, I would like to also express my doubts towards the term 'expanded', which I find quite ambiguous — because, in my opinion, it tends to flatten practices and their relation instead of sharpening them. For example, if we say that an 'expanded' understanding of choreography may also include dramaturgy, we seem to suggest that dramaturgy and choreography can, from a certain view, become something similar. This blurs both practices. If we insist, however, on treating both choreography and dramaturgy as distinct terms and practices, we can arrive at more insightful observations about how one can assist the other. In this sense, we do not talk about one practice included in another but more about different practices we are involved in while we work that help us shift perspectives and modes of (re)searching — practices that shift our dominant positions as we pass, or maybe exactly *because* we allow ourselves to pass from one to the other. Allowing in this way also another look on those dominant positions, too ...

EP — Absolutely. And I think this is how we approached the relation of dramaturgy to other terms and practices, when asking guests in the roundtable discussions, for example, to consider the suggestion of dramaturgy as 'working on actions' from within their own practices (as performance makers, choreographers, dramaturgs, writers, curators, theorists, and others). Given that we have further claimed in the book that this suggestion may be extended from the field of performance to other artistic fields, dimensions of practice, and aspects of life, this is a good moment for me to ask how you each 'work on actions' from whichever perspective you work. And how does this 'working on actions' make your practices relate to (or help create) specific relations to conditions, contexts, frames, and institutions?

DT — I am thinking now of the form and function of the 'open letter'. Maybe because it is quite popular lately in my environment, given the recent 'open letter' exchanges between Jan Fabre and the Greek artistic community on the topic of the artistic directorship/curation of the Athens and Epidaurus international festival.[5] An open letter is written to someone specifically but is addressed to him or her publicly. What interests me here is exactly this delicate balance between the private and the public. In this case, the addressee becomes a representation more than a specific person with a concrete identity, but still not someone abstract. This is exactly what, for me, makes the open letter an action in the way that Hannah Arendt has described it: something that appears and places itself in the public sphere in order to act upon the world. In this case, we could see the open letter as an action of correspondence that has the potential, sometimes even the power, to change a decision, to cause an immediate effect, to have an impact. I would say that it is in a similar way that I relate to how I 'work on actions' in the research, artistic, and educational contexts I am involved in. In all these cases, I somehow try to construct encounters as open letters addressed to those (collaborators, students, et cetera) that I work with and beyond. I do this perhaps via the opposite movement, which I still find similar. I try to address people or things in a public manner even within more private settings (such as a class, a rehearsal studio, or a conversation). Starting always from the specific bodies or institutions involved, the particularity of their functions and needs, my aim is to create 'open letters' that articulate concerns, questions, and processes and those in turn aim to reach much farther than the specific context they appear in, to deal with the ways in which we meet, exchange, and work together at large. I guess here, through this metaphor, I am trying to point to the way our work can be affected when we use the potentiality of public addressing and positioning as a motive, also in more intimate, private encounters. What is the driving force of what we do? Where does this work stand in its context? What does it attempt to do within this frame? What does it ask (back)? How are bodies placed in it? How do they enter or exit this encounter? To ask such questions not in an abstract way, but with the direction that an open letter has is what for me turns something into an action — a force that every time, with each single step it takes (be that during a rehearsal day in the studio, in a class, or otherwise), demands and achieves a small change, a shift, a displacement, an activation. It needs a lot of effort and it does not always work, I know...

KG — The discussion around 'activation' is very crucial for our take on 'working on actions'. Activation can namely aim for small changes, but also for bigger ones. Such bigger changes are often aimed for by activist practices, for instance, that have not been extensively addressed in this book, although we are clearly concerned with the political implications of 'action'. I am now reminded of a performance I attended recently,[6] where audience members were asked by other audience members various questions about who they are as political, biological, and social subjects, and one of these questions was, 'Are you an activist?' My immediate response to that question was 'no', since I am not systematically trying to raise awareness on specific urgent problems and in this way inflict change.[7] Nor am I producing artworks, which would be another possible way to consider artistic practice by means of artistic activism.[8] When thinking about 'action' in a more expanded way, however, and more particularly about processes of 'working on actions' that we have outlined in this book, the question of 'being an activist or not' rather suggests shifting one's focus towards identifying and then further 'working on' the public and plural aspects of action that one is already engaged in. In other words, *how, what, when,* and *why* one is engaged with actions (in the Arendtian sense) become more relevant questions. So, it makes sense for me to link the question of how I 'work on actions' to Simon Bayly's 'intentionally myopic preoccupation' that he proposes in his text here, rather than 'far-sighted preparations of events' that would be effective and ingenuous. This leads me to two aspects of my work, really: our collaboration since 2010, and my work in higher education. On the one hand, and as it has, it is hoped, become clear in the Introduction of this book, our collaboration has been since the very beginning engaged in various institutional and contextual 'affairs' (although not so consciously) — attempting to understand, intervene, and reconfigure conditions of working and modes of production in theory and in the arts by staying 'under the radar', as we have explained. We have thus been busy with 'setting into motion' processes that concentrate and interfere with particular contexts and conditions, rather than aiming for big changes on a larger scale. On the other hand, as an educator I similarly find it crucial to keep on figuring out, together with my colleagues, ways of creating critical platforms for students to engage with artistic practice and discourse while paying attention to how these are situated and produced by various contexts, and how they participate and/or interrupt processes of knowing, experiencing, and understanding the world.[9] In either case, I think it is important to understand 'working on actions' by means of Arendt's attributes of action that also correspond to the principles we have outlined in this book. Setting into motion, plurality, unpredictability, mobilizing questions, commoning, and alienating have by now become principles that I seek to identify, locate, take under consideration, and further operationalize in how I engage with my role as educator, theorist, and researcher.

EP — Let us dwell a little bit on those principles for dramaturgy then, and consider them in the context of our working together. For a very long time during this project we resisted reflecting upon our 'collaborative modes' — my sense is that we preferred 'just doing it'. I remember two occasions, however, in which we did: the first time was at a meeting in Brussels midway through the project, when a certain anxiety arose about how we were sharing work (load), whether we were conscious about any inequalities or injustices in the way we were dealing with administrative and financial issues, how we were prioritizing this project alongside other work and life commitments, and how we were communicating (or miscommunicating) those to each other (given the specific conditions of among other things living and working in different countries/contexts). The second time was in public, when we were invited to present on 'how we work together' at a conference in Giessen, Germany,[10] towards the end of the project, when we decided to speak individually about our collaboration, and shifted between the anecdotal, the self-reflexive, and more critical accounts of our working modes. In fact, we had often been encouraged to reflect on the politics of our working modes and it is only after this presentation that we were able to articulate it as we have in the Introduction, where we speak about the dramaturgy of our collaboration. Looking back at the three principles for dramaturgy that we have offered here — mobilizing questions, alienating, and commoning — and although we refer to these as arising from the workshops, I would like to test the hypothesis that they were actually principles we were practising in our collaboration — or, were they? What kind of collaborator (or co-worker, to try to avoid the problematic dimensions of collaboration that we have already highlighted in the book) do such principles make us? Or how may they help us think through specific modes of co-working, as we may have practised them during this project and in the writing of this book?

DT — I recently caught myself thinking that the three of us somehow constitute a whole organism. I don't mean this in any sense of flawlessness, but more in the sense that

I believe that each one of us brings very different qualities to the work that none of the other two can bring: for instance, when one works more smoothly with abstract ideas, arriving slowly and attentively at new articulations, another one is working in more explosive ways, coming out of the blue with concrete new ideas about projects and when and how these could take place, while a third one ensures a clear and insightful articulation of things and processes, continuously making sure that everything is in place. If one would then put such working qualities together, nothing would be repeated and everything would be completed, I think. It is in this sense that we constitute a whole organism. Now, when breaking this organism in three different bodies, one gets three quite queer co-workers, I would say. Queer maybe in the way that Jasna Jasna Žmak and Joachim Robbrecht discuss it, as a process of constant reconfiguration of what we think we may already know or do via what the other knows or does. In our collaboration, at least as I experience it, one has to look at things from three different perspectives at the same time (Andrea Božić and Julia Willms' 'divided attention' also comes to mind here), or one works from a constant 'what if' of another perspective (in my case, I would need to think, what would Konstantina think here, or how would Efrosini react in this case, and so forth). This became quite clear to me when I had to facilitate a workshop on my own in Barcelona, where I realized that I acted in certain instances as Efrosini would have acted, something I wouldn't have done if she were there. Shifting between one's self and others, between familiar habits of one's own and habits of others that become equally familiar through the proximity of work, is something I find myself often doing in the frame of our collaboration. Rudi Laermans' notion of the 'collaboratory' comes also to mind now, which he has discussed as a mode that 'repeatedly subverts "the subjective"'. As he has described, 'through cooperation those partaking become other: they experience processes of de- and re-subjectification'.[11] Undoing my 'self' through the other to only re-turn to a different 'me' is how I would also describe myself in our collaboration.

But to address also specifically the question about the three principles we discuss in the book, I think that they are constantly present in what we do. It then becomes a bit like the 'chicken-or-egg' question, though: did the principles make the work or did the work make the principles? I know that chronologically what we do happened first, as an urgency to act together in our common field of operation (performance) via our respective different roles. As we have already stated in the Introduction, this is the way that we prefer to work in general. We don't presuppose hypotheses that we then simply test or execute, but we reflect on what it is that we do as we go along detecting its main modes of operation. In this sense, it was through our work that the principles emerged. At the same time, though, I don't think that the emergence of these principles was coincidental and that they were absent in what we did before, although not articulated explicitly. Maybe it would then help to try thinking of what was consciously there in their place before we arrived at them as such? If I try to trace things back I would arrive at starting points, questions, or concerns such as the following: whom do we invite in our work, how, and why? Where, when, why, and for how long does this invitation take place? How do we spend it/ waste it together? What is different, has changed, moved forward in our work after this invitation? What do we take with us from it as we continue to work?

KG — In order to avoid falling into the trap of the 'chicken-or-egg' question, I will thus start from the assumption that the three principles are indeed constitutive of our working together. I would even go on to suggest that there are many more principles that are at play that we have not (yet) identified, which relate to disagreement, tension, complicity, play, the anecdotal, and so on. In any case, I do not think that I can find a satisfying adjective to describe the work that happens 'between us three, plus more', which could be another principle. I can, however, describe its 'doing' as an excess, as a production of surplus that cannot be sufficiently regulated. Here I refer to the 'actual' surplus of ideas, meetings, people, writings, notes, and time of being together, which has administrative implications. But there is also a more symbolic and conceptual level to this surplus, which is that everything we do happens between us and is in effect triggered by this 'between-ness' and, hence, the work that we do exceeds our individual capacities for regulation. Karen Barad's notion of 'intra-action'[12] is helpful to consider here, which points to such aspects of between-ness seen from the perspective of 'action'. Intra-action namely shifts attention from an attempt to understand entities to an understanding of relationships between agents that are not viewed as bound to their pre-existing capacities, and in this sense do not preexist the relation or the action that occurs. As she has explained, contrary to 'interaction', which assumes that there are separate entities interacting with one another, intra-action points to the prioritization of the relationship between components that do not preexist that relation. Barad's approach is in the end a post-human one that is also clearly echoed in Augusto Corrieri's text here, which seeks to re-scale dramaturgy outside anthropocentric framings of theatre and of the world at large. So, perhaps, the excess that I find quite compelling in our working together possibly has to do with such a post-human and relational dimension of action, which could be interesting to further consider through our collaborative research.

DT — It is interesting that you refer here to the post-human also as the relational and not solely as the outside of the anthropocentric. Seeing the intra-human as part of the discourse on post-humanism is an approach that particularly stresses the ethical and political problems but also potentialities involved in the topic, much more effectively, in my opinion, than doing this mainly through a focus on technology, genetics, space, or other non-human aspects related to the anthropocene.[13] This is an approach that I have also followed in the research I have been conducting for the last two years on the notion of social imaginaries, the way we imagine our future on Earth, and the contribution of art and artistic research to such acts of imagination.[14]

Especially in relation to the latter aspect, I would like to share some concerns, which relate also to this project.

Artistic research is what I consider myself having worked on quite intensively for the last eight years, and I place 'Dramaturgy at Work' in the same frame of work. A conference on artistic research that I attended recently though, left me somehow utterly indifferent towards the term and the questions that relate to it, in a way that made me question the nature and the value of what it is that we do. There is something quite irrelevant, I find, in questions that have to do with how we do artistic research, what we mean by it, who should do it and who shouldn't, how it relates to 'good' artistic work, how it should be evaluated, and so on. At the same time, nevertheless, I do recognize the need to create a certain frame especially when we talk about it in educational terms, since I also see the risk of naming anything 'artistic research' in order to exploit it accordingly. Given the fact that all three of us are involved in educational institutions as well, I was wondering if we could reflect on the way possible frames for approaching artistic research could come out of the way we developed 'Dramaturgy at Work'. What if, for example, we would consider the following few paragraphs as a micro-conference on artistic research in its own terms and see what may emerge? If the abovementioned questions are indeed irrelevant, which questions could replace them? In other words: What are the questions to ask in/of artistic research (if we should ask any questions at all, instead of just doing it)?

KG — For me it is of great importance to acknowledge where artistic research is happening, whether this is an educational institution, or a residency, or a theatre venue, or whether it is institutionally independent at that moment. Given my work within the educational context of artistic research, however, the first questions that come to mind seem to be articulated from the perspective of an educational institution. And from this perspective, I would probably ask the artist-researcher: Why is it important for you to make artistic work? What do you think is 'at stake' today and how do you think your work deals with that (or not)? Where do you make your work public and how do you decide what places and contexts are relevant and what are not? What are you searching for (if anything)? What is the role and function of writing in the work that you do? Do you need an educational diploma in order to find a more stable job/income? Do you consider yourself operating inside or outside institutional frames, and if yes, which ones?

EP — First I should also underscore that by artistic research I mean research that happens through artistic practice, wherever that takes place (that is, not research on the arts or about the arts, so not, for example, performance analysis). In this sense, it concerns a deeper understanding and articulation of the type of thinking that is enabled through artistic work, which has the capacity, however, to inform how one learns and develops work in other fields, too. In the workshops that were part of our project, for example, we attempted to unfold ideas, concerns, dynamics, and issues as those emerged through the practices of participants; these were mostly artistic, and then in cases where they were not, I still feel we encouraged participants to approach their work as such (see how Nienke Scholts describes this in her text, for example). Artistic research in this sense allows one to ask questions such as those Konstantina poses above, which request of the researcher to be more reflective about what they are doing, why, and for whom, to pay attention to the ethical and other implications of their practice, and to position their work within larger socio-political and economic structures. And it is not that other types of research do not do this — for example, a sociological approach or a philosophical consideration of artistic work may also reveal such aspects — but artistic research does this as its primary mode of enquiry. This is where its significance lies for me, within educational institutions in particular, where it can offer new paradigms for knowledge production. And this is why in my work within educational institutions as well, I am not so much eager to promote so-called 'practice-as-research' (a similarly exhausted term, and a great example of a term that has perfectly been exploited, particularly by the UK educational system), but to test out how different approaches to knowledge, which I may have arrived at through artistic research, can be shared across subjects and modes of learning.[15]

KG — Our various institutional positions and affiliations are quite determining in how we speak and in how we position ourselves in the field of performance. Since we ultimately move beyond performance making in how we understand and propose the practice of dramaturgy in this book, I am wondering whether this perspective needs to become more concrete while also remaining speculative, now that we have arrived at the Epilogue. I refer here to dramaturgy as an 'infrastructural affair' so to say, or as a 'systemic' type of practice as Una Bauer has argued here — that is, as an affair with institutions, with various other sectors, with funding bodies, and so on. Differently put, considering the political implications of dramaturgy today, I think a lot about (counter) movements, affiliations, conspiracies, (dis)connections, and interventions on an infrastructural level. I am also thinking of sabotage, posthumanism, contagiousness, queering, anxieties, and cosmology, as these have been suggested by the guest authors in this book. Taking into account the political dimension of dramaturgy as an 'infrastructural and systemic affair', as well as the contributions of the guests in this book, what are your 'concluding thoughts'? Or, to put it in a more task-based manner, can you write a paragraph that, according to you, could be the last paragraph of this book and in which you would address dramaturgy from this perspective?

EP — I hope that I am not copping out of the challenge here, but I would suggest that the way in which we have worked on this project and have subsequently developed the book already contains to a certain degree elements like the ones you identify through which we may consider dramaturgy as an 'infrastructural and systemic affair': (counter) movements, affiliations, conspiracies, interventions, sabotage, et cetera. Let me return for a moment to Danae's initial question about our current interest in dramaturgy, and approach my 'concluding thoughts' through a confession. Perhaps I should have added earlier on that dramaturgy did not only function as a shared field of enquiry for us in research terms, but it also served some other seemingly secondary purposes: because of the fact that 'dramaturgy' implies a field that undoubtedly touches on theatre, dance, choreography, performance, theory, and philosophy — in short, a field that so perfectly incorporates and speaks back to our respective fields of practice — we have been able by presenting the project as a *dramaturgical* one to draw support for it from institutions and organizations that each one of us is connected to (and that similarly position themselves within these distinct areas) across Europe. In a similar way, we have been able to reach out to colleagues as well as other artists, writers, and thinkers with whom we have fruitful dialogues — and some of whom have equally drawn on their own institutional affiliations or 'jobs' to make possible their participation in our project, regardless of whether dramaturgy is their particular field of practice. I do not think that all of this is purely strategic or opportunistic; it's not just about 'ticking the boxes', but goes much beyond that. It proposes ways of practising research (on dramaturgy, in this case) within the infrastructural. In fact, it suggests bending the structures to fit purposes and, in this way, I would claim, it reaffirms the possibilities that can be afforded by institutions, funding bodies, and so forth, rather than undermines them. I consider this a powerful move, a 'working on actions', and one that has indeed been embraced by the guest authors of the book who have in turn suggested, as you say, their own tactics or examples of tactics for such a politicization of dramaturgy.

DT — If I understand the task correctly, what it asks me is to discuss the social and political connotations of dramaturgy. What does dramaturgy, especially as discussed here (through inefficiencies, mobilizations, disorientations, alienations, and more) have to offer on an infrastructural level? If I were to do this task (and I also hope I am not copping out here), I would copy-paste all or parts of the section 'In Collaboration' from the Introduction. Or maybe only its last paragraph. I think that the suggestion there is quite clear: a more effective construction of actions on the social and political level seems to be possible only when passing *through* the dominant neoliberal and post-Fordist modes of work and production. Acting as a smooth-operator in a sense, slowly shifting things from within, one step at a time, under the table. Exhausting, overusing, outgrowing systems that aim to exploit. In order to do that, one has to pretend following the flow, while becoming the tidal wave that overturns it. What may take the form of flexible, temporary, always available, quick efficient work (all typical characteristics of post-Fordism), actually produces ongoing, strong, and concrete 'inefficient' acts that cannot easily become capitalized and commodified by neoliberalism. If I had to put it in two to three lines (to make your task even stricter, since we generally like playing with rules in our workshops and beyond):

On an infrastructural level, dramaturgy as we have explored it in this book suggests creating actions that act in disguise, balancing between two movements at the same time, 'moving in mysterious ways' while seeming to move 'properly'.

Notes

1 From 2003 to 2010 I was working with choreographer Apostolia Papadamaki, who is based in Greece.

2 See the announcement of the conference 'Conference: Expanded Choreography. Situations, Movement, Objects' at MACBA, Barcelona, March 2012: www.e-flux.com/announcements/conference-expanded-choreography-situations-movements-objects.../.

3 See Spångberg, 'Dance and the Museum', www.movementresearch.org/criticalcorrespondence/blog/?p=8100.

4 See, for example, the artistic project *The Friend at Work*, which I initiated in 2014: http://thefriendatwork.wordpress.com.

5 Performance and visual artist Jan Fabre was appointed in February 2016 by the Greek Ministry of Culture to curate the Athens and Epidaurus international festival (http://greekfestival.gr/en/home). He resigned from this position in March 2016 only days after his first press conference where he announced his plans for the years 2016 to 2019. This was in response to an 'open letter' the Greek artistic community wrote to him in which they reacted strongly against Fabre's curatorial plans. Fabre and his collaborators replied with another 'open letter' to the Greek artists a few weeks later.

6 Here I refer to the performance *Anonymous P.* by Chris Kondek and Christiane Kühl, which I attended at Frascati Theatre in Amsterdam, the Netherlands on 15 January 2016.

7 Duncombe and Lambert ('The Art of Activism', p. 26) have explained how the most common approach towards change among activists is 'CHANGE= PEOPLE + AWARENESS'.

8 'Artistic activism is a hybrid practice combining the aesthetic, process based approach of the arts with the instrumental, outcome focus of activism ... Artistic activism blends the affective and the effective'. Ibid., p. 34.

9 For instance, in the context of a course entitled 'Writing Dancing' that I teach at Utrecht University, the Netherlands, students got involved as 'dance journalists' in the festival Moving Futures in the Netherlands (2015 to 2016), being asked to produce critical and collaborative writings that would become public in the frame of this festival.

10 For more information: http://theyesconference.tumblr.com.

11 Laermans, *Moving Together*, p. 389.

12 Barad, 'Posthumanist Performativity'.

13 I refer here to the term that emerged particularly in the last five to six years to describe the era that begins when human activities started to have a significant global impact on Earth's geology and ecosystems – the era we are currently placed in.

14 My two-year artistic research on the notion of social imaginaries has so far resulted in the creation of one stage piece (*One Small Step for a Man: Hello, Goodbye*) and a performance lecture (*Something Dreamy*). Currently, I am in the making process of a second one-to-one performance that attempts to act as a speculation of our future life on the planet (*Earth in 100 Years*). For more information on all projects see: www.danaetheodoridou.com.

15 See also a text I published on *Bellyflop Magazine*, which resulted from a panel conversation at London's University of Roehampton's Centre for Dance Research on 13 March 2015: http://bellyflopmag.com/blog/artists-as-scholars-seriously-part-1

Bibliography

— Barad, Karen. 'Posthumanist
    Performativity: Toward an
    Understanding of How Matter Comes
    to Matter'. *Signs: Journal of Women in
    Culture and Society* 28, no. 3 (2003),
    pp. 801–31.
— Duncombe, Stephen and Lambert,
    Steve. 'The Art of Activism'. In *Truth
    is Concrete: A Handbook for Artistic
    Strategies in Real Politics*, ed. by
    Florian Malzacher et al., pp. 16–30.
    Berlin: Sternberg Press.
— Laermans, Rudi. *Moving Together:
    Theorizing and Making Contemporary
    Dance*. Amsterdam: Valiz, 2015.
— Protopapa, Efrosini. 'Artists as
    Scholars: Seriously?' *Bellyflop
    Magazine*, 2015. http://bellyflopmag.
    com/blog/artists-as-scholars-seriously-
    part-1 (accessed: 18 April 2016).
— Spångberg, Mårten. 'Dance and
    the Museum: Mårten Spangberg
    Responds'. *Movement Research*,
    2014. www.movementresearch.org/
    criticalcorrespondence/blog/?p=8100
    (accessed: 16 April 2016).

Acknowledgements

Since March 2014, when the research project that led to this book started, we have had invaluable conversations and exchanges with artists, writers, dramaturgs, pedagogues, theorists, and curators who participated in workshops that took place in Belgium, the Netherlands, the United Kingdom, Greece, Spain, and Croatia. How does a research project lead to a book? How can the findings of workshops be reflected therein? Should they be? How can the encounters that take place in a workshop situation be reinvented through a book? The first thanks thus goes to all of the participants for sharing their time, ideas, concerns, and feedback, and for giving us in advance, with such great generosity and trust, their permission to use material from the workshops in any way that serves this publication. Many on numerous occasions expressed how much they are looking forward to reading this book and we are glad to now be able to share it with them. Similarly, we would like to thank all our invited guests in the roundtable discussions for their insightful views and perspectives. Some of them have worked attentively on an elaborated version of the statement they presented in those encounters for this publication. They have approached our feedback in a careful and thorough way and we are grateful to them for their patience and dedication.

A heartfelt thanks goes to Pascal Gielen who, from the very start, showed great trust in our work. He supported our project in many ways, not only by organizing one of our workshops, but also, and most importantly, by securing funding for this publication, inviting us to include it in the 'Arts in Society' series, and offering his insightful feedback. We are deeply grateful to him for providing us, in such a discrete and generous way, the ideal conditions for making this book happen.

The whole project could not have been realized without supporters, organizations, and individuals who facilitated and hosted the workshops and roundtable discussions that led to this book, discussed the details of the project with us, and provided suitable frameworks for our work in many countries throughout Europe. We especially want to thank: Christel Stalpaert and the Doctoral School Council of Arts, Humanities and Law of Ghent University, Belgium; Charlotte Vandevyver and workspacebrussels, Brussels; Guy Cools, Research Group Arts in Society and Dance Academy of Fontys School of Fine and Performing Arts, Heleen Volman and DansBrabant, Tilburg, the Netherlands; Centre for Dance Research at University of Roehampton, UK; Kirsty Alexander, Siân Goldby, Fiona Millward, and Gitta Wigro of Independent Dance, Eva Martinez and Richard Cross at Sadler's Wells Theatre, and the Bonnie Bird Choreography Fund in London, UK; Marianthie Paschou and the Institut français de Thessalonique, Martha Katsaridou, Dafni Moustaklidou, and the Hellenic Theatre/Drama & Education Network (TENet-Gr), Thessaloniki, Greece; Syndesmos Chorou and occupied theatre Embros, Athens, Greece; Nicole Beutler, Andrea Božić, Marijke Hoogenboom, and all the organizers of the WE LIVE HERE Academy, Amsterdam; Goran Sergej Pristaš, Darko Lukić, Jasna Jasna Žmak, and Academy of Dramatic Art of University of Zagreb, Croatia; and Elena Carmona, Graner, and Mercat de les Flors, Barcelona, Spain.

Throughout the writing process Ric Allsopp supported our work with the utmost insightfulness. A deeply felt thanks to him for the incredible ways in which he took care of us during a writing residency at Falmouth University, UK, in June 2015, for the playfulness and enthusiasm with which he engaged in our task-based modes of working, and for pointing out to us the catalytic function of our work during a wonderful working session at the Olive Grove on a sunny afternoon in Falmouth, as we had just embarked on the writing process. Later on, as we developed the book, Ric continued offering feedback and challenging what we do, often by overturning our plans and encouraging important shifts. This publication, in its general approach, structure, and tone would have been very different had it not been for his input and advice. He has been a great mentor for us in many ways and we are forever grateful.

Other people with whom we have had dialogues during the research and writing process have contributed to this publication in multiple ways: Joe Kelleher challenged us to think about 'what is at stake' in dramaturgy today and offered his invaluable feedback on early drafts of the book; Bojana Kunst prompted us to consider how our practice is a politicized one; and Janez Janša was the one who first referred to us as 'mafia', offering a new perspective to the ways in which we frame and operate within our working processes. We consider them all continuous interlocutors and our partners in crime, and we feel very fortunate to have had their ongoing and invaluable support in this and other projects.

We wish to extend our thanks to colleagues from various fields who attended our roundtable discussions and with whom we have shared inspiring talks. We have tried to include some of those heated negotiations, reflections, and concerns in this publication. Readers, it is hoped, will be able to perceive the dynamics developed through such exchanges and our attempts to explore the potential of ideas when shared and multiplied.

Last but not least, our warmest thanks goes to our families and close friends, those who have been by our side for the past couple of exciting and challenging years, supporting us throughout this project in their own extraordinary ways.

Konstantina Georgelou
Efrosini Protopapa
Danae Theodoridou

About the Authors

Una Bauer (b. 1978) is a Senior Lecturer at the Academy of Dramatic Art in Zagreb. She obtained her PhD at Queen Mary, University of London. Her interests lie in dance and theatre practices, history of ideas, affect, social media, networked publics, community, death, public sphere, crime fiction, and travel writing. Her first book *Priđite bliže: O kazalištu i drugim radostima* (*Come Closer: On Theatre and Other Joys*, 2015) is a collection of essays on theatre and everything else. Bauer lives and works in Zagreb (HR).

Simon Bayly (b. 1965) is currently a Reader in Drama, Theatre and Performance at the University of Roehampton in London, with a background as an independent theatre maker. His teaching and research interests include practices of participation and cooperation within contemporary art and social movements and he is currently undertaking a study of the face-to-face gathering as an overlooked but ubiquitous organizational form. Recent publications include essays on meetings, waste, and the artistic 'project' as the contemporary configuration of work for the journals *Angelaki* and *Performance Research* and the book *A Pathognomy of Performance* (2011). Bayly lives and works in London (UK).

Andrea Božić (b. 1970) is a choreographer. She studied comparative literature and English at the University of Zagreb. She also studied at the School for New Dance Development and the Amsterdam Master of Choreography, both at De Theaterschool in Amsterdam. Her work reorganizes perception combining the conceptual with the sensorial and the physical, creates paradoxical situations, and asks questions about the effects of attention and imagination, perception of presence, politics of viewing, presentation of reality, and distribution of authorship. Recent projects include: *The Cube*, Spring Festival, Stadsschouwburg, Utrecht (2016); *Spectra*, Vienna Art Foundation (2015); and *Day for Night, ARE YOU ALIVE OR NOT?*, De Brakke Grond, Amsterdam (2015). Božić lives and works in Amsterdam (NL).

Nicola Conibere (b. 1977) is a choreographer and scholar. She studied at Cambridge University and Trinity Laban Conservatoire of Music and Dance in London. She is currently a Senior Lecturer in Dance at Coventry University, London and teaches at Trinity Laban Conservatoire of Music and Dance. Her research explores what choreographic practice offers to the politics of spectatorship and the notion of publics, with a particular interest in theatricality and the generative potentials of bodies. Her work *Assembly* was shown as part of the 20th Biennale of Sydney in 2016, and recently her work has been shown at venues across the UK and Europe.

Guy Cools (b. 1964) is a dance dramaturg. Recent positions include Associate Professor at research institute Arts in Society in Tilburg and Guest Professor at Ghent University. He has worked as a dance critic and curator and as a production dramaturg, with amongst others Koen Augustijnen (BE), Sidi Larbi Cherkaoui (BE), Danièle Desnoyers (CA), Lia Haraki (CY), Akram Khan (UK), Arno Schuitemaker (NL), and Stephanie Thiersch (DE). His most recent publications include *The Ethics of Art: Ecological Turns in the Performing Arts* (co-edited with Pascal Gielen, 2014) and *In-Between Dance Cultures: On the Migratory Artistic Identity of Sidi Larbi Cherkaoui and Akram Khan* (2015). Cools lives in Vienna (AT).

Augusto Corrieri (b. 1980) is an artist, a writer, and a Lecturer in Theatre and Performance at the University of Sussex in Brighton. He focuses on the crossover between ecology and an expanded understanding of performance. His first book is *In Place of a Show: What Happens Inside Theatres When Nothing is Happening* (2016). Between 2006–2012 he made several performances within a dance framework, including *Photographs of a Dance Rehearsal* (2008), commissioned by London's Camden Arts Centre, and shown again at Vienna's Tanzquartier. Corrieri currently lives and works in Brighton and London (UK).

Konstantina Georgelou (b. 1981) is a performing arts theorist, currently working as a Lecturer in the Master of Theatre Practices at ArtEZ University of the Arts, Arnhem and at Utrecht University. Her research spans over the areas of dramaturgy, choreography, artistic research, and philosophy, with a specific focus on the ethical, social, and political aspects of performance. Her ongoing engagement with modes of production in theory and in the arts takes different experimental formats in primarily collaborative projects. Her recent publications include: 'Syros: A Bet on the Potentiality of Co-Operation' (co-edited with Efrosini

Protopapa and Danae Theodoridou), special issue, *Maska: The Performing Arts Journal* 29, no. 169–171 (2015); 'The Art of Lawlessness' (co-edited with Eva Fotiadi and Manolis Tsipos, Institute for Live Arts Research), *Performance Research* 19, no. 6 (2015); and *Inventing Futures* (co-edited with Emilie Gallier and João da Silva, 2013). Georgelou lives in Amsterdam (NL).

Ivana Müller (b. 1972) is a choreographer, artist, and author. Through her choreographic and theatre work (performances, installations, text works, video-lectures, audio pieces, guided tours, and web-works) she rethinks the politics of spectacle and the spectacular, revisits the place of the imaginary and imagination, questions the notion of 'participation', investigates the idea of value and its representation, and keeps on getting inspired by the relationship between performer and spectator. Her pieces include: *Edges* (2016); *We Are Still Watching* (2012–2015); *Positions* (2013); *In Common* (2012); *Partituur* (2011); *60 Minutes of Opportunism* (2010); *Working Titles* (2010); *Playing Ensemble Again and Again* (2008); *While We Were Holding It Together* (2006); *Under My Skin* (2005); and *How Heavy Are My Thoughts* (2003). They have been produced and presented in major theatre festivals and venues in Europe, US, and Asia. Her work has occasionally been shown in visual art contexts including the 56th Venice Biennale (2015).

Betina Panagiotara (b. 1980) is a journalist, dance theorist, and currently a PhD researcher at the University of Roehampton in London. She looks into contemporary dance in Greece during the present sociopolitical turbulence, focusing on emerging artistic practices and collective working modes. She holds a BA in communication, media, and culture, and an MA in dance histories, cultures, and practices. She collaborates with festivals and artists in research and production, and works as a journalist for international media. Her research interests are in artistic production modes, dance ethnography, politics and history, and animation in performance. Panagiotara lives and works between London (UK) and Athens (GR).

Efrosini Protopapa (b. 1979) is a choreographer and scholar. She works as a Senior Lecturer at the University of Roehampton in London. Her research interests lie in experimental and conceptual practices across dance, theatre, and performance, and her latest work focuses on notions of negotiation, thinking, friendship, disagreement, and encounter in/as performance. Recent performances include *The Friend At Work* (supported by Arts Council England) and *Disputatio* (a commission by Siobhan Davies Dance). Publications include 'Syros: A Bet on the Potentiality of Co-Operation' (co-edited with Konstantina Georgelou and Danae Theodoridou), special issue, *Maska: The Performing Arts Journal* 29, no. 169–171 (2015) and articles for *Performance Research* and *Contemporary Theatre Review*. Protopapa lives in London, and works both in the UK and abroad.

Joachim Robbrecht (b. 1979) works as a writer and director for performance and as a performer. He studied at the University of Ghent and Amsterdam University of the Arts. His artistic work revolves around current socially relevant themes, approaching theatre from a post-disciplinary stance. In addition to his own productions he collaborates with andcompany&Co., Moeremans&Sons, Dood Paard, De Warme Winkel, and Toneelgroep Oostpool. Recent productions include *The Great Warmachine* (2015), *Black Bismarck* (as collaborator of andcompany&Co., 2013), and *Figaro Desire Machine* (2012). Recent texts include *Crashtest Ibsen: Ik zie spoken* (for Moeremans&Sons, 2016) and *Bromance* (for Toneelgroep Oostpool, 2015). Robbrecht lives and works on the axis Brussels-Amsterdam (BE-NL).

Jonas Rutgeerts (b. 1986) is a dramaturg and performance theorist. He studied philosophy at KU Leuven and dramaturgy at the University of Amsterdam and is currently working on a PhD on choreography and philosophy at KU Leuven. His main research interests involve choreographic processes, social choreographies, and the relation between movement and politics. As a dramaturg and researcher he collaborates with among others Labo21, Ivana Müller, David Weber-Krebs, Sanja Mitrović, ICKAmsterdam, and Clément Layes. He is the author of *Re-act: Over re-enactment in de hedendaagse dans* (2015). Rutgeerts lives in Leuven (BE) and works internationally.

Nienke Scholts (b. 1984) works as a dramaturg, currently at Veem House for Performance, and with several artists. She is a researcher at DAS Research in Amsterdam, where she looks into new organization models of artistic practices. She lectures in the MA Scenography programme at HKU University of the Arts Utrecht, and is a co-founder and editor of Platform-Scenography (P-S). She is interested in co-developing methods/practices invoked by new forms of art, and applying dramaturgy to other realms than performance alone. Recent publications include *Current Movements, Future Landscapes* (co-edited with P-S/Research Centre Performative Processes, 2016). Scholts lives in Utrecht and works both in the Netherlands and abroad.

Arabella Stanger (b. 1982) is a dance and performance theorist, currently a Lecturer in Dance at the University of Roehampton in London and from 2017 a Lecturer in Theatre and Performance at the University of Sussex in Brighton. Her work explores the social and political dimensions of performance, with a particular focus on space and spatiality in choreographic practice. Recent publications include: 'Heterotopia as Choreography' (*Performance Research*, 2016); 'The Choreography of Space' (*New Theatre Quarterly*, 2014); and 'Merce Cunningham's Ensemble Space and the Black Mountain Principle of Community' (*Black Mountain College Studies*, 2012). Stanger lives and works in the UK.

Danae Theodoridou (b. 1978) is a performance maker and researcher. She completed her PhD in dramaturgy at the University of Roehampton in London and teaches in various university departments and art conservatories of theatre and dance in Europe. Her latest work focuses on contemporary dramaturgical practices and the notion of social imaginaries. Recent performances include *Earth in 100 Years* (2016) and *One Small Step for a Man: Hello, Goodbye* (2015). Recent publications include '"I'm Sleeping": The Metaphor of Sleep as a Dramaturgical Directive In Performance', *Performance Research 21.1* (2016) and 'Syros: A Bet on the Potentiality of Co-Operation' (co-edited with Konstantina Georgelou and Efrosini Protopapa), special issue *Maska: The Performing Arts Journal* 29, no. 169–171 (2015). For more information: www.danaetheodoridou.com. Theodoridou lives in Brussels (BE).

Julia Willms (b. 1974) is a visual artist. She studied visual communication at Maastricht Academy of Fine Arts and Design and media art at the University of Applied Arts in Vienna. Her work deals with the nature of perception, the very act of viewing itself, and the shifting position of the spectator within the proposed environment. Recent projects include: *The Cube*, Spring Festival, Stadsschouwburg, Utrecht (2016); *Im Raum mit_*, BNKR, Munich (2016); *Spectra*, Vienna Art Foundation (2015); *Skyward*, Altana Kulturstiftung, Bad Homburg (2015); and *Cité de l'image*, Clervaux (2014–2015). Willms lives and works in Amsterdam (NL).

Jasna Jasna Žmak (b. 1984) is a dramaturg and writer. She studied in the Department of Dramaturgy at the Academy of Drama Art of the University of Zagreb where she is now an Assistant Researcher. Since 2010 she is a board member for the Center for Dramatic Art in Zagreb as well of the editorial board of the performing arts journal *Frakcija*. She is currently writing a PhD thesis on lecture-performance. Recent publications include *Moja ti* (My Y♀U) (2015), *The Other at the Same Time* (2013), and *samice* (Solitaries) (2012). Žmak lives and works in Zagreb (HR).

Index

Colophon

The Practice of Dramaturgy
Working on Actions in Performance

Editors
Konstantina Georgelou
Efrosini Protopapa
Danae Theodoridou

Authors
Una Bauer
Simon Bayly
Andrea Božić
Nicola Conibere
Guy Cools
Augusto Corrieri
Konstantina Georgelou
Ivana Müller
Betina Panagiotara
Efrosini Protopapa
Joachim Robbrecht
Jonas Rutgeerts
Nienke Scholts
Arabella Stanger
Danae Theodoridou
Julia Willms
Jasna Jasna Žmak

Antennae Series N° 23
by Valiz, Amsterdam

Part of the Series
'Arts *in* Society"

Copy Editing
Laura Booth, Janine Armin

Proof Check
Els Brinkman

Index
Elke Stevens

Design
Metahaven

Paper Inside
Munken Print 100 gr 1.5

Paper Cover
Bioset 240 gr

Printing and Binding
Ten Brink, Meppel

Publisher
Valiz, Amsterdam, 2017
www.valiz.nl

ISBN 978-94-92095-18-3

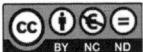
The authors and the publisher have
made every effort to secure
permission to reproduce the listed
material, illustrations and
photographs. We apologise for any
inadvert errors or omissions. Parties
who nevertheless believe they can
claim specific legal rights are invited
to contact the publisher.

Distribution:
USA/Canada/Latin America: D.A.P.,
www.artbook.com
GB/IE: Anagram Books,
www.anagrambooks.com
NL/BE/LU: Coen Sligting,
www.coensligtingbookimport.nl
Europe/Asia: Idea Books,
www.ideabooks.nl
Australia: Perimeter Books,
www.perimeterdistribution.com

ISBN 978-94-92095-18-3
NUR 675

Printed and bound in the Netherlands

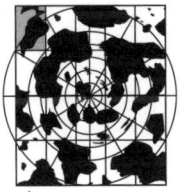

Antennae